Vincent

THE LONG SILENCE,
A STORY OF THE GREAT WAR

DEREK McCANN

ILLUSTRATED BY SIMON McCANN

ISBN 978-1-66781-724-8 (Softcover)
ISBN 978-1-66783-282-1 (Hardcover)
ISBN 978-1-66781-725-5 (eBook)

Table of Contents

VINCENT

A quiet man, one might say,
Keeps himself to himself most of the day.
But in his dreams, he returns to that place
of ancient memories he cannot erase.

Of blood and mud and cold and rain,
Of fear and fatigue, hurt and pain.
Of many fine men, whose lives they gave,
lying far from home, in a sodden grave.

How could he talk to those at home?
Who could not know what he had done,
The constant struggle to survive
The road through hell and stay alive.

That is why he can never tell
Of the times when his comrades fell,
Of the stench of death and the guilt as well,
That he came through when others fell.

That, my friend, is the reason why,
He came across as quiet and shy.
To his children it had never made sense,
Why he'd kept that long silence?

Introduction

My eyes were heavy as I yawned for the third time. The brilliant sunset in the rearview mirror signaled approaching darkness. I needed backup in my losing battle with fatigue, and prudence dictated I pull over. But I wanted to get home; my mother-in-law and my wife's aunt slept in the back seat, snoring in gentle harmony. My mother sat in the passenger seat beside me, a privilege she always claimed and to which I always gave way. Behind her back, the family knew her as "She Who Must be Obeyed". Well, now she was going to have to earn her front-seat status.

We were returning from a day in San Antonio, where I was worn out traipsing around the shops and touring the Alamo with my three companions. San Antonio had been a "must" on all our itineraries, but we'd left Houston at eight in the morning and now, twelve hours later, I was feeling the strain.

The three of them had come over to visit from Ireland. This was one of several day trips we'd taken, packing in as much of the Texas "experience" as possible. I knew my mother would probably never come back—particularly as the airlines had banned smoking, and there was no way she would ever do the ten-hour flight without getting through at least a pack of Rothmans.

I chose to resolve my fatigue by asking my mother to start talking and not to stop until we arrived home. That's what she did, recalling her life story. As it turned out, I learned a good deal about the relationship between my parents on that trip. Listening to her revelations, I had no trouble staying awake!

The story I'm about to tell concerns my father, who, although he was a good and gentle man, rarely spoke to his children, except to tell us to finish our homework or clean up after dinner. There's no doubt he loved my brother, myself, and our three sisters, but a gap in age amounting to two generations left a chasm between us. Also, he was away a good deal, and when he was home, we kept a safe distance. We didn't really know him. But, curiously enough, I don't believe my mother knew him that well either.

While my *Mama* and *Dada*, as we called them, did love each other deeply, it wasn't always as rosy a path as we children thought it to be. Their life together began with the purchase of a house that was beyond their humble means, and after five years of financial stress, they were obliged to sell and move to a somewhat less desirable, but more affordable, place.

Dada also had a drink problem. In his job as a Customs Preventive Officer, he frequently had occasion to board ships on their arrival in Dublin Port, where he was stationed, and the visit to the captain's cabin to examine the manifest usually entailed imbibing a glass or two of Jameson's—maybe even three. One dark night as he steered an erratic course home on his bicycle, in his somewhat inebriated state he made a small but critical error of judgement, the result of which found himself lying on the side of the road. Though the bike lay on top of him, the front wheel still spinning, he was feeling little pain. But it gave him pause to contemplate the wisdom of his actions. That was a turning point, and he swore off drink for the next twenty-odd years.

The last problem was they had their rows, like any couple I suppose; but while Mama cooled down and was ready to kiss and make up the next day, he would carry his ire swathed around him like a dark cloak for the next couple of weeks and not speak a word. I can only imagine how deeply this hurt her, as she, being of a somewhat garrulous nature, was left with a one-sided conversation.

She called these periods of marital iciness "The Long Silence".

Dada was long dead when I signed up for Ancestry.com and typed his name in the search box. To my amazement, and no doubt to the horror of his spirit looking over my shoulder, up came his army number and all his records. This was fortunate as nearly two-thirds of 6.5 million soldiers' records were destroyed when the War Office Record Store at Arnside Street in London was hit by an incendiary bomb in September 1940—one of the early casualties of The Blitz. The surviving records were mostly charred or water damaged and became known as the "Burnt Documents". In the late 1990s they were microfilmed and permanently preserved in the National Archives in Kew, London, my father's papers were among them. A further serendipity was the discovery that the National Archives had also digitized the war diaries, kept by every unit of the British Army during World War I, and in those, I found the diaries of Dada's company: the 75th Field Company, Royal Engineers. A third and equally valuable source of information was the digitized Trench Maps used by the military during the war, with which, using the map references given in the diaries, I was able to pinpoint the exact location of the company on a day-by-day basis.

The story that unfolded was not one of my father's personal activities, for he left no remembrances, neither written nor verbal.

The war diaries rarely mention individuals. It is about the war he experienced; of people who shared his limited domain, and events he would have been witness to. The war and the Spanish Flu pandemic that followed it were apocalyptic events that enveloped the entire planet, but each participant witnessed only a tiny aspect of the whole, seen from his or her own perspective.

This book, *Vincent: The Long Silence*, is about Vincent McCann's war.

When my father enlisted in September 1914, like most other recruits he probably thought it would last only a few months—this is what they were told. His short service contract was for three years, or until the war ended. Prior to that, he had worked for Harland and Wolff shipyard as a fitter. This was when the *Titanic* was under construction, and after that ship was launched and subsequently sank, the yard lost a lot of orders and cut down on the workforce drastically—such was the business of shipbuilding.

In those days there was no protective welfare net such as unemployment benefits, so if you lost your job, there was no money to buy bread. Maybe he was among the unemployed and needed work, which was not an easy thing for a Catholic in Protestant Belfast. In any case, the army might have been a good option, and they were recruiting. Or, maybe he was still working as a fitter in the yard and just saw posters with Lord Kitchener pointing his finger, telling him his country needed him.

Either way, he made the decision to enlist.

My father told my mother that although he did join up, he was underage, and *his* father bought him out and brought him home.

That was a lie—two lies in fact. He was not underage when he signed up, nor did his father buy him out. He served with the 75th

Field Company Royal Engineers on the Western Front until he was demobilized in March 1919.

What Vincent McCann knew and experienced went with him to the grave, and the stories in the ensuing chapters are taken from the 75th Field Company's war diaries, letters, and accounts from other soldiers, and the results of many in-person visits to the locations where his company had been stationed. In many instances I adopted some license and have fleshed out the brief facts stated in the diary to give body to the story.

It may or may not have happened the way I've depicted it, but, as they say in the movies, this is "based on a true story."

Prologue

He was cutting my hair. The dull scissors gave the odd tug, forcing a wince.

Regardless, I was happy. It was a rare occasion of contact with someone I loved but could never know.

Shy and deeply Victorian in his upbringing, with tragedy entering his life early, like a thief, stealing his childhood, and the endured horrors of a long-forgotten war were sealed in his mind, not wanting to be shared. Two generations of different cultures separated us like the Berlin Wall. The mold he grew up in formed a father I could never reach. No one, not even my mother, was privy to his inner self.

Yet, he had much to tell.

Since he couldn't, I'll endeavor to do it for him.

Let's wind the clock back to 1902, to a small village in County Louth, Ireland, when life's calloused hands were already shaping Vincent McCann.

His mother was dying. The family had grown used to her cough. She would stop her work at the sink, holding on to the edge, the other hand on her chest. It was a dry cough, not boding well.

Being so taken up with their own lives, as children are, they didn't notice her get weaker and paler, as Tuberculosis sucked the life from her. When she took to the bed, it was a shock—who would look after them?

Vincent was only eight years old.

After she was gone, the effort of keeping the house together took its toll on his father. He became withdrawn and edgy, morose almost. For a long time afterwards, a mantle of sadness enveloped the family. They had to learn to look out for each other and share the daily chores of a busy household.

In 1910, just sixteen years old, Vincent got an apprenticeship at the Belfast shipyard—a chance to learn a good trade and transition to the world of adulthood.

"Vinnie," as he was called, was glad to go to work and get out of the house. As an apprentice fitter in Harland and Wolff, he absorbed himself in using his hands and learning the skills he was taught. In the vast engine shop, he embraced the camaraderie of his fellow apprentices. It was an exciting place to work, watching the giant skeleton of the *Titanic* grow on the stocks alongside her sister ship, the *Olympic*.

He dreamed of one day going away on one of these giant liners as an engineer. A romantic vision, though somewhat removed from reality. Dreams got him through the day.

They might even have all come true, if it hadn't been for a single gunshot in faraway Sarajevo, precipitating the "War to End all Wars".

The year was 1914. He was a journeyman fitter in the yard, and they still talked about the "Great Ship"—the *Titanic*—having sunk two years past. How stunned they all were when the news came out, and now war had broken out on the continent, with an unwilling Great Britain sucked in. At twenty-years-old, he found it exciting, and wanted to sign up. His father felt otherwise, but there was no stopping him.

At the recruiting station, they thought he was a fine speci-men—healthy as a horse, ready and willing.

He was a soldier now.

CHAPTER 1

The Last Post

MENIN GATE, YPRES
October 2017

As the sweet, sad notes of *The Last Post* rang out in the still evening air, a chill enveloped me; tears formed in my eyes. At first, I tried to stifle them—Irish culture frowns on men showing emotion—but my stoicism abandoned me and the tears rolled freely down my cheeks.

The high walls of the Menin Gate had tens of thousands of names inscribed on them. Fifty-five-thousand ghosts mingled with visitors from all over the world who had come to witness their sacrifice. The spirits of the young men, whose dreams were stopped violently in their prime; denied the chance to say goodbye. They come back each night to mingle with the visitors, waiting to see if their sweethearts, mothers, and siblings had come to bid them farewell. They were the ones who were never found.

Missing in Action. "A soldier of the Great War."

Each name on the walls had once been a tiny baby held fondly in his mother's arms, christened with love. He had grown up strong and healthy, for only the sound of wind and limb, were chosen to come out here to these killing fields, now covered in red poppies, to be fragmented into unrecognizable pieces of flesh, bone, and viscera, their last sensation a shock wave.

He lay so soft in his mother's arms,
New life, so sweet and innocent,
And grew to childhood with quiet charm,
His heroic dreams yet nascent.
As a youth he was his father's pride,
He won the heart of every lass
Until dark clouds of war did bode
A grim future that would come to pass.
Off he marched to pipe and drum,
Immortal and so full of pride,
By Christmas he would soon return
They said... but he never did.

(Derek McCann. "A Soldier of the Great War")

My wife, Terry, and I, words failing us, walked silently away.

• • •

We had recently purchased a barge with a few friends, and had taken delivery in the port of Nieuwpoort, Belgium. Our first trip brought us to the town of Veurne, and then we proceeded along the Lo Canal to the River Yser. The whole area is rich with the history of World War I.

While we travelled at a leisurely pace along the canals, my brother-in-law Pat regaled us with the story of how the Belgians flooded the whole plain to prevent the Germans capturing the towns on the coast. As he talked, we turned into the Ypres-Yser canal, which terminates in the charming Belgian town of Ypres. This pleasant market town played a major part in the war, being the center of a salient[1] on the front line, hotly contested throughout the war.

---

1 A bend in the front line encircling the city.

One can't visit this town without learning a great deal about the "War to End All Wars". There were gates to the town, dating back to when it was a walled, fortified city. One of these was the Menin Gate, which opened onto the road leading to the small town of the same name. Thousands of troops passed through this gate on their way to battle, and it was here the tradition of sounding the Last Post was established to commemorate the soldiers of Britain and the Commonwealth who gave their lives defending Belgium. The ceremony takes place every day at eight in the evening, come rain or shine. The names inscribed on the walls are those who were listed as "missing".

It was while visiting this town I began to think about the idea of writing a book to honor my father's contribution to that war—something he had never taken any credit for.

The following day, we cast off our moorings and steered the barge away from the dock. Gliding peacefully along the canal, we slipped by the Essex Farm Cemetery where, just over a century ago, the men buried there laid down their lives along with those whose names are remembered on the Menin Gate. The sheer number of young lives lost leaves one speechless.

At that time in 2017, I knew my father—or "Dada," as we called him—had taken part in the Great War, but little else. A few years earlier, I had found his army records online, and then got copies of them from the National Archives in Kew, London. It felt like there was a spirit moving me, guiding me along a trail of discovery to reveal young Sapper[2] Vincent McCann's early experiences, which his tight-lipped Victorian reticence forbade him to speak of around me while I was growing up.

---

2 He was with the Royal Engineers, where the equivalent of Private was "Sapper."

Several serendipitous events followed my decision to put them to paper.

Every evening, from the day they were mobilized to the day his company was demobilized, the company commander had sat down in dark, claustrophobic dugouts, lit only by candle, or occasionally in more comfortable billets behind the lines, licking his lead pencil and scribbling the doings of the day.

These were the *75th Field Company's War Diaries.*

After the war, these documents languished on dusty shelves for one hundred years, waiting for discovery and the miracle of digitization. This opened up the activities of the group of men my father fought alongside. Vincent's story was waiting for me to put it down on paper. His family thought he'd never taken part in the World War, and I felt that what he did, needed to be understood. The three and a half years he spent on the Western Front probably did more to make him the man he was—the father he was—than any other event in his life.

While writing the diaries, the company's daily location was precisely jotted down by the commanding officer, using mysterious numerals and letters that I later understood to be coordinates on the trench maps they used. Then, the final piece of the puzzle, the trench maps themselves, were revealed to me. The National Library of Scotland had digitized them, so I was able to pinpoint my father and his company's location each day, and usually where they worked. These provided me with a structure around which to write.

Gradually, the story of Vincent's experiences, and those of the soldiers around him, evolved.

But to get to the man he was, let's go all the way back to the beginning, as the nineteenth century merges into the twentieth…

CHAPTER 2
Military Necessity

"Where the pools are bright and deep,
Where the gray trout lies asleep,
Up the river and o'er the lea,
That's the way for Billy and me."

(James Hogg. "The Boy's Song")

TALLANSTOWN, COUNTY LOUTH, IRELAND
November 1906

The coolness of autumn had settled in; showers tempered the heat of a long, warm summer. As the year drew to a close, the farmers felt smug with another abundant harvest; the kind one remembers in later years:

"Ah, yes, oh-six was a grand harvest, that year we had just enough rain and just enough sun, and sure by the end of October, the barns were full."

Life in the small Irish village went on as it had done as far back as anyone could remember. Even during the famine years, the Plunkett family had treated the tenants well. Few now had any memories of those terrible times, though Louth in the relatively drier Northeast of Ireland suffered less than the wetter West and South coasts.

The cackling of crows in the bare trees overhead went unnoticed by two young lads walking along the path towards the old stone bridge, survivor of countless winters and wars, joining the two halves of Tallanstown across the river Glyde. The boys were deep in conversation as they kicked a stone between them, scattering the dead leaves covering the path, scuffing their boots, inviting a scolding from their parents at some later stage.

Vincent McCann and Billy McCardle were both 12 years old, and as they reached the bridge they met with their other classmate, Mick Nugent. The three were all the same age and in the same class at the national school. Not quite past the age of playing, at the same time they were on the cusp of manhood, and shared many common interests, the foremost two being girls and fishing, or fishing and girls, one couldn't be sure which was the correct order.

The river Glyde, in full flow now from the autumn showers up in the hills, rushed past the police station where Vincent's father was sergeant. On each side, old elms and willows drooped down to kiss the waters gurgling past. Near the barracks stood Saint Peter's Catholic Church and the national school. Across the road were the estate workers' cottages with more recent additions on the opposite side of the river, most occupied by the laborers and tradesmen employed by Louth Hall.

Vincent lived in the house adjoining the barracks with his widowed father and siblings; Joe, aged 15, was the oldest at home, Jim having left for the Christian Brothers training college in Dublin. Edith, at 11, was already fulfilling the duties of housekeeper in addition to her studies, helped by Mina, who was 7. Leo was 10 and Wilfred 8. At times, because of the shortage of rooms in the small house some of the lads often stayed with their grandmother, Anne Jayne, in the nearby village of Mansfieldstown.

Leaning over the parapet of the bridge, oblivious to the damp moss, the mesmerizing waters of the river captured the boys' full attention. They chatted idly, mostly about girls. Vincent's eyes glazed a bit as he thought of Mary Coghlan, who at the vastly superior age of 14, looked down her nose at him. But that wasn't deterring his ardor. Being generally a reserved person though, he wasn't getting very far and had yet failed miserably to make his feelings known. The other two were doing no better, so eventually the conversation drifted to fishing for trout, a subject on which they had considerably more expertise, and their plans for Saturday. They were thinking of going to that sweet spot they knew on the river, where, outside the village they could enjoy being away from adult scrutiny. The bend in the river made a still pool where the fish sometimes gathered, and they had in fact managed to land a small trout a week ago.

"And frisking in the stream below
The troutlets make the circles flow,
And the hungry crane doth watch them grow
As a smoker does his rings."

(Francis Ledwidge. "Behind the Closed Eye")

15

While making their plans, they were all talking at the same time until Vincent was startled by a shout from his father to come and help get the tea ready. He reluctantly said goodbye to his pals and ran home. The other two lads went off to the row of houses they lived in on the other side of the river. The evening was closing in and one of Vincent's jobs was to light the oil lamps and trim them—by now the house was nearly in darkness. He enjoyed this task and took pride in getting the blue lamp flame trimmed, just so, that there was the brightest light with no smoke. The smell of fresh baked soda bread filling the small house and mixing with the sweet oily odor of the paraffin lamps would remain a memory with him for years to come, and comfort him during times of almost unbearable stress which lay ahead in his future.

The village of Tallanstown was small, by any comparison, and a handy station for their father, Patrick, who had plenty to cope with besides his job and was nearing retirement. He was saving to buy a small farm back in Cavan where he was born, but bringing up a pack of hungry kids kept the little money he put aside to a bunch of dreams in a jar.

Their cozy milieu was about as remote as a village could be in Ireland, surrounded by woods and farmland, the trees now shedding their leaves to make a soft brown carpet over the roads and along the riverbank. The nearby Louth Hall estate employed most of the tenants in the cottages on each side of the bridge. This, and nearby Mansfieldstown where their grandma lived, were the only places Vincent knew, apart from a rare visit to the big towns of Belfast or Dundalk. Down the road just around the bend were the gate lodges to the manor, where Lord and Lady Louth lived—the 14th Baron and Baroness Louth.

Often on a winter's evening, the family sat around the kitchen table in the warm glow of the oil lamps, having finished their tea, just talking. Sometimes their father would tell them ghost stories or tales about the goings on in the country around them; as a diligent policeman, there was little that went on without his knowledge. One evening, he talked about the "Big House", as they called Louth Hall. Patrick slowly lit his pipe as he recalled the story of the Louth family.

The family name was Plunkett, going way back in the depths of Irish history to the Norman invasion. He told them how a Norman knight, Sir Hugh de Plunkett, came over to Ireland in the time of King Henry II and purchased large tracts of land in Counties Louth and Meath. The Plunketts came to Tallanstown in the late 1400s and built a tower house there, which was later extended into the present rambling property. One of Sir Hugh's descendants, Oliver Plunkett, was created Baron of Louth by Henry VIII in 1541. Though they remained loyal to the Crown, they also developed connections with the old Gaelic culture, and they remained Catholic despite pressure from the Crown to transfer their allegiance to the Church of England.

In 1670, a relative of the Plunketts, Oliver, who had joined the priesthood, was appointed Archbishop of Armagh, and during a period where the penal laws were relaxed somewhat, he returned from exile in Rome to take up his duties. He founded a seminary in Drogheda, which was later demolished as anti-Catholic sentiment returned. During this time in Ireland, he secretly stayed with the Plunketts at Louth Hall. Eventually he was tried for Treason by the English and sentenced to death. In 1681 he was hung, drawn and quartered—a most gruesome execution as one could imagine, which Patrick described in detail, laughing at their squeals of horror. In the 1700s the Plunketts became Protestant but returned to the Catholic faith in the 19th century and remained staunch Catholics ever since.

Every Sunday the family would take their place in their special pew in the church.

They were a world apart from the people in the village. They spoke differently, were better educated, and above all else, privileged. Their son Otway was only two years older than Vincent, but they may as well have come from different planets. Yet they were as one with the community and their kindness respected. Once a year on a summer Sunday, all the village trooped up to the garden party which was held on the Manor grounds where they ate and drank—occasionally too much—played games and sang as the stout loosened up their inhibitions. The abundant food was laid out under a marquee on long tables with white linen cloths—different from the wax cloth table cover in most of the villager's houses.

Life in that small village had a sweetness and tranquility, which the children took for granted, but experiencing it in their most impressionable years, it shaped their lives forever.

It was only four years since their mother, Wilhelmina—or Minny, as she was known—had died after a long illness and the family was still trying to cope with the tragedy. The doctor's diagnosis was tuberculosis, which was rampant throughout the country and seemed to have no real cure. A leaden heaviness lay over the household for a long time. Each grieved in their own different way. Even now, Vincent missed her terribly—he was only eight when she passed away, an age where he badly needed a mother. When his friends talked about their mothers, he felt the tears well up, an ache in his heart and had to turn away. He'd developed a way of coping by withdrawing into himself, incommunicado as it were, which other people found irritating, but it was his method of grief management.

But, as time wore on, a routine settled in where they all helped out and kept the household running smoothly. Then just over a year prior, his oldest brother Jim, with his mop of black hair, always getting up to hair-raising scrapes—the one they all looked up to—left for Baldoyle in Dublin to start his training as a Christian Brother.[3]

As their father brought Jim to the college in Baldoyle, he felt a loss that only a parent knows, when the first child spreads their wings and leaves. He felt sure Jim wouldn't make it through the training, wild individual that he was. In fact, he did complete it. The lanky young man with the penchant for talking his way into trouble, and then back out, proved to be a diligent student and was very popular with the other pupils and teachers. On Christmas Day, 1905, Jim became a member of the Order. They sent him to Carlow to gain teaching experience but earlier in the year he was taken ill and had to be brought back to Dublin. The news sent a shiver down his father's spine, the memory of his young wife's fatal illness still fresh in his mind. But Jim was improving, according to his last letter and he enjoyed teaching in Synge Street School. The medical treatment up in Dublin was better and his strong constitution was fighting back. His letters were full of stories about the students and the shenanigans they got up to. It was obvious that although they missed him, he had found his niche in life.

It was a tight little family. Edith and Vincent were close, both having the same droll sense of humor and calm personality. Their younger sister Rita, who was now four years old, had been fostered out with the Blackwells, a childless couple who lived down the road. Mary Blackwell was Rita's godmother and stepped in when Minny died. Patrick just couldn't cope with a young baby. Mr. Blackwell, or Uncle Robert, as the kids knew him, was a small wiry man with skin like leather from the sun; he worked as a carpenter on the estate and on occasion sneaked the lads in to see the big house when the family

---

3 A Catholic religious order devoted to teaching and missionary work.

was away. He was a kind man and, in his shop, he taught Vincent how to work with wood, using a saw and plane. Vincent, who was good with his hands, learned basic techniques in carpentry that stood to him in later years. Leo and Wilfred were always up to some mischief together, constantly in trouble with their older brother Joe. Though the kids argued a fair bit, when trouble came from outside, they closed ranks and looked out for each other.

Vincent didn't like school—he just wanted to get out into the "real" world and learn a trade and start earning some money, but his father was determined he would finish his education first. That meant another few years yet, which at that age stretched a lifetime away. That's not to say he disliked all subjects. There was reading and drawing, which he loved, and he wasn't too bad at arithmetic. In fact, he was a voracious reader, devouring books in the little free time he had between household chores and fishing with his pals. Joe made sure he did his share of these jobs and then of course, there were his lessons.

Groan...

The national school they all attended was one of many built after the founding of the Commission for Education in 1831. The copy books the children used were those designed and produced by Mr. Vere Foster,[4] a philanthropist who devoted most of his life to improving the lot of teachers and education in Ireland. This good and kindly man devoted his not inconsiderable wealth to bettering the lot of the Irish people in the post famine years. His copy books for writing and arithmetic resulted in a generation of well-educated scribes. Vincent's own handwriting was a testament to this.

---

4 Vere Foster was a remarkable individual, who devoted himself to helping the education of Irish Children after the famine years. His story is briefly described on the book's web page. http://www.thelongsilence.com

Although he enjoyed doing carpentry with Mr. Blackwell, Vincent's real ambition was to go to sea as a ship's engineer. The genesis of this idea goes back to an early spring day, that same year, when Vincent had a bad dose of whooping cough, which was proving very stubborn to clear up. His father had to go to Belfast on police business, and he took his son with him. After visiting the R.I.C. Headquarters, they had some lunch and then went down to the docks; the premise being that they would walk around the gasometer, a giant cylindrical tank where the town gas was stored. It was said the fumes would clear up the congestion. Whether it worked or not, it was a great trip, and Vincent had his father all to himself for a day. They looked at the ships lying alongside the docks, hatches open and dockers busily loading and unloading the cavernous holds, shouting, and cursing, ignoring the tall mustached man and his little boy standing there taking it all in.

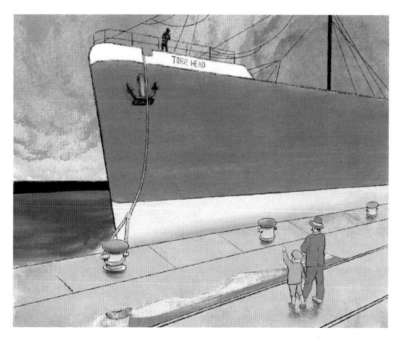

Ships have their own smell—paint, cooking, coal, and steam. Vincent inhaled that along with the gasometer fumes, cough forgotten. His father spied a large steamship tied up alongside the dock, which he recognized as the one where his old friend Jimmy McKay was chief engineer. It was one of the Head Line ships—Belfast's own shipping company—the *SS Torr Head*.

They went on board and sure enough Patrick's friend was there. After they'd chatted and caught up on their respective news, Jimmy brought Vincent down the engine room for a look around. The boy was *gobsmacked*[5] as he stared down at the giant triple expansion steam engine and the huge boilers with gaping furnaces, giving him his first glimpse into what seemed like Hell. The heat, the noise and hiss of steam, enthralled him. To a boy whose whole life had been spent in a quiet country village, this was jaw dropping. The desire to be one of these men controlling this giant beast grew in his gut. The sight of the polished brass gauges, the sweating stokers feeding the boilers, the smell of steam and oil would stay with him forever.

The romantic in Vincent led to daydreams of traveling to far off exotic countries and exploring foreign cities which, in turn, inspired his studies with a goal worth working for. Books on the sea took over his reading and filled his mind with dreams of life on a steamer like the *Torr Head*. Jack London, Herman Melville, and Josef Conrad became his heroes. He painted a mental picture of himself in white uniform walking along the harbor of some tropical port, listening to unfamiliar accents and languages while strangely dressed people stared at him. The lovely innocence and sense of immortality of youth filled his mind with nothing but optimism. These dreams began to fill the void in his "Long Silences."

---

5 English slang for 'amazed'.

"Let him enjoy it while it lasts," his dad had muttered sagely. His brother Jim, from an early age, was resolved to be a missionary and had filled Vincent with stories of the Far East and its mysterious ways while he listened with eyes the color of a tropical ocean, bright with anticipation. He couldn't wait. At age 12, a wonderful, trouble-free, adventurous life stretched out ahead of him.

It just so happened that there *was* a path Vincent could take. Mr. McKay had told him he'd worked in Harland and Wolff Shipyard for six years as a fitter before getting a job with Head Line. This prompted Vincent to pester his dad to get him an apprenticeship there too. The harassed father who was already regretting bringing his young son down the docks rolled his eyes and said he'd see what would happen—"...but you have to finish school first. Ye'll get nowhere without a good education son." *Yet*, he thought, *an apprenticeship in the yard would be the beginning of a fine career for the boy, if he'd stay at it.* He hoped he wouldn't lose another son to the mystique of foreign adventures.

Patrick went about enrolling Vincent in the Christian Brothers school at Hardinge Street in Belfast, where his brother Joe was just finishing his education. This was a fine school, where the brothers trained the lads in various trades, while at the same time completing their academic education. The next year, Vincent and his father boarded the Belfast train at Drogheda, and so began a new journey in the boy's life.

• • •

BERLIN, GERMANY
November 1906

Around the time the boys were planning their fishing trip, eight hundred miles away in a different country and a very different world, two men stood, with their hands behind their backs, staring at a large wall map of Europe. The lights had long been lit, but the men were oblivious to the late hour, as they worked in the wood-paneled room in the German War Ministry in Berlin.

General Helmuth Von Moltke, German Chief of Staff, stocky and ramrod straight, typified the Prussian militarist with close-cropped hair and handlebar moustache. He was a close friend of the Kaiser, Wilhelm II, a principal advisor to the arrogant old cousin of King George V of England. Beside him, his colleague and predecessor, General Albert von Schlieffen, a fellow Prussian, taller and older than his friend, took a thoughtful pull on his cigar. He was fanatical about detail, well known for preaching *"Der Teufel steckt im detail,"*[6] to his subordinates. The details in this case revolved around the timing of his plan. If everything went like clockwork, they would achieve their years-old ambition—the demolition of the French army. The two old soldiers ruminated over the plan painstakingly developed over the previous two years by von Schlieffen, who, to give him his due, was a brilliant military strategist. In theory at any rate. In practice nothing goes like clockwork in a war, and he should have known this.

Von Schlieffen's focused ambition in life was to defeat and humiliate France along with Russia, who between them consti-tuted a mortal threat to the continued survival of the newly fledged German State. To this end he had worked on a plan that would, by his reckoning, lead to the rapid annihilation of the French military, followed by deployment of his armies to the Russian frontier and the defeat of their ponderous forces, introducing a long-yearned-for German hegemony in Western Europe. Von Schlieffen had held von Moltke's position until January 1906, when he was forced to retire after being kicked in the head by a horse (one is inclined to feel sorry

---

6 "The Devil is in the details."

for the unfortunate horse whose hoof met that iron Prussian skull). Although he had been retired, the bewhiskered old Prussian had not yet finished with his detailed and intricate game of chess that would solve for good the threat posed by the French.

Ever since a treaty had been signed in 1873 between Russia and France guaranteeing mutual support in the event of either being attacked by Germany, the German military leadership felt threatened. Bitterness rankled between Germany and France following the latter's defeat by the Prussians in 1870, ceding to the Germans the provinces of Alsace and a large chunk of Lorraine, including its rich iron ore deposits. As the threat from their neighbor grew, the German generals felt the urgency to act, quickly and decisively, and leave France on its knees before Russia could come to their defense. To achieve this, they would also have to defeat Russia, and therein lay the problem.

While Russia could put together a massive army, they would be slow to mobilize with their antiquated rail system and vast tracts of land to traverse, before reaching the German frontier. The plan necessitated the defeat of the French over a period of no more than six weeks and then they could tackle the Russians. A strict timetable was essential.

Von Schlieffen was coming to some final conclusions about how they could accomplish this. He drew four well-manicured fingers across Belgium, like the Four Horsemen of the Apocalypse, wheeling them across the country, with his thumb representing two armies holding the French in Alsace-Lorraine.

He muttered to his colleague, "We will have to encircle them. That leaves us with no choice but to go through Belgium, it is the only way... the only way."

His fingers left a slight groove in the cloth map, representing burned villages, orphaned children, trampled crops, and a trail of destruction and untold human misery across a country that simply wanted to live in peace, safe in its neutrality.

The fact that Belgium was neutral, a pact that was guaranteed by several nations—including Germany and the United Kingdom of Great Britain—eluded the arrogant old generals, who felt the British would not want to get involved. Her entirely volunteer army was small and spread out across the empire. This would be a land war, and the Royal Navy, though the biggest in the world, would be of little use. Germany, as well as France, had conscription, which meant they could assemble a huge force of well over one-million men. Britain on the other hand, relied on a volunteer army numbering about three quarters of a million all told, relying on the navy for protection. Had the generals realized the horrific slaughter and destruction their plan would let loose on Europe and the rest of the world, even they may have had second thoughts. But in their minds, it would be a quick and decisive war, leaving Germany the victor.

The plan called for the largest group of German armies to attack through Belgium and into the North of France.

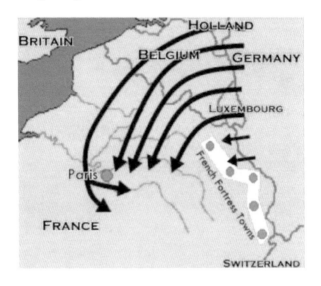

The tiny Belgian defense force would have no choice but to let them through. About twenty percent of the total forces would be kept back to hold off the Russians on the Eastern front when they mobilized. Another German army would be facing the French in the Ardennes corridor in the Northeast of France, but the main and much larger group of armies, represented by von Schlieffen's four fingers, entered Belgium in the North and wheeled south and across the French border, taking the French army on its left flank and rear. Caught in the jaws of a giant pincer, the French troops would be crushed. After France was conquered, the Germans could then concentrate on the Russians, who would be no match for their highly mechanized and efficient armies.

"The invasion of Belgium," von Schlieffen explained, as if Moltke needed any explanation, "will be a *military necessity*," and was thus justified in Von Schlieffen's mind. The German generals felt that Britain would be preoccupied with Her own troubles in Ireland, which was on the brink of civil war between the Unionists and the Irish Volunteers over the looming possibility of Home Rule[7] for Ireland.

To think that the little boy chatting with his friends on this cool November evening would be drawn into that grizzled seventy-three-year-old German general's plans many years later would be unimaginable. Throughout the following years, both would follow their different paths leading toward Belgium, though Von Schlieffen never did get to see his plan in action, as, presumably to his chagrin, he died in January 1913.

• • •

7 Ireland was promised Home Rule (i.e. self-government within the United Kingdom) by the Parliament of the United Kingdom in 1914. It was then postponed until the end of the War, and in fact was never implemented.

BELFAST, IRELAND
September 1907

Vincent's first day at the Christian Brothers' school on Hardinge Street was a difficult and transforming experience. He felt uncomfortable in the uniform, the stiff shirt collar rubbing his neck had him poking his finger behind it in a vain effort to relieve the irritation. He also had to cope with the Belfast accents and idiom of the pupils, harsher than his gentle Louth vernacular. But the sheer number of the classes astonished him. In addition to the Mathematics, English and Irish he had learned in the National School, he would now be studying Science, Metalwork, Drawing, and French. It was indeed a far cry from the National School with the earnest tutelage of the only teacher, Mr. Traynor. A frisson of excitement ran through him when the Head of the school, Brother Craven, showed the class around the newly built science lab and metal workshops. It was going to be good here; he felt an inner conviction that this school would give him an opportunity to make his way in the world.

A year later Patrick McCann retired from the RIC and the family prepared to move to Belfast. There, he would take up a job as a warder in Crumlin Road Gaol. He had found a little red brick house on Bedeque Street that was within a short walk of both Crumlin Road Gaol and Hardinge Street School; this would be their home for the next ten years. Life was going to be very different in the bustling city, with its thriving linen, engineering, and shipbuilding industries. The sooty town was filled with constant noise and chaotic activity, which seemed like bedlam after the quiet of the village the children had grown up in.

They adapted quickly, however, and the young ones made new friends at school. Joe by that time was well into his apprenticeship as an electrician. In the autumn of 1910, Vincent began an apprenticeship in the workshops of Harland and Wolff as an engine fitter. He felt that he was beginning his much dreamt-of career as a marine engineer. In the machine shops he'd be helping to build massive engines, like those that had awed him on the long-ago visit to the *Torr Head*.

The yard's biggest ship ever built was a growing skeleton on slip Number Three. The giant hulls of the *Titanic* and her sister ship, *Olympic*, dwarfed the men working on them, reducing them to the significance of ants. It was awe inspiring, and the men of the yard rightly felt the accomplishment they were taking part in.

They took great pride in what was then the state of the art in naval architecture. It was an achievement for a young Catholic boy to be part of that, especially as an apprentice, but he'd been fortunate in getting into Hardinge Street School—a stepping-stone to the apprenticeship. When he finished, he would be ready to go to sea and leave the grimy streets of Belfast for exotic foreign climes.

As it happened, the sea in question turned out to be a sea of mud, and the foreign climes were not exotic Far East islands, but the devastated battlegrounds of France and Belgium.

CHAPTER 3

The Lure of Lord Kitchener

"Far and near, high and clear,
Hard to the call of War!
Over the gorse and the golden dells,
Ringing and swinging of clamorous bells,
Praying and saying of wild farewells:
War! War! War!"

(Robert W. Service. "Rhymes of a Red-Cross Man")

BELFAST, IRELAND
December 1889

Discarded on the living room floor, the *Belfast Evening Telegraph* lay open on page three. The main article on the page was of scant interest to either of the occupants of the room—Minnie McCann and her mother Anne, preoccupied as they were with the impending birth of Minnie's first child.

Describing the battle of Toski in southern Egypt the previous August, the story waxed on in typical Victorian verbiage, about an aspiring young major who led the Egyptian cavalry against the Muslim Mahdi army. His name was Horatio Herbert Kitchener, an Irishman, albeit of the aristocratic kind, born in Ballylongford, near Listowel in County Kerry, Ireland. While of little interest to the two ladies, H.H. Kitchener would in years to come, have a direct influence on the life of Minnie's fourth child. But that would be many years hence.

A companionable silence lay between the two women, disturbed only by the click of knitting needles as they contentedly worked on a growing collection of baby clothes. The glowing coal fire was heating up the small room, adding to the warm light of the oil lamps, easing the early December chill. The smokey fog outside almost blotted out the light from the gas street lamps and Minnie had decided she'd stay the night in her mother's house, rather than brave the gloomy streets. Patrick, her husband of less than a year, was on night duty at the R.I.C. police barracks where he was a constable and had suggested she stay with her widowed mother till morning. The "two up, two down" redbrick terraced house was well kept and neat, with the curtains drawn in the living room keeping out the cold, damp smog that had lingered over Belfast for the last week.

Minnie sat across from her mother, watching as Anne's hands moved expertly with the knitting needles. They chatted from time to time about the baby, the focal point of their interest. Minnie had realized she was pregnant the previous June, and so far, apart from early bouts of morning sickness, all was going well. Just now she could feel the baby moving and not for the first time she felt a sense of wonder that there was a live human inside, a little foot kicking away as if to assure her that all was well.

"I think he's going to be feisty," she said with a smile, breaking the silence. Somehow, she knew it would be a boy, maybe because of the energetic movement she could feel, as if he wanted to get out and start his life long before she was ready for it.

"Have the two of ye definitely decided on a name yet?" her mother asked in her soft Antrim accent.

"We have," Minnie answered. "If it's a girl we're calling her Wilhelmena. If it's a boy, and I feel it's going to be, it'll be John, after Pat's daddy," she said, with a firmness precluding any further suggestions her mother might make.

"Aye," Anne replied, giving her daughter an old-fashioned look, and kept her peace.

Just over a month later, on the 26th of January 1890, three days before their first wedding anniversary, Minnie gave birth to a healthy baby boy—John James McCann, the first of a growing family that would keep her busy over the next ten years. After Jim, as he became known, came Joe, Cecil and then in 1894 on April 29, Vincent arrived, with a wide smile on his puffy little face. Over the following six years, as the century faded out, Patrick and Minnie's family grew to include Edith, Leo, Wilfred, Mina, and finally Rita.

• • •

During that same decade, H.H. Kitchener became Governor-General of Sudan. The great man's career was as impressive as his bushy moustaches and piercing eyes, spanning South Africa, India, and Egypt. Despite, or maybe because of the fact he rarely set foot in England, his popularity with the people never waned. So much so that on the outbreak of war in 1914, Prime Minister Asquith asked him to take up the position of Minister of War. No doubt he was hoping this would improve the image of the government in the public eye. Kitchener reluctantly took up the post, leaving his aides to carry on the administration of Egypt.

As the twentieth century rolled into its next decade, the United Kingdom maintained a professional army which, though battle hardened in the Boer war, and well trained, was less than half the size of the huge forces put on the field by Germany and France.

In August 1914 when war broke out in Europe, the government was sure it would be a short one, concluding by Christmas, with victory over Germany.

Lord Kitchener[8] thought otherwise, declaring the war would continue for at least three years and he adamantly maintained that position much to the annoyance of his cabinet colleagues. He was ultimately proven right. He was a career soldier, after all, who had fought in many conflicts and knew a lot more than most of the civilian cabinet who'd never set foot on a battlefield. He knew that it would require a lot more troops to maintain the conflict and pushed for a volunteer army to support the regular troops. In the end, the government caved, and the push began for a major recruitment drive. The nation responded to Kitchener in a way they would never have answered the call by the dry and somewhat stuffy Prime Minister, Asquith. The now famous posters of the heavily mustached Earl, pointing an accusing finger at eligible young males, appeared everywhere.[9]

On the eve of war, both France and Germany had conscription for many years and were putting up an army each with about 4

---

8 General H.H. Kitchener was elevated to the peerage in 1898.

9 Picture of poster from Wikipedia Commons public domain, courtesy of Imperial War Museum.

million men; already in the opening days of August 1914 they were mobilizing. Britain's meagre contribution, which she felt obliged to send over on the invasion of Belgium, was 6 divisions—later reduced to 4—or about 100,000 men. This was the BEF.[10]

• • •

At the engine works in Harland and Wolff, on a hot August afternoon, Vincent and his mates were having lunch in the engine shop. Over steaming mugs of tea and sandwiches they crowded around him as he read the Wednesday edition of the *Belfast Newsletter*. The main stories were about the BEF retreat from Mons, which began two days earlier.

It had been their first encounter with the German army and though they had to fall back, along with the French, they did put up a good fight against superior numbers. It was the 26th of August, and three days earlier, on Sunday the 23rd, the Germans had overrun Mons.

The front page was full of the heroic fighting of the British troops, in particular the Royal Irish Fusiliers, who had held Nimy Bridge while the remaining troops began the retreat. The BEF was small, but they were very professional and well-trained soldiers, many of them battle hardened in the Boer War. The newspaper gave long accounts of the German barrage against the troops holding the Mons canal, and how they fought back until they were overwhelmed and began a long and slow retreat into France.

Excited talk about joining up consumed the group until the foreman shouted at them to get back to work. Enlistment would mean a break from the humdrum life in Belfast and the incessant religious politics. Over in France, they would all be the same, Catholic

---

10 The "British Expeditionary Force."

and Protestant, fighting a common enemy. The irresistible lure of the unknown and the excitement of war captured their minds, while the idea of possibly getting killed or maimed didn't occur to most of them. They thought they were invincible. Back at work, they continued to talk, and the seed was sown. At first, Vincent felt he should stay where he was, hold on to what he knew best for a few more years. He'd never travelled at all in Ireland, far less on the Continent. He had already made his plans for a seagoing career.

But the main reason was his family. Since the death of his mother, they'd been a tightly knit clan. His father had admitted to him and Joe one day that he deeply missed their brother, Cecil, who died when he was only five years old, and their little sister, Rita, who went to live with her godmother. They never saw her now, after they'd come to Belfast. Then Jim had left, and the little clan was getting smaller.

Now, how would it be if he announced he was going away... to war?

As his foreman, John McDougall was helping him to set up the big lathe, he asked him, "Mr. McDougall, I was thinking about ... *em* ... the war, you know ... what do you think of all this talk about signing up?"

"Son," his old mentor said, "I've taught you all I know about iron working, and I'd hate to see it wasted on a battlefield." The old man took off his paddy cap[11] and scratched his few remaining grey hairs. "But to be honest," he continued, "if I was your age, I would probably sign up. Someone has to stand up to those bloody Jerries." He paused for a minute, thinking, then added, "But see here, if you do take the King's shilling, ask to go with the Engineers, and at least you'll be keeping up your trade. You might even learn something."

---

11 Flat cap.

With that, he gave Vincent a wink, patted him on the shoulder and went over to help one of the other apprentices. Vincent stared after him, deep in thought.

As August came to an end, on an afternoon coming home from work, Vincent saw another poster with the mustaches and finger pointing at him, cleverly placed near the shipyard gates. He continued walking, lost in thought, a frown deepening under the lick of dark brown hair that covered his brow. He knew his father wouldn't be happy with it and that worried him—his dad had suffered a lot of loss in his life, and he didn't want him upset again. But the seed had germinated. He looked up and saw the recruiting office on the street corner and hesitated, crippled with indecision. Then turning, he crossed the threshold and went over to the line of men waiting to be signed up.

As he stood in line, still agonizing if he was doing the right thing, he saw a familiar head of curly red hair. It managed to distract him from his dilemma while he tried to remember who it was—then it came to him. He'd seen that red hair and protruding ears in Hardinge Street School. The owner had been a class ahead of him, and if he could remember rightly, his name was Kelly. After signing up, everyone was told to report the following day, and then ordered to disperse. Vincent and Kelly nodded to each other and went their separate ways.

"Why?" his father asked. "Why would you join up? You don't have to, there's no conscription."

"Because I believe it's the right thing to do," Vincent answered. "And, if we are fighting alongside the Protestant Ulstermen, maybe we might bury our differences and learn to live together."

"I don't believe that will ever happen," his father said, "it goes too deep for that. I grant you, in the short term if you're fighting alongside them, it will be different, but once you all come back here, the old wounds will open up again."

"But if enough Irishmen join up, maybe they might consider bringing in Home Rule for the Island," Vincent said. "Besides, they say it won't be a long war, they're saying it'll be over by Christmas."

"*Pshaw!*" his father bridled. "Listen, Vincent, I'll buy you out, you don't have to go. Just think about it." Although he knew that once Vincent had made up his mind, that was it.

With a stubbornness that characterized him throughout his life, and no doubt helped him survive the coming years, Vincent held his ground. An innate sense of adventure beckoned, and he was determined to go through with it.

The following day, his dad brought up the topic again, and again Vincent stood his ground.

Patrick, sitting at the head of the breakfast table, remembering how he felt at that age, shook his head and said, "If you have to do it son, just make sure you do a good job and I'll be rightly proud of you."

The outcome was that Vincent found himself in a queue of other young and not so young Ulstermen going for their medical exam, and once again he bumped into his former schoolmate, Kelly.

Vincent was 20 years of age, and at 136 pounds, five-feet-eight-inches tall, he was fit and healthy. Now that he'd made his decision, he looked forward to a world that held opportunities unavailable to a young Catholic man in Protestant-dominated Ulster.

To him it was a good choice. He signed up with the 122nd Field Company of the Royal Engineers. The recruiters, seeing his skills as a fitter, assigned him that trade and the rank of "Sapper" and the description of "Iron Turner, Skilled". This required a test, which he passed comfortably under the supervision of John McDougall, at his engine shop. He would continue doing what he did best. Next, he was given his uniform, and as was the ubiquitous practice at the time, had his photograph taken.

He reported to the training camp at Clandeboye, Co. Down. As fortune would have it, Kelly and Vincent ended up in the same company of Royal Engineers, 122nd F.C. The former, who was a carpenter by trade, also worked in the shipyard. He introduced himself as "John", and, in the course of their conversation, Vincent found out that he came from the Short Strand district of Belfast. Opposites attract, they say, and this guaranteed a close friendship between the two.

Vincent was dark haired, almost black, with an untidy lock always hanging across his broad forehead. He was quiet in demeanor, some would say soft; he was soft in the way a tree bends with the wind, but never breaking.

John was a bit taller than Vincent, with a mop of curly red hair; his freckled face reflected good humor, but he had a short temper too, which got him in a lot of trouble.

Vincent's innate calm, perfectly balanced John's impulsiveness, while John's quick thinking got the pair out of many a scrape.

Not long after they arrived at Clandeboye, the first fly appeared in the ointment. Most new recruits there were UVF[12] men—devoted to protecting Protestant Ulster from Home Rule—or "Rome Rule", as they called it—with the rest of Ireland at any cost. From the start there was a tension between them and the Catholic recruits, resulting in frequent and sometimes violent conflict. John Kelly, with his quick temper, was usually to be found in the middle of these battles.

After Vincent had pulled his mate out of one too many fights with the "Prods," the officers in charge of training decided to transfer the two lads and a few other "Sinn Feiners"[13] to a training center in the South of Ireland. They were reassigned to the 75th Field Company Royal Engineers which was based at a training camp in Kilworth, near the town of Fermoy in County Cork.

• • •

When the train with the transferred soldiers arrived at Fermoy[14] Station, it was already dark. They were met by a lorry with a sergeant sitting next to the driver. He jumped out and got them organized with their kit into the back of the truck. There were six of them—in addition to Vincent and Kelly, there was Andrew Beale, one of the older recruits at 27, Sam McLaughlin, Kevin Collins, and Dan Dooley.

All were from Belfast and its environs.

It was freezing cold, sprinkles of snow covering the wooden seats in the back, which was open to the air. Try as they might, they couldn't keep warm, and by the time they arrived at their quarters,

---

12 Ulster Volunteer Force; set up by Edward Carson, a Northern Irish politician, with the intention of preventing by armed force the introduction of a self-governing United Ireland.

13 Sinn Fein, meaning "We Ourselves" in Gaelic was a political party founded in 1905, whose manifesto was the assertion of Irish National Sovereignty and self-determination. The UVF was in direct opposition to them.

14 Fermoy is a town in County Cork, Ireland.

their extremities were numb. Regardless of their discomfort, the sergeant jumped out and shouted for them to form a line and come to attention. He introduced himself as "Sergeant Pring" and would be their training sergeant for the next six months. He was a short, stocky individual, veteran of many wars, whose brown, wrinkled face gave little away. After five minutes standing there in the snow, with no sound but their chattering teeth, a figure marched out of the hut, and approaching them, walked along the line inspecting each one with a glittering eye. Not a word was spoken. Pacing up and down, with hands behind his back, the martinet suddenly turned to face them.

Walking right up to Kelly, he went nose to nose with him and shouted in a broad Dublin accent, "Do you know what 'nemesis' means, you bloody Belfast bastard?"

"Er...no sir!"

"Well, I'll tell yez, ya carrot-haired piece of ratshit!" he said, spittle forming at the corners of his mouth, as he warmed to his harangue, steel blue eyes two inches from Kelly's. "Nemesis," he said, head swiveling from left to right, "was the Goddess of Vengeance. Retribution if you like. And *I'm* going to be your fucking Nemesis!"

As the martinet looked to the left, a voice to his right muttered, "Some goddess."

Ignoring the comment, he went on, his face still in Kelly's, who was choking on whiskey fumes from his breath, "I'm CSM[15] Elliot," he said, resuming his pacing. "If you didn't like it in Clandeboye, you're going to fucking hate it here. I'm going to turn you bunch of weeds into soldiers if it kills me, but it'll probably kill yez all first."

The group studied the CSM as he stood there, letting his words sink in. He was about Vincent's height, and everything about him was ramrod straight. His back was, "Like someone shoved a poker up his arse," Beale, one of the other recruits, later remarked. His bushy, greying eyebrows were straight, his nose was straight, and his thin-lipped, steel-trap mouth was straight as well. When he addressed them, he leaned slightly forward as if he was going to jump right inside them and devour them from the inside out.

"Christ," Vincent thought. "I'll take Clandeboye any day."

Without another word, Elliot saluted Pring, turned round and stamped off. Both Elliot and Pring were Boer War veterans—men who knew and understood the horrors of war, who were determined their recruits would be as prepared as possible to endure what would meet them in France. They were opposites in temperament, Pring being softer but still firm; between them they would mold these young men into professional soldiers.

Pring marched them to their quarters, a concrete block hut that was only slightly warmer than the sub-zero temperatures outside. There was a coal stove lighting in the center and not surprisingly the beds either side of it were already occupied by recruits who had joined

---

15 Company Sergeant Major.

two months ago. Pring introduced Corporal Ned Duggan, who was in charge of the section. Duggan was a small, skinny fellow, fair in color, and if it was not for his thin nose, his eyes would have touched, they were so close together. They later discovered he had family in nearby Fermoy and would contrive to slip away home every opportunity he could. He showed them where they could hang up their wet gear, and having done that, they got under the few blankets laid out on their cots and lay shivering until gradually they warmed up.

At six the next morning, Reveille sounded, bringing Pring bursting through the door and thus their day began.

For the first two months, it was all drills, musketry, classes, and every weekend, route marches. As the weather began to improve, they focused more on the engineering work, trench digging, laying wire by day, and then, by night, carrying their equipment in silence over broken ground in the dark, building temporary bridges, cutting wire, and honing all the skills they would need in France when they got there.

They were kept busy building a system of trenches, dugouts, and machine gun posts that were going to be used by the Irish Guards company training alongside them. Even though he was signed on as a fitter, Vincent didn't escape the hard manual labor that was expected of them all; in a time when mechanical diggers were unheard of, the shovel and pickaxe were the only tools available for digging.

As time went by, Vincent and John made friends among the men they would remain in company with for the next four years, though beyond doubt they would lose some of them too.

They spent the spring and early summer of 1915 at Kilworth training camp, missing the BEF's first retreats in front of the German onslaught. Names like Liege, Ypres, Namur were coming through in the newspapers; all collapsing in the path of the mighty German war machine. The Belgians' heroic defense of Liege and Namur were no match for the massive howitzers brought up to flatten them. Atrocities were committed by the vengeful German army, who found they needed to fight hard instead of the easy passage through Belgium they had anticipated.

Things weren't looking too good for the allies, nor for the Germans as their progress ground to a slow halt only 30 miles from Paris. In fact, it began to look like the engineering company's training in digging trenches might come into good use. At that stage a few butterflies were starting to flutter in the trainees' stomachs at the idea of finally coming eye to eye with the hardened Teutonic warriors facing down British and French armies. But they were young men, secure in the belief that they could handle anything the Germans could throw at them.

• • •

However good or bad the life in Kilworth training camp was, with leave in Fermoy and enjoying the fine bars there, it came to an end on the 19th of June.

The first entry in the 75th Field Company's War Diary by company CO, Major A. Rolland, was this:

Moore Park, Kilworth.
19/7/1915;
75th Field Co. R.E. received orders to mobilize.

CHAPTER 4

Mobilization

"To be willing to give when there's no more to give
  To be willing to die so that honor and justice may live."

(Mitch Leigh. Lyrics from "The Impossible Dream")

HOUSTON, TEXAS
April 2003

Dog tired, we opened the front door of our Houston home to the welcome smell of baked salmon and roast potatoes. Our eldest son, Simon, had prepared a splendid meal, which we washed down with a nicely chilled bottle of Chardonnay.

We had just finished the three-day drive from San Diego, where we had gone to see our youngest son, a US Marine, off to war. He was among the earlier troops deployed on Operation Iraqi Freedom. Never a pleasant time for parents. Simon, a self-taught culinary artist, was staying with us while he went to college. After the meal we sat down to relax, never suspecting a thing.

Then he pulled out a card from his shirt pocket and handed it to his mother, Terry—an ID for Private Simon McCann. He'd joined the army. This, when the U.S. had just gone to war with Iraq. Dear God, what are these kids thinking? At least James had joined the Marines before 9/11 and war fever took a hold. While Simon's motives were altruistic, that was scant consolation to parents who were planning to send food parcels to one son already at war. Now we faced the prospect of two sons going to the battlefield and hoping day by day that they were OK.

The point is, young people don't overly concern themselves about their parent's feelings, when they decide to do something that seems to them like a great idea.

In truth, Vincent *had* been concerned about how his father would take it, but he felt that he had to go and do his bit. They were told it would be over by Christmas. His father, reading the news every day, had followed the retreat of the BEF from Mons and the terrible casualties they suffered. The Battle of the Marne was in full flow with about 50,000 soldiers on each side, dead or injured. Stories of this and other battles filled the newspapers, and the prospects looked grim for both sides. The "Brilliant Strategist" General Schlieffen's plan was in tatters. The Entente[16] forces had only just managed to recover from a disastrous retreat. This was shaping up to be a long, costly, and very deadly war—not the three months escapade governments predicted it would be. Nobody knew who would win, and what the final casualty toll would be like. Patrick tried reasoning with his son, but the deed was done.

Vincent was Sapper McCann, Royal Engineering Corps, regimental number *57563*.

• • •

The dark face of warfare had changed; regrettably not always recognized by the upper echelons of military command. These

16 Britain, France, and Russia were known as the "Triple Entente" and Germany, Austria-Hungary, Bulgaria etc. were known collectively as the "Allies."

lessons would be learned to their cost, and more tragically, to the cost of their soldiers, and those waiting at home for them to return. Since the Boer War, the automobile and its commercial cousin, the truck, had come onstage. In many other ways warfare had become more mechanized. Although the machine gun had been around for a long time, it had been developed to where it was used to devastating effect against the traditional lines of soldiers marching across the battlefield. Small arms had improved accuracy and range. Artillery was bigger, more precise, and effective. Motor and steam-driven transportation had arrived on the scene, creating mobile armies that could cover greater distances faster; extending lines of supply. Railroads enabled huge amounts of ammunition and supplies to be brought quickly to the front. Aircraft were making their debut over the French and Belgian battlefields. The battle tank would later make its appearance at the Somme. These modern armies were forced to adapt quickly and rely heavily on their engineering battalions.

Without the Engineers there would have been no supplies to the armies; they maintained the railways, roads, vehicles, water supply, bridges, and transport. There would have been no communications, because the Engineers on both sides maintained the telephones, wireless, and other signaling equipment and indeed, the first flying corps also came under the Royal Engineers. Cover for the infantry and gun redoubts for the artillery depended on the companies of engineers attached to each division. It fell to their technical skills to develop responses to chemical and underground warfare. Little wonder that the Royal Engineers supporting the British army grew into a large and complex organization. Vincent was a small cog in this very large machine.

• • •

MOORE PARK MILITARY CAMP, KILWORTH CO. CORK, IRELAND
July 1915

Rumors and gossip were common currency in the camp. Training had soaked up their lives for the last eight months and at this stage they despaired of ever going to war. The repetition of drills and exercises was getting on everyone's nerves, resulting in a palpable tension. In the heat of July, reading about the battles fought at Mons and the Marne, Gallipoli and on the Eastern Front, the lads all wanted to be part of it. If they had to sweat digging trenches, then they'd rather do it for real.

It wasn't just the men who were training. The subalterns were mostly young men fresh out of college or who may not even have finished. They had no leadership experience, beyond maybe being captain of the cricket team and lacked the other requisite skills needed to command a section of sappers in battlefield conditions. In addition to laying wire, learning trench and dugout structure, and other tasks, they had to learn navigation using the trench maps supplied by the ordnance corps.

This latter was proving a problem for Second Lieutenant Ure.

Henry Ure was tall, a tad under six feet, loose limbed and a bit on the awkward side. Nonetheless, he was very popular with both the men in his section and the other officers. But he did have a problem, which he did his best to conceal. Henry had directional dyslexia. When he needed to turn left, he turned right, often resulting in confusion during drills, with his section going one way while he marched off in the opposite direction. There are people like that who function perfectly well in every respect, except when it comes to navigation. Major Rolland, the CO, suspected things were not quite right when Ure's section arrived back after a navigation exercise, two hours after all the others came in. After that he would put one of the experienced NCOs with him—usually sergeant Adams.

Despite small problems like this, they became a well-coordinated unit, eager to try out their skills on the battlefield, but at times they felt the army had forgotten them. Still, it had its advantages, especially the excellent level of hospitality in the nearby town of Fermoy, of which they availed most weekends.

• • •

You could have cut the fug of cigarette and pipe smoke with a knife in Fitzgibbons Bar, where Sergeant Pring, his ruddy face growing more rubicund with each fresh bottle of porter that appeared in front of him. He was regaling the table with the story of "The Angels of Mons", as if he'd been there on the battle line himself when the spectral warriors came to the rescue of the retreating British troops. The other lads around the table were in thrall. Pring knew how to tell a great story, and rarely had to buy his own beer.

"There we was … " He gazed into space, recalling the scene he had gleaned from the newspapers. "An' Fritz were pushing towards us, while we dragged our dead an' wounded to safety. This was it, we thought, this is the end of the game … " A master of the dramatic pause, Pring looked around at the expectant faces, and continued. "When suddenly we saw these ghostly figures on white horses, armed wi' bows 'n arrows, charging the Hun, who stopped and then turned and ran for their fuckin' lives … " Another pause. "We was able to get ourselves rallied, and pulled back withou' no interference from the Jerries. Ah, Jaysus, ye shoulda seen it. A whole army of ghosts."

They'd all heard it before, but Pring, an old hand and expert raconteur, was the embodiment of the old *sheanchaidhe*.[17]

---

17 Traditional Irish storyteller.

It was well attested that during the fiercely fought battle, while the outnumbered and exhausted British troops were retreating to the south, fighting their way through trees and brush, a mysterious group of ghostly horsemen were seen charging towards the enemy. They advanced against the attacking Germans, scattering them and allowing the weary soldiers to get away. As another bottle of porter was brought to the table, he took a long pull, warming to the tale of these spectral angels, mounted on snorting battle horses, armed with short bows.

"Did they have wings, Sarge?" asked one lad from Dublin.

"Aye lad, some say they did; proper angels they were," replied the Sarge, stifling a smile. Then, *maybe they did have bloody wings,* he thought.

This story of the "Angels" had been popular in the British papers and helped build morale after the long retreat south, almost to the suburbs of Paris. Strange things happened on the battlefield.

Vincent and John sat at the table with their drinks, smoking a Capstan[18] and smiling at the old campaigner earning his beer. They were tired after another day's labor. In addition to the usual route marches and drill, they had built a network of trenches and mock strong points, developing a realistic battlefield in the Irish countryside.[19] They worked in their undershirts in the summer heat, sweating and complaining, developing the expertise that would be used over the next four years. They were young lads, and they wanted to get out of here and move on to where the action was, to the real trenches. One can only take so much training while other soldiers are on the front line in the thick of the action.

18 These were Vincent's favorite cigarettes.

19 This was used for units of the 16th Irish Division, who were also training at Kilworth.

As they walked the three miles back to the camp in the waning light, Vincent savored the soft damp smell of the Irish country air, with its hints of honeysuckle and gorse, bringing back memories of his childhood. He sensed in his gut that that childhood was over now, and his life was about to change.

That was Saturday, July 17, 1915.

• • •

The following Monday dawned bright and sunny. At noon, the men were ordered to assemble on the parade ground. They stood around, singly and in groups, smoking and chatting. In the July heat their jackets were off, collars undone, the mood one of relaxed expectation. The buzz of speculation slowly died as their commanding officer, Major Rolland, came out of his office, the orders slip in his hand, and a silence descended on the men.

Looking around him, Rolland saw a group of soldiers, whom he, his officers, and his NCOs had brought from rough to multi-faceted diamonds.

But, he thought, *the final polishing won't happen until they get to France.* He drew a deep breath, relishing the drama of the moment and announced that their company was to be mobilized and would leave for France in August.

Going back to work, Vincent absently pulled a cigarette out of a pack and offered one to John. They stood together; hands cupped around the match as they lit up.

With the smoke curling up around his eyes, Vincent said, "Well now John, what's going on in your mind?"

"Mmmm … I'm thinking we're going to be putting all this trainin' to use at last, Vinnie, but no doubt laddie, it'll be tough," he replied. Then, lifting his cap, he scratched his head and stared at the cloudless blue sky, continuing pensively, "I wouldn't wonder that some of us won't be coming home after it."

"I've been reading the newspapers too, and the 'Killed in Action' pages are getting more 'n more," Vincent said morosely, sucking nervously on his cigarette.

"I know, but there's no point 'n worrying about the future, is there, when we don't even know where we're going. Which reminds me, I must send a few lines to me mama…"

John stubbed his fag[20] out on the ground, seeing CMS Elliot approaching with a murderous look on his face, and the two of them got back to work, their brows creased in thought.

They all wondered what would happen when they got out there. The vision they had was colored by the dramatic newspaper reports coming back from the front, which were sometimes a long way from reality. Vincent felt they would see action in the very near future. A sudden frisson caused the hairs to stand up on the back of his neck.

News was coming back about the fighting in Ypres, a small town in Belgium none of them had ever heard of. Would they be sent there? There was talk about a new Guards Division being formed and they would be part of it. The Guards were elite fighting men, though to be honest, most had been killed or wounded in the earlier fighting, and the ranks were filling with more and more raw recruits like themselves. But their discipline and training were legendary. The men talked about little else, provoking a sense of anticipation that altered the mood throughout the camp. They stood in little groups chatting and the different personalities began to show themselves. Some—the less imaginative, probably—were excited, some fearful, some apparently indifferent, standing around scratching their arses wondering what they were doing here. There was much bravado on

---

20 British slang for cigarettes.

display. None had any idea that those who survived would be out there for almost four life-changing years.

As the warmth of July merged into the thunderstorms of early August, the men were kept busy doing drills, training, and getting equipment and horses ready for the arduous journey ahead. CSM Elliot's shouts were heard all over the camp, as he cajoled and threatened, pushing the already stressed men to the limit. A few quietly disappeared over time, regretting their impulsive decision to join up, and melted into the Irish countryside. "Good riddance," Sergeant Pring would say, they weren't worth going after, though the military police were out searching for them. Drills for entraining[21] and detraining were carried out with great precision, for the logistics of moving a company of men, animals, wagons, and machinery was complex.[22]

The company was organized into two groups: mounted (including the CQMS, farrier, shoeing smith, bugler, 3 NCOs, and the drivers and batmen), and the rest were dismounted, which included trades such as blacksmiths, bricklayers, carpenters, fitters, clerks, masons, painters, plumbers, surveyors, draftsmen, wheelwrights, engine drivers, and others. They still relied a lot on horse-drawn wagons for transport and had an establishment of seventeen riding horses for the officers and NCOs, plus fifty-five draught horses and four pack horses or mules. Increasingly, mechanized transport was

---

21 The military term for getting 200 men, with their horses, wagons, and equipment, smoothly and efficiently onto the train.

22 In 1915, each infantry division included two or three field companies of engineers. There were about 200 men in a company; the CO was usually a major, sometimes a captain as second in command, with four lieutenants, each in charge of a section. There were twenty-three NCOs (Company Sergeant-Major, Company Quartermaster Sergeant, Farrier Sergeant, six Sergeants, seven Corporals, and seven 2nd Corporals—a rank peculiar to the engineers. There were 186 other ranks (OR) consisting of one shoeing smith, one bugler, 138 sappers, thirty-seven drivers, and eight batmen. In France they would also have an interpreter attached to the company.

being brought into use. Wagons accompanied them, carrying the diverse equipment needed for their work, ranging from shovels and picks to lathes and drilling machines. Except for the bugler, all the ranks were armed as infantrymen with the SMLE (Lee Enfield .303) rifle. They were expected to fight when called upon, and in many instances did in fact join the infantry in action. In the same vein, the infantry had their own labor squads known as "Pioneers," who often worked with the Engineers with the sappers supervising.

On Friday, August 13, they left Kilworth Camp and entrained at Fermoy. The station was full of uniformed soldiers, sweating in the heat, cursing those that got in their way, loading their packs and gear on the train. It seemed to be an uncontrolled melee, but in fact there was an orderly boarding of the carriages, as the engine hissed and puffed, building up steam for the journey to Dublin. There was much muttering about leaving on Friday the 13th, but nonetheless, off they headed, packed like sardines into the stuffy train. John and Vincent managed to get a seat for themselves and looked across at each other. They just smiled and raised their eyebrows. Nothing more needed to be said.

CHAPTER 5

Saying Goodbye

They shall not say I went with heavy heart:
Heavy I am, but soon I shall be free,
I love them all, but oh I now depart
A little sadly, strangely, fearfully,
As one who goes to try a mystery.

(Robert Nichols. "Farewell")

FORT BRAGG, NORTH CAROLINA
December 14, 2006

Our son, Simon, was leaving on his first military deployment to Iraq.

He was packed into a bus, which would take them to the airfield, with the rest of his company. He'd managed to get a window seat at the back. We were standing there ready to wave goodbye. The window had steamed up with all the body heat and he wrote in the foggy window with his finger—"Somebody's farted," followed by a smiley face. Simon could always bring a bit of humor into any grim situation.

It was a similar situation that his grandfather endured on the train from Fermoy to Dublin, packed with troops, on a hot August day, smoking, farting, laughing, and fooling around. The whole group was tense with nervous excitement. Young Irish lads, some of whom had never left their hometown, were now off to war.

As Simon told me after he came home, "You're filled with a feeling of no control over what will happen to you in the coming months, you just get carried along."

• • •

DUBLIN, IRELAND
August 1915

Arrival at Dublin was followed by detraining and marching to the North Wall docks. On board the troopship, they continued their journey across the Irish Sea. For many, including Vincent, it was their first time on a ship at sea. Luckily, it was relatively calm. They arrived at Amesbury Station on the Salisbury Plain on the night of the 15th of August and marched to their camp at Rollestone. The following week was taken up with drills and preparing equipment and wagons for transport to France.

On August 22, they entrained for Southampton. There they marched along the docks and boarded the ship awaiting to bring them across the English Channel to France.

There was a feeling of anticipation in the air as they marched in orderly file on board the steamer, surrounded by the smells and noise of the docks, humming with wartime activity, as Kitchener's "New Army" was being mobilized to fight in France. Dockers were shouting and cursing as they loaded crates of weapons, food, and munitions. Farriers and drivers struggled with frightened horses leading them on board the SS Queen Alexandria, while black smoke belched from the ship's three funnels as the Engineers built up steam for the trip across the channel. The decks were crammed with sweating khaki-clad bodies jostling for a space to put their packs down. Finally, the gangway was lifted off and the crew busied themselves with letting go the moorings. With the last line cast off, water churned up at the stern as the turbines picked up speed and the black water between the ship and the berth widened, the bow pointing south towards Le Havre and the war.

Vincent and John leaned on the rail at the stern, watching mesmerized as the wake foamed behind the ship.

The latter looked down at the freckled backs of his hand and turned to Vincent with a smile. "This is where the fun starts Vinnie."

Vincent grinned back at John and replied, with his customary droll humor, "Aye ... I wonder where it'll end?"

After a while, they could feel the ship begin to roll gently in the swells coming up the English Channel, and the two of them walked unsteadily over to where they left their packs, and where they would spend the night.

For many, this would be their first time on the continent. The men settled down in tired groups, smoking, playing cards, anything to pass the long night. Fortunately, the weather was good, with just a low southwesterly swell causing a gentle roll as the ship ploughed its way towards France. They hoped the German submarines were hunting somewhere else. Many didn't feel like sleeping; others, who could sleep in any situation, found a quiet corner and curled up with their pack as a pillow.

Le Havre, bathed in the morning sun, greeted them as the ship glided through the piers of the outer harbor. For the first time they heard the French language spoken as the dock workers rushed on board to get the equipment off. Foreign smells greeted them as they disembarked, tired after sleeping with their heads on their packs, jammed between the huddled bodies of their comrades.

The horses were skittish after the sea crossing, so Vincent and John turned to help one of the drivers guide his two down and hitch them up to the machinery wagon. They had a vested interest, as this wagon contained equipment they'd be using later, and they wanted to see it get safely to their destination—wherever that may be. Vincent stayed with one horse, his hand on the bridle, calming it, empathizing with the animal. He threw his pack of equipment on the back of the wagon and walked along chatting to the driver, who rode on the other.

The Farrier Sergeant rode over and looked at what Vincent was doing and nodded approval.

"You stay with that horse, sapper. You've a way with him," he said, then turned and rode off up the train of carts.

"Beats marching with the others," Vincent thought, smiling to himself.

"I've seen yer around," the driver said as the horses moved forward. "Wot's yer name?"

"Vincent, though a few of them call me 'Vinnie.'" He looked up at the driver, sitting straight backed, moving gently in rhythm with the horse. He was a well-built lad, a few years older than Vincent, country bred, not showing that pasty look city dwellers had.

"What about you, then?" Vincent asked.

"My name's Basson," the driver said. "Billy. I'm from a place called Welford-on-Avon. It's on the River Avon 'n I'm sure ye've heard about Stratford-on-Avon, haven't ye? You know, where the poet Shakespeare lived?"

"Aye indeed, I have."

"Ah, it's a lovely little town. Grand pub there," he said, a dreamy look in his eyes. "I'd go there evenings after work and 'ave a pint. It's called The Bell. The story goes that Shakespeare was 'avin' a pint there wi' 'is friend Ben Johnson; ye 'eard of 'im haven't ye?"

Vincent nodded, though he hadn't a clue who Ben Johnson was.

"Well, the oul' bard was walkin' on 'is way back to Stratford, y'see, an' 'e caught a cold or pneumonia or sumpin', and next thing, 'e was dead!" Billy said it with some satisfaction at this claim to fame for his hometown. Then he looked at Vincent and quoted a well-remembered verse: " … *an' never to know for whom the bell tolls; it tolls for thee.*" Billy grinned at Vincent, relishing the play on words. "That was written by a chap called John Donne," he said. "Lovely poetry that fella … Shakespeare was well gone when that was written."

"I like a bit of poetry m'self," Vincent said. "In fact, I brought a book of poems by Robert Service with me. It's called *Rhymes of a Rolling Stone*. My father sent it to me a month ago … some say it's not real poetry, just doggerel, but I don't care, it's good enough for me."

The conversation went on—poetry, their homes, their families, and of course the war itself. A few hours had slipped by when they suddenly realized they were at the camp, as the progress slowed in front of them. The roads were dry, and they were covered in dust, hot and sweaty, though the evening was cooling down. They hadn't eaten since breakfast, but the kitchen wagon would be getting food ready. In the meantime, they had to feed the horses and bed them down for the night.

"C'mon and we'll get these nags tied up and fed," Billy said, co-opting Vincent as an unofficial driver. The latter didn't seem to worry and the two of them got to work.

It was evening by the time they got to Camp Number Five, which was up near the cliffs overlooking the port. They only managed a few hours' sleep before they were roused again at just after three in the morning to march back to Le Havre and board a train which, according to the scuttlebutt, would take them to Lumbres.

There they would join up with the First Guards Brigade.

• • •

LUMBRES, NORTHERN FRANCE
August 24, 1915

They spent the night bivouacked in a field beside the station. Vincent, John, and Billy shared a tent. After they had put their gear away and eaten, there was a bit of time where they were able to sit and chat.

The scent of the late summer evening lingered, and insects were drawn to the tilly lamp as they smoked and talked quietly about their lives before they joined the army.

"What'd y'do before you signed up?" John asked Billy.

"Horses mostly, worked for different farriers. Stables too, some farm work… anythin' I could get." Billy smiled—he had a grin that lit up his round face. "I like animals, would've been a vet if I'd 'ad the schoolin', but this is the first full-time job I've 'ad." Then, looking down at his feet, he said, "I wish I'd list'n'd to my mum though. She wanted me to go on in school, but I was mad keen t'work." Then he looked at them. "But this," he waved his hand around. "S'truth, I wouldn't miss it fer anything."

"What'd you lads do?" he asked, and John told him all about the shipyard.

"Vinny was a fitter," he said, "working on the big engines for the ships. I was a carpenter. I worked in the shop mostly."

"Bloody hell," Billy said. "That must've been interestin'. Were ye's there when they built the Titanic?"

Vincent wasn't saying much, having drifted once again into a reverie, leaving most of the talking to John and Billy. He was a thinker really, just sat there looking at the others, staying on the edge of the conversation, wondering what it must have been like for Billy, working on the farms like that.

Stubbing his ciggy out, he stood and stretched, feeling his calves ache, and said, "We should turn in lads, it'll be an early start tomorrow." And he was right.

Starting in the morning of the 25th, they marched to Ècuire where they joined up with the First Guards Brigade.[23]

---

23 Just for the record, there are around 400-500 men to a battalion, and four battalions formed a brigade. Three brigades formed a Division and two divisions an Army Corps.

FORMATION OF GUARDS DIVISION IN 1915

Lord Kitchener sat down and gave some thought,
As to exactly how, this war be fought,
There's not enough troops and not enough guns,
To do battle right now, with the terrible Huns.
So, he scratched his head, and picked his nose,
Put his chin in his hand in a Rodin like pose,
He twirled his mustache, then it came in a flash,
The Guards, the Guards, derring-do and panache.
They're fighting men, courageous and brave,
Brought together in France, the country they'll save.
I'll go to the King, and his blessing I'll ask,
To give to these men this honorable task.
By Jove, with the Guards, we'll trample the Bosche,
With General's French and Haig, Joffre and Foch,
We'll chase them, erase them, show them who's tough,
With the Guards at their heels, they'll soon cry "Enough!"

(Derek McCann. "The Guards")

In July 1915, nearly a year into the war, His Majesty King George V approved the formation of a Guards Division on the advice of his Minister of War, Lord Kitchener. The latter, whose brainchild this was, went ahead with the arrangements without any discussion with the war cabinet or the Commander-in-Chief of the BEF. Kitchener named the Earl of Cavan, Field Marshal Frederick Rupert Lambart, as the commander of said Guards Division.

On the 16th of July, as the 75th Field Company was being mobilized, Kitchener ordered the 3rd and 4th Grenadier Guards, 2nd Irish Guards, and 1st Welsh Guards battalions to be prepared for overseas service. They were to move to France immediately, where they would join those battalions already in service. The Guards' Division was composed of highly experienced soldiers, which would prove an advantage in the fighting in France and an example to the other newly minted troops of "Kitchener's 2nd Army." In August 1915 the divisions were formed at Lumbres, near St Omer, France. Each had three companies of Royal Engineers attached to them, and the 75th, 76th, and 55th Field Companies found themselves with the 1st and 2nd Brigades of Guards.

The 75th Field Company remained billeted at Ècuires until September 10, by which time the blisters on their feet had healed and they were enjoying the hospitality of the little French town. There was a degree of mutinous muttering when they got orders to move on to Herbelle and were put in new billets there. Here, they actually got to work for the first time and were kept busy in lining out trenches around the town of Herbelle and neighboring villages, putting their Irish training into practice. On the 19th of the month, they marched back to their billets in Ècuires.

There was a lot of marching—there were a lot of sore feet.

75th Field Company War Diary
September 22, 1915.
Company marched to Audington.

September 23, 1915.
Company marched to Nedonchelle where they were billeted.

September 25, 1915.
Arrived and bivouacked at Neoux.

September 26, 1915.
Company left Neoux and arrived at Vermelles.

• • •

On September 25, the Battle of Loos began.

CHAPTER 6

The Western Front

"This war, like the next war,
is a war to end all wars."

(David Lloyd George. British Prime Minister. 1916)

On the 1st of August, 1914, with threatening thunderstorms and the generally unsettled weather matching the mood of the politicians, Germany began its ravishment of Western Europe.

Hordes of grey-clad troops marched across the border into the town of Troisvierges, in Luxembourg, taking the railway station; though hardly a major accomplishment, this was essential for them to move supplies into France.

Three days later, at precisely 8am, the armies of Generals Alexander Von Kluch and Karl Von Bülow, in accordance with the Schlieffen Plan, marched into Belgium, leaving the British government with no option but to declare war on Germany. The plan's strategy, displaying unparalleled Prussian arrogance, erroneously assumed the Belgian army would peacefully allow the Germans to march through their country, offering no resistance.

The Belgians thought otherwise. What followed resulted in the all-critical timetable of the plan being delayed to where six weeks stretched into four years.

A miscalculation of this magnitude on the chess board would have gotten a chess master merely laughed at, but on the checkerboard of Europe, the consequences were catastrophic and began a conflict that dragged on interminably, costing millions of young men's lives, wrecked the German economy and changed the World Order forever. For the Belgians, under their plucky ruler, Albert I, gave a spirited resistance initially centered at the fortified town of Liege. It was no match for the giant rail-borne 400-millimeter mortars which were brought in and installed around the forts surrounding the town. But it slowed the massive German troop movement down, ruining the rigid and inflexible timetable.

After flattening the several feet thick, reinforced concrete structures at Liege and Namur, the Germans marched through Belgium, meeting further resistance from the newly arrived British Expeditionary Force at Mons, whom they forced into retreat and continued to gain control of the vital industrial regions of Belgium, and Northern France. The seemingly unstoppable Teutonic Armies in grey were only 40 miles outside Paris before their advance came to a grinding halt.

The German troops had over-extended their supply lines to where they couldn't get food, munitions and all the other supplies needed to keep an army on the road. The nearest railhead was 80 miles to the rear in Belgium, and horse-drawn transport could not adequately bridge the gap across the muddy battlefields. The Schlieffen plan had failed.

The increasingly exhausted German troops faced stiffening resistance as the French used their well-developed rail network around Paris to assemble a new army to protect the capital. The government even commandeered all the Paris taxis to ferry the troops to the front line. A division of men needed about 1,000 tons of supplies per day, which would mean two trains with almost 50 wagons. The two armies pushing back the British and French had about thirty divisions between them. With a gap of 80 miles to bridge, the supply chain broke down, leaving no option but to retreat. In addition, the Belgians had continuously sabotaged the communications system, so much so that the separate German armies were unable to consult with each other. One didn't know what the other was doing.

It was time to regroup. The chastened invaders had to turn their back on the ultimate prize, Paris, and march back the way they came, until they dug in at the River Aisne.

The tide of the German advance was dramatically turned with the Battle of the Marne—a river in Northern France flowing roughly east-west, where the French and British rallied and both sides fought each other to a standstill. The outcome was that the Germans entrenched themselves in a line stretching from the Swiss border with France, up into Belgium as far as Ypres and the canal connecting the city to the coast. This was followed by the "Race to the Sea," wherein the armies of both sides tried to outflank each other, trying to gain command of the North Sea coast of Belgium and France. Both sides remained dug in along a meandering line of fortified trenches, which changed little until late 1917 and into 1918.

It was like a stalemate in chess. Had common sense prevailed at that point, millions of lives would have been saved.

• • •

General Sir John French was Commander in Chief of the BEF in 1915 when, with the French army under Général Joseph Joffre, an attempt was made to drive back the Germans from their heavily fortified trench system and breach the front line.

The plan was for the British army to support the left flank of the French, who were carrying out a major offensive in Champagne and Artois. Joffre felt the numerical superiority of his army would affect a decisive breakthrough in the German Front Line. While the French were focusing their efforts on the heights of Vimy Ridge, the British were expected to advance into the coal basin below, in the sector of Loos-Hulluch.

Having walked the trenches, Generals Haig and French had serious doubts about the wisdom of attacking the Germans in such a well defended position. However, they were told to go ahead by Lord Kitchener, who in turn had been persuaded of the importance of a British attack in this sector by Joffre. They had six divisions, exhausted by the fighting earlier in the year and hampered by an insufficient supply of shells. Munition production in England had not kept pace with the consumption in France.

But the attack was to go on, at any cost. It became known as "The Big Push", or the Battle of Loos. Several days before the attack, a continuous preliminary bombardment began showering 250,000 high explosive shells on the German lines. The intention was to terrify the enemy and tear up the protective wire in front of the trenches. Neither plan worked that well. Though the defending Germans were stunned, the tangles of barbed wire remained, in most areas, very much intact, which the attacking troops only discovered when they were charging across No-Man's Land.

25th of September 1915:
"In many places British artillery had failed to cut the German wire in advance of the attack. Advancing over open fields, within range of German machine guns and artillery, British losses were devastating.

The British were able to break through the weaker German defenses and capture the town of Loos-En-Gohelle, mainly due to numerical superiority. Supply and communications problems, combined with the late arrival of reserves, meant that the breakthrough could not be exploited."
    —Edmonds' *History of the Great War* (1928) pp 163-167

CHAPTER 7

The Generals

With their bristling moustaches
And their arrogant pride,
They strode with panache,
While the soldiers died.

(Derek McCann. "The Generals")

CHANTILLY, FRANCE
September 1915

Officers stood around in small groups, chatting animatedly, in the "Salle à Manger" of the Villa Poiret, where Général Joffre had his personal quarters. The genteel mansion was only a short walk from the Grand Quartier-Général (GQG) and was the venue chosen to discuss the forthcoming push against the Germans.

Conversations stopped abruptly as the door swung open to admit a man of generous proportions, whose round, humorous face, radiated imperturbability and "*cran*",[24] qualities so admired in the French military. The chair, at the head of the long mahogany table groaned in protest as the general sat down heavily. Covering the table from end to end was a detailed three-dimensional diorama of the

---

24 French word meaning "grit".

front line, stretching from Loos to Arras. Engineers had been busy, using modeling clay for the topography and bits of wood representing buildings—even trees were shown. Being an engineer himself, he was meticulous with detail, and he had no intention of anything going wrong this time.

At sixty-two, Joseph Joffre, or "Papa Joffre," as he was fondly known, was in overall charge of the French Army on the Western Front. Chunky of build, his large belly was at least partly responsible for his sobriquet; bushy grey eyebrows overhung hooded eyes, which gave him a sleepy appearance, but it would have been a mistake to underestimate this tough survivor of many battles, both military and political. His popularity with the French Government had waned since the failure of the French and British attacks during the second battle of Artois, and its companion assault further south in the district of Champagne during the summer.

Standing attentively opposite the diorama, Général Victor d'Urbal, commander of the French 10th army, looked tired. Things hadn't gone well during the summer, and now they were about to go through the same ordeal again. Aides-de-camp and senior commanders kept politely to the rear, while the two generals went over the battle plan.

The chief objective was to capture an escarpment about eight kilometers northeast of Arras, known as Vimy Ridge. Just below the ridge, on the model, was the small village of Souchez, represented by a matchbox with a 9mm bullet acting as a church spire.

After some silence, while he studied the diorama, Joffre ponderously stood up, and, leaning forward, rested his hands on the table and spoke.

"Gentlemen, this time we must take the ridge back. Let's not make the mistakes of last May. Général, how much artillery do we have available this time? And let's look at its disposition."

D'Urbal followed up with a display of heavy and light artillery, artfully using cigarettes to mark the different gun batteries. He ended by assuring Joffre that it would definitely be enough to cut the wire in front of the German defenses.

"I just hope the British do as well at Loos," Joffre remarked. "Believe it or not, they didn't want to attack there at all," he said in a tone of utter astonishment. "Haig and French said they would sustain too many losses. Do they think this is a tea party?" His voice went up half an octave. "*Au nom de Dieu, qu'est-ce qu'ils pensent?*[25] Our left flank would be at the mercy of the Bosche!" His mustaches quivered at the vehemence of his frustration.

"Hmph," was the utterance that summed up d'Urbal's contemptuous reply. "What was the outcome of that; will they attack?" he asked.

"*Oui … Oui*, they will … they will. I have spoken to Kitchener, and he has told them. But it is imperative we coordinate with them."

$$\bullet \; \bullet \; \bullet$$

25 "In the name of God, what do they think?"

CHATEAU PHILIOMEL, BEF ADVANCE HEADQUARTERS
September 24, 1915

The chandeliers were lit, even though it was ten in the morning. Little sunlight came through the tall sash windows; the somber effect enhanced by the book-lined walls surrounding the rich mahogany conference table. At one end stood a blackboard with an enlarged trench map, number 36c, NW, on a 1:20,000 scale. The top left portion showed the town of La Bassée, with its canal running east-west. Then, three miles to the south, Hulluch. In between was the formidable Hohenzollern Redoubt, a veritable fortress built on a huge slag dump, and occupied by the German 6th Army after the fighting in May. Further south was the town of Loos, also occupied by the Germans, and a little to the east another high point, Hill 70.

All around Loos, a coal mining town, were slag heaps, making excellent defensive positions for German machine gunners. Apart from these elevations, the surrounding countryside was as flat as the crêpes the occupant of the room enjoyed for his breakfast.

71

FIELD MARSHAL SIR JOHN FRENCH

Standing at the window, peering absently at the horses grazing in the pasture, Field Marshal Sir John French took out a cigar and clipped the end.

The same age as Joffre, he looked older, perhaps because of his cavalry background, and too much exposure to the sun in various African campaigns. His face was squarer, a strong jaw showing a determination which had brought him to the position of Commander in Chief of the BEF.

FIELD MARSHAL DOUGLAS HAIG

There was a knock on the door, and a soldier came in with a tray of freshly brewed Jamaican coffee, the Reed and Barton silver service and china cups a far cry from what the troops were using in the trenches twenty miles away. The servant was followed by General Sir Douglas Haig, commander of the British First Army, and General "Wully" Robertson, Chief of Staff of the BEF.

"Good morning, gentlemen," Sir John greeted them. "Coffee?"

After pouring the coffee, and some small talk, he offered them cigars, lit up his own and puffed to get it going. Then they got down to business.

"As you know, it appears Joffre will get his way, and we'll have to attack at Loos." French said, in his clipped Harrow[26] accent, waving a hand at the map. "I've had dispatches from Kitchener telling us to get on with it." As his face went a shade redder, he exclaimed, "Bloody Hell! Our hands are tied behind our damn backs, working with the French."

"Hm, I know, I know, and we'll undoubtedly suffer for it," Haig said mournfully in his Scottish brogue. "We do have one card up our sleeve though," he remarked, "but that depends on the weather, doesn't it?"

"Chlorine," Robertson supplied, unnecessarily, for it was the elephant in the room.

Haig stood and went over to the map. "I had hoped to keep the attack, if it comes to it, on a very narrow front, so we can concentrate our artillery fire. As you know, gentlemen, we're desperately short of shells." He said this looking at Robertson, who nodded in agreement.

"Y'see," said Haig, his vernacular coming out as he got more enthusiastic, "we're constrained by the start date. Joffre insists we attack on the 25th, which is understandable, as that's their planned

---

26 Harrow is one of the more prestigious boarding schools for boys in England.

date. But I don't know what the damned weather will be like. I don't know if we can use the gas."

"Perhaps Kitchener could ask the King for a westerly wind?" Robertson remarked with a smile.

"Um, yes," Haig said, his dour temperament intentionally missing the joke. "I've decided on two plans for the battle, depending on the conditions. If the wind is from the west, or southwest, I'll use the gas on a wide front, which should immobilize the enemy." He paused to let it sink in. "And if it doesn't cooperate, we'll keep the attack to a narrower front," he said, pointing with his cigar along the shorter section of the line. "At a later date, when the wind is suitable, we can use the gas, and widen the front."

He pulled on his cigar, and emitted a cloud of smoke, which blew conveniently across the map, like a cloud of gas, choking the German troops behind their lines.

"Either way, though, the attrition on our side will be terrible."

Robertson, who was one of the very few senior officers in the British military who rose up from the enlisted ranks, leaned back in his chair and said, "As far as logistics are concerned, we're facing a shortage of shells, which you just mentioned sir. I think we can have between 250,000 and 300,000 hauled up to the front all told." He went on to outline the different quantities of each size of shell. "Production is just not keeping up," he said. "But that's something that needs to be attended to."

French then spoke up. "As far as reserves are concerned, I'm going to use the Cavalry Corps, The Indian Cavalry Corps, and Haking's XI Corps." Both other men knew that the latter were mostly untried troops of Kitchener's "New Army." "You know the new Guards Division will be with Haking, and we should use them for the back up."

"I'm still shocked by the way Kitchener never even told us about the formation of the Guards Division," Robertson said. "The way he goes on, one would think he's running the war on his own."

"Do you mean I've no control over the reserves?" Haig asked, shocked.

"I'd rather keep that card in my hand for the moment," French replied, ignoring Haig's rolling eyes.

The meeting broke up after a couple of hours wrangling over the reserve troops, which the French insisted on holding control over. Haig and Robertson left just after noon, the former muttering under his breath, about the Commander-in-Chief's abilities.

As it turned out, the reserves were greatly delayed by the congestion on the roads combined with the desperately slow going in the rain and the quagmire the roads had become. This was to have a critical effect on the outcome of the battle.

• • •

HINGES CHATEAU, FORWARD HEADQUARTERS
September 25, 1915

The air in the room at two o'clock that morning was thick with enough cigar smoke to poison the entire German army. But the atmosphere of tension in the room was equally thick, passing from man to man, emanating like an invisible energy from the tall figure pacing up and down—too restless to sit for a moment.

On General Haig's shoulders rested the terrible responsibility of releasing hundreds of tons of chlorine gas, which, if the wind blew in the wrong direction, would annihilate his own troops instead of the enemy. On the other hand, if he didn't use the gas, his men would have to cross open ground, in full view of German machine guns on the surrounding slag heaps. They would be wiped out anyway.

What made it more galling was that the whole situation was not of his choosing; to the contrary, he had strongly advised against it.

Douglas Haig, son of the owner of Haig and Haig, distillers of fine Scotch whisky, was a cavalryman. He'd led charges with lance and sabre in Sudan and the Boer War. He'd come into the Twentieth Century skeptical of the use of machine guns and artillery.[27] Now, the windows of the chateau shook with the continuous thunder of howitzers just miles away, pounding the German defenses. The idea of using gas he found obnoxious, but he was forced into a corner, from which he couldn't escape. Either way he'd be damned.

Dawn would break at 6:30.

In the corner of the room, the ticking of the large Coromandel grandfather clock and the general's boots pacing on the wooden floor were the only sounds that broke the silence in the room. They were waiting for the weathermen to arrive. Just as the clock struck the half hour, the door was opened by an orderly and two subalterns walked in. Soaked and disheveled, realizing that everyone in the room was waiting for them, they reported to Haig.

"Sir. The wind is coming from between west and southwest, and, at the moment, it's quite steady …" the young officer recited as he consulted his sodden notes. "That said sir, it's likely to change a bit and go more to the west but will drop off some." Looking up, he paused nervously, then continued, "My feeling is that when the rain stops, the wind will change to the south, or die off altogether … That's what I'm thinking … Sir." His hand shook as he folded the notes and put them away.

---

27 Haig's boss, General French wrote in his book *1914;* "I feel sure in my own mind that had we realized the true effect of modern appliances of war in August, 1914, there would have been no retreat from Mons, and that if, in September, the Germans had learnt their lesson, the Allies would never have driven them back to the Aisne. It was in the fighting on that river that the eyes of all of us began to be opened."

Haig turned to the gas advisor, an R.E. major, who stood staring at a map on the table.

"What do you think, Major; if the wind changes, they won't let it off, will they?"

"Sir, as far as I know, unless you give an order to the contrary, we are to go ahead, that's our orders sir. That's what we understand. It's … *em* … General Gough's[28] orders …" he said, tapering off uncomfortably.

"Well, what do you advise?" Haig asked, turning to the weathermen again.

"Mm, er, sir, it's not really our job to advise *you* …" the senior of the two said, wishing the ground would open beneath him.

"Dammit," said Haig, "Somebody's got to make the decision—" He stopped suddenly, realizing they were all looking at him.

The uncomfortable weatherman went on, "Eh, I think, sir, that in view of the conditions, it should be as soon as possible, in view of the conditions, like, the wind being from the west now, an' all."

The worried general left the room without a word, and the occupants relaxed, sat down and lit fresh cigars.

As he walked up the stairs, Haig continuously remonstrated with himself over his indecision, but he had to know what the conditions would be. At the top he came to a heavy wooden door, which led to the outside, onto a tiled floor surrounded by a parapet. He was oblivious to the rain falling on his uncovered head and lit a cigarette. His throat was dry, from smoking and tension. He noticed the smoke was drifting towards the east, towards the enemy trenches.

He stared into the darkness and then said to himself, "We'll go with the gas." Turning, he stomped back down the stairs, went into the conference room, officers hastily jumping up from their chairs,

---

28 General Officer Commanding 1st Corps, in Haig's 1st Army.

and said to the messenger, "Tell General Gough …" He paused, not for dramatic effect, but giving himself one more chance to hold off. "To go ahead with the gas. Let it off at 5:50."

Then, turning abruptly, he left the room.

All during the day of the 24th, and into the night, it had been lashing rain, mostly from the west or southwest. This created a mess of mud and wet grass the troops had to run across. The ground was flat and the Germans occupied the little high ground there was.

At 5:50 in the morning on the 25th the wind was very light from the west and southwest when the gas was released.

The rain had stopped.

Dark green clouds of chlorine emerged from the cylinders as the Engineers, wearing heavy green box respirators, opened the valves; the gas moved slowly towards the German trenches and then lingered over No-Man's Land; to the north of the Hohenzollern Redoubt, it began to drift back over British trenches, choking the soldiers even before they could climb out of the trenches, causing hundreds of casualties on the British side. In a few places, it did have a devastating effect on German defenders.

At 6:30 the soldiers climbed out of the trenches and walked into a hail of machine gun fire. Just as General Haig had predicted. They did have successes, in some areas, capturing the town of Loos (9th Scottish Division),[29] but in other areas they were beaten back.

The losses were horrifying.

---

29 Scottish troops played a major role in capturing the town of Loos and Hill 70.

CHAPTER 8
A Great Deal of Nonsense

From wrath-red dawn to wrath-red dawn,
The guns have brayed without abate;
And now the sick sun looks upon,
The bleared, blood bolstered fields of hate
As if it loathed to rise again.
How strange the hush! Yet sudden, hark!
From yon down-trodden gold of grain,
The leaping rapture of a lark.

(Robert W. Service. "The Lark")

NORTHERN FRANCE
October 23, 2019

We were late. Again.

"S'truth," as driver Billy Basson would have said, we can never seem to get our act together regarding the planning of a journey. But this time, it was a bit critical; it was nine at night and dark for the past hour, as we negotiated the narrow streets of Lilliers in Northern France.

My driving had been hampered by frequent thunderstorms that had turned into a steady downpour. We'd sent a message ahead to the Chateau Philiomel that we were delayed, but there was no reply; the website said that after nine, there would be no one to check in guests. Finally, we were guided by the GPS along a dimly lit road to the place marked on the screen with the checkered flag. We stared in disbelief as the headlights, piercing the slanting rain, picked out two tall, gaunt, stone gate posts surrounded by tall trees; heavy iron gates led into a narrow driveway edged with untended grass. It looked abandoned. We were looking for a brightly lit French chateau, overlooking elegant gardens; instead, it seemed in the dark and rain like something out of a Hollywood horror film. The driveway seemed to go on forever, as we carefully negotiated our way. Then, as we rounded a bend, a man stood there with a large flashlight, holding an umbrella, waiting for us, and behind him a beautiful old-world chateau. Laughing with relief, we got out and introduced ourselves. All apologies.

Chateau Philiomel, headquarters of General Sir John French during the early part of the First World War, turned out to be everything we expected it to be. It was built in the early 19th Century by the great-great-grandfather of the man who welcomed us—Frédéric Devys.

The great-grandfather of Frédéric was in residence when the British requisitioned it and from where the General orchestrated the clash of imperial titans that was the Battle of Loos. It was just far enough behind the lines not to have been destroyed by shellfire, which is why it is still a usable building, and being run as an exclusive guest house. I thought, quite rightly as it turned out, that this would be a good place for us to stay while doing our research into the Battle of Loos.

Frédéric guided us inside and proudly told us the history of his family and the chateau, particularly its involvement in "*La Grande Guerre*". It took little imagination to hear the echo of military boots up and down the wooden central staircase, the clipped accents of officers waiting to meet with the general, and to sense the frisson as the battle raged twenty miles away. The high-ceilinged period decorated rooms retained their 19th Century mystique, drawing the occupant away from the accumulated stress of cellphones and laptops. After Frédéric left, we found ourselves the only human occupants, but the ghosts of past residents offered ample company; one could hardly tell if the creaks and groans were the old building resettling itself to the cool of the night air, or was that a footstep…?

The following morning, after a superb breakfast prepared by our host, we stepped outside through tall wooden doors. The aging and slightly neglected portico with its tall columns, revealed a large pasture with horses grazing, edging a large pond. On the left of the driveway, lay a wood of autumn-tinged, mature chestnuts and elms vying for space.

• • •

NORTHERN FRANCE
October 24, 2019

Winding its monotonous way through flat countryside, the D943 in Northern France hardly presented the most exciting drive, apart that is, from avoiding suicidal French drivers. The two-lane road brought us from Bethune toward the small town of Lens. As neatly tilled fields flashed by, we watched farmers busy harvesting the sugar beet crop, their huge tractors and trailers loaded with beet blocking the roadway. The picture of prosperity belied the muddy fields, wrecked villages, and impassable roads that the soldiers faced in 1915.

Before arriving at Lens, a lesser road veered to the left, taking us toward the small town of Loos-En-Gohelle. The surrounding countryside stretched to the horizon, the only variations in topography being two giant pyramid-like slag heaps which appeared on the horizon and the silhouette of a pithead. This used to be coal mining country. It was a cool and sunny mid-autumn day, small cumulus clouds passing overhead, alternating light and shade. Coming up on our left-hand side, we saw a war cemetery and pulled across. These cemeteries dot the countryside in Northern France and Belgium, a reminder of the slaughter that took place here and all along the Western Front, just over a century ago.

"Why did we have wars?" one has to ask oneself, looking out over the neatly lined white headstones. This question always comes after the conflict, never before it. Stimulated as they are by arrogance, pride, greed, stupidity; inherent in all of us, the answer unfortunately is, "There will always be wars."

These grim repositories of what remained of youthful hopes and dreams are beautifully kept by the British War Graves Commission, a tribute to the sacrifice made by so many young men. As we entered, a terrible sadness overwhelmed us. It was the deep, palpable grief, as dense as the clouds of green gas that lay over the battlefield, left behind by bereft families who had come to visit their loved one. The walls, lined with plaques inscribing the names of those who were never found, gave us shelter from the biting wind, which blew across the unobstructed countryside. Acres of uniformly laid, pure white marble markers; all identical, until upon individual inspection, it became clear that here lay a young man—somebody's son, husband, brother, or father—who had been cut down in the prime of life; a young man who would never be able to grasp the opportunities to fulfill his ambitions, raise families, and do all the things we take for granted, thanks to his sacrifice.

About half the graves were unidentified; these had the simple inscription: "A soldier of the Great War." Their loved ones would never find closure.

Walking around the cemetery examining the headstones, one startling fact became clear. With just a few exceptions, all of them had the same date. The 25th of September 1915. That date marked the first day of the Battle of Loos.

• • •

Just over one hundred years ago, as that wet and windy Saturday of the 25th of September drew to a close, the fields around were littered with the torn and mutilated bodies of these men. The advancing troops did not have time to stop and offer help or succor to their comrades, who's piteous cries for help, or just a drink of water, could be heard as they moved forward across the torn and muddy ground. There are so many accounts by men whose orders were to keep advancing, ignore the wounded, who later agonized over this. Eventually help would come for those who were left alive, but too late for most.

It took months to bury all the dead.

• • •

In 2010, twenty bodies were found in a mass grave and were buried in this cemetery. Only one was identified: Pte. William McAleer, of the Royal Scots Fusiliers. The others lie under a stone marked "A Soldier of the Great War."

The graveyard was named "Dud Corner Cemetery"—so called because of the many unexploded shells found in the area.

As we drove away, not a word was uttered.

• • •

LOOS, NORTHERN FRANCE

September 25, 1915

Before sending the infantry over the top, the British released 140 tons of chlorine gas from 5,000 cylinders placed on the parapet of the front-line trenches. This was the first time they had used gas, and the first time it had been used since the Germans started this unsavory method of fighting at Ypres the previous April. However, a change in the wind blew a lot of the gas back into the British lines, killing a number of men and putting 2,500 out of action before they even had a chance to climb over the parapet of the trenches.

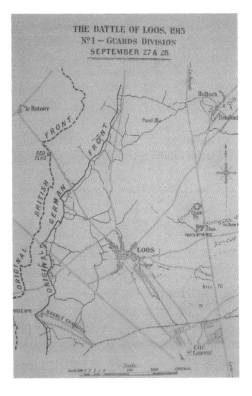

THE BATTLE OF LOOS, 1915
No 1 — GUARDS DIVISION
SEPTEMBER 27 & 28

The attack went well in the southern sector, where the Scottish regiments took the village of Loos and Hill 70[30]—a low hill just to

---

30 See accompanying map.

the east of the village. But to the north, where a vast complex of underground shelters and machine gun nests called the Hohenzollern Redoubt faced them, progress was considerably slower and more costly.

Just on that one day, as Vincent and his company were still marching to the front line, 8,500 men died on the battlefield. General Haig's concerns had been right. It was the single greatest carnage since the beginning of the war. The following day, the numerical superiority of British troops, which Haig had so much relied upon, was badly eroded by the arrival of huge numbers of German reinforcements to fill the gaps caused by the bitter fighting the previous day.

As German reservists and seasoned troops began to take control over the lost ground, the Guards Division, including the 75th Field Company Royal Engineers, arrived at Vermelles. The village by that time was a heap of rubble.

• • •

NOYELLES-LES-VERMELLES, MAP 36B NE
September 26, 1915

It was raining almost continuously, soaking the men and creating a sea of mud which they had to slog through. As they dragged aching legs through the sticky mess, heavy packs[31] weighing them down, they cursed quietly and sometimes not so quietly, the people who had sent them over here. Frequent roadblocks had slowed progress to a snail's pace, caused by stalled wagons, war damage and returning troops trying to get back to the rear with their wounded. Ambulances from the Casualty Clearing Stations crawled past, full of filthy, bloody

---

31 A pack carried: 150 rounds ammunition, overcoat, 2 prs. socks, one pants, one shirt, ground sheet, emergency rations, 24 lbs ordinary rations, Mackintosh, mess tin, cleaning kit, soap, towel, plate, mug, tobacco; then there was a satchel over the shoulder with 2 smoke helmets, and of course the rifle and bayonet.

soldiers, many of them gassed by their own side.[32] The line of troops was stalled again while two horses with their limber[33] were being pulled out of a shell hole, up to their bellies in the mud.

So, on they struggled towards Vermelles.

Vincent pulled a reluctant horse by the harness, whom he'd decided to call Herbert after the Minister of Defense.[34] There were two horses pulling the wagon, but Herbert's partner, Horatio, had driver Billy Basson riding him. Vincent's empathy with the animals was put to good use now. Talking gently to the horse took his mind off his aching feet, which were being sucked down into the goo churned up by thousands of troops and artillery moving to and from the front.

The weather, which had been reasonably dry up to now, had broken, and the leaden skies were dumping rain on them, adding to the misery of blistered feet. They'd been marching for days now—Écurie, Audincthon, Nedonchelle, and the night before at Neoux. Drips from the incessant rain flowed from Vincent's sodden hat down the back of his neck; his heavy raincoat felt like a ton of weight. He well understood the animal's reluctance, with the noise of gunfire and the sharp smell of cordite mixed with the stench of chlorine gas getting closer. There was another stink in the air that really made the horse nervous—it was the smell of death that pervaded the battlefields of the Western Front. The big draft horse, sensing Vincent's empathy, worked hard to pull the heavy wagon of machinery through the mud. They were getting closer now to the battle zone. The number of wounded and walking wounded was increasing, their haggard faces telling the tale of destruction they had witnessed. The

---

32 Fielding R. *War Letters to a Wife*. The Medici Society Ltd. 1929.

33 A short wagon used for carrying ammunition.

34 Herbert Horatio Kitchener.

sappers were getting their second wind, talking with each other and exchanging comments with the soldiers going the opposite way.

Up ahead, Vincent heard one young Irish sapper asking a bandaged Scotsman, "Is it always like this?" To which the dour Celt replied, "Och, no Paddy … Only on fucking Saturdays." His further derogatory comments on the level of Irish intelligence were thankfully lost in the noise of an ambulance passing by.

Vincent, still leading the horse, had fallen into a walking sleep, he was so tired. He shook his head and looked up to see buildings ahead.

Someone shouted, "Vermelles! … Looks like we're there." But then they turned to the left and it was another half hour before they finally arrived at the camp. They were all exhausted, hungry and soaked to the skin, ready for a night's sleep.

More than ready.

Despite his weariness and aching back, for he was still exhausted from a recent bout of malaria, Major Rolland had to continue on while his second in command organized the billets and food preparation. He rode the several miles to La Rutoire, where the Guards Division Headquarters was located in a large farmhouse. He dreaded the orders he was going to receive when he got there.

The First Guards Division and the Engineers had arrived at their bivouac near Vermelles in a state of exhaustion. The evening was spent getting the animals fed and settled down, erecting tents, preparing food, and stowing their gear. Tired after six hours marching—if wading through mud could be called that—their feet throbbed, backs ached, and shoulders burned from the straps of their packs. They were soaked, hungry, cold, and covered in mud from the march.

General French's long-awaited reserves had eventually arrived at the battlefront, but not quite in pristine fighting condition.

• • •

"*A great deal of nonsense ...*" wrote Major General Richard Hilton, a former observation officer, "*... has been written about Loos.*"

He continued:

"*The real tragedy of that battle was its nearness to complete success. Most of us who reached the crest of Hill 70, and survived, were firmly convinced that we had broken through on that Sunday, 25th September 1915. There seemed to be nothing ahead of us, but an unoccupied and incomplete trench system. The only two things that prevented our advancing into the suburbs of Lens were, firstly, the exhaustion of the 'Jocks' themselves (for they had undergone a belly-ful of marching and fighting that day) and, secondly, the flanking fire of numerous German machine-guns, which swept that bare hill from some factory buildings in Cite St. Auguste to the south of us. All that we needed was more artillery ammunition to blast those clearly-lo-cated machine-guns, plus some fresh infantry to take over from the weary and depleted 'Jocks'.*

But alas, neither ammunition nor reinforcements were immedi-ately available, and the great opportunity passed."[35]

---

35 Warner, P. (2000) [1976]. The Battle of Loos (Wordsworth ed.). London: William Kimber.

CHAPTER 9

The Missing Lieutenants

"It is my painful duty to inform you that
a report has this day been received from
the War Office, notifying the death of ..."

*(First line of standard War Office telegram,
advising of the loss of a loved one.)*

Disbelief greeted Major Rolland's announcement; he had just returned from the Division HQ at La Rutoire and informed them they had to leave now to put up wire and sandbags in front of the British trenches between Loos, Hill 70, and the Hohenzollern Redoubt, which the British had failed to take the previous day. It would be impossible to work in daylight, what with the constant German shelling and machine-gun fire, so they had to get the wire set up during the dark.

The land in between the trenches had been the scene of bitter fighting the previous day. The thick mud was littered with mutilated bodies lying soaking in the drenching rain, where a few stretcher bearers were creeping around like ghouls in a cemetery, ignoring the bodies while they searched for the wounded. Going out of the trenches at all, was risking becoming one of those bodies. Yet they had to do it. Major Rolland had given orders for all sections to be employed on this work.

This was their first time going into action.

Fumbling in the dark, Vincent helped two other sappers pull a roll of wire over the parapet. Sweating from fear and exertion, he pondered the wisdom of signing up. His father had been very much against it, but some rebellious quirk in his personality made him go ahead. Now he wondered if he'd ever see his dad again, and he felt a wave of sadness sweep over him, as he realized that he might not. But he was here and all he could do was keep going forward. There was no time for self-pity. The roll of wire was heaved up with much grunting and cursing and they started laying it out.

The ground was slippery and muddy where it had been torn up by shellfire and thousands of British army boots. Body parts, clothing, shoes, personal belongings, and abandoned weapons littered the ground.

Worse, there were thousands of wounded, who were unable to move but were crying for help, some lying in shell craters where they had crawled to for comparative safety. It was essential to consolidate the forward lines before the next day, and there was no time to aid the wounded or remove the bodies—they were under strict orders to ignore them and keep working. It was a living nightmare for the young lads of Vincent's company, who were all visibly terrified. Shaking with fear, they stumbled around in the dark trying to pay out the vicious barbed wire, tearing at their clothes and exposed skin. The very real smell of death around them was stomach churning, the cries of the wounded and stretcher bearers trying to find them was like a scene from *Dante's Inferno*:

"Abandon all hope who enter here

For this is where all things are left behind …"

Vincent saw several of his companions throw up their dinner. His own half-digested meal had already been heaved up, traces of it on his sleeve where he had wiped his mouth. Every so often the sky was lit by a German flare, and they were shouted at to get down and lay absolutely still. As they struggled in confusion with the wire, fighting panic and the urge to run, a figure came running toward them, bellowing encouragement, and helping them get the wire run out.

It was CSM Elliot.

This was a different Elliot; gone was the martinet of the parade ground, replaced by a battle-hardened, mud-covered warrior, delivering the inspiration they desperately needed. They needed a leader, and this man knew what to do, calming their nerves with his coolness and self-control. They turned to with a new will to get the job done, the battle noise receding as they focused on working as a team, running out the coils of wire that had to be in place before daylight.

75th Field Company War Diary
September 27, 1915.

On return at 5.40 am received orders to send 5,000 sandbags before daylight to 3rd Coldstream. Tried to get through but limber was stopped by a brig. Gen R.A. and sent back as it was too light to get through. Sandbags delivered about 7 pm. At 1pm received orders to obtain trench bridges to be found at Sailly la Bourse and convey them to Le Rutoire. Obtained them, delivered them, and they were put across trenches beyond Le Rutoire by No. 2 section by about 6.30 pm. No casualties.

Since the 75th Field Company had arrived on the 26th of September, they had labored and sweated getting down the protective wire on the new trenches to prevent the inevitable counterattacks getting near them. The men were well past dog tired and were, if anything, on a second wind. Grabbing something to eat when they could, snatching a catnap here and there, they worked on, doing what they did best.

After the wire had been laid, the old British trenches had to be crossed by the attacking infantry, using trench bridges, and roads were cleared to allow them, and all the paraphernalia that was needed—ammunition mainly—to be brought up to the new front. They also had their own wagons to get up there with the rolls of wire. They all worked together in the mud in teams. As they worked to bridge the trenches and get the rolls of barbed wire and sandbags across, wounded and exhausted soldiers struggled to get past, going in the opposite direction. The noise and confusion were blotting out the orders of the NCOs and shells from the German artillery were landing all around them. Yet all through the twenty-seventh, into the evening when the Guards moved forward, they managed to lay down the sandbags and wire and the wagons were sent back to Vermelles for more supplies.

• • •

With the Guards Division finally under Haig's command, the 1st and 2nd Guards Brigades began to relieve the two forward divisions with orders to consolidate the line. Lieutenant Harold Macmillan, the future Prime Minister of England, who had arrived a few weeks earlier with the 4th Grenadier Guards, recalled the Corps Commander's address prior to the move up to the front line:

"Behind you all Gentlemen, in your companies and battalions, will be your Brigadier: behind him your Divisional Commander, and behind you all—I shall be there!"

And then came a voice from the ranks facing him: "Yes, and a long way back too!"

Despite the confusion as the Guards moved forward in the darkness on the night of the 27th, the relief was completed by dawn on the 28th, and they succeeded in making themselves as safe and comfortable as was humanly possible in the captured German trenches. Early that afternoon, the Earl of Cavan was ordered to consolidate the British line with the 2nd Guards Brigade, capturing Chalk Pit Wood and Puits[36] No. 14 on the Lens—La Bassée road. The 3rd Guards Brigade captured Hill 70, while the 1st Guards Brigade protected the left flank.[37]

The three objectives could be clearly seen from where Brigadier General John Ponsonby, commanding 2nd Guards Brigade, issued his orders. The ground was flat, and the area beyond the road was totally exposed to German machine-gun and artillery fire. It was a particularly bleak and unattractive view, not rolling countryside with conveniently placed cover, but a stark coalfield dotted with odd

---

36 Puits No. 14 was one of the many coal mines dotted around the countryside.

37 The 75th Field Company was with the 1st Guards Brigade.

buildings and slag heaps. Puits No. 14 was a pit head with a fragile-looking gantry for the winding gear silhouetted on the horizon, described by the special correspondent of *The Times* as "*a conspicuous and ugly building with the usual lofty chimney*".

Two companies of 2nd Irish Guards moved off at four in the afternoon and reached Chalk Pit Wood with only a few casualties, having been protected by a smokescreen laid by 1st Guards Brigade. They then joined 2nd Scots Guards as they advanced in open order and doubled downhill under very heavy fire of shrapnel…

75th Field Company War Diary
September 28, 1915.
Bivouacked at Vermelle. No. 4 section, under 2nd Lt. Bousfield obtained material for 2 more trench bridges to take wagons. Took them to Le Rutoire and placed them across trenches near that place. One casualty—very slightly wounded at duty.

• • •

The British trenches had become dangerous obstacles for the troops moving forward, in many places capturing German trenches, which then had to be "turned around", fitting parapets on the rear side. Though the notorious Hill 70 east of Loos had not yet been taken, Loos was occupied and the push was on to take the Hohenzollern Redoubt. The sappers were working to bridge the old trenches just east of La Rutoire.

• • •

A platoon from the 2nd Guards waited to pass over the trench bridge the sappers had just installed, while they hammered securing pins into the soil.

Sapper William Dooley sat on the edge of the trench and, lighting up a sodden cigarette he pushed his hat back and wiped the sweat off his forehead, leaving muddy streaks.

"Who're you fellows with?" he asked, curious.

"We're B company, Second Irish Guards."

"And what's yer name… sir?" asked Dooley, remembering his manners.

"Kipling … er, Lieutenant Kipling," the young man replied.

"You'se any relation to that poet … em … Rudyard Kipling, isn' it?" he asked, looking at his mate, Jimmy Doyle for confirmation. Doyle nodded.

"Er, yes, actually. He's my father."

Doyle, ever the great reader, said, "His ole' man wrote *The Jungle Book*."

"I'll be damned," said Dooley, shaking his head at this discovery, and seeing the discomfiture of the boy in soldier's uniform, hoped to encourage him by adding, "Give those Fritz a good hiding," and then, grinning, waved them across the bridge, which was now ready.

"Okay, lads, the bridge is ready, walk careful on it though, ya don't want to end up in the trench, do yez."

With that, Doyle stubbed his cigarette out and, grabbing a crowbar, jumped back into the trench, Dooley was close behind him. The last thing they saw was the platoon walking into a smoke screen set down by the 1st Irish Guards. They were heading into an area known as Chalk Pit Wood.

Lieutenant Kipling was never seen again.

JOHN KIPLING

On the south coast of England, the hay was ready for gathering and in the fields around the pretty little village of Rottingdean; farm workers were busy raking it in and piling it into neat stacks, while the weather permitted. In a large Georgian house, facing the village pond, the sun glanced off the upstairs windows, from which the mewling of a new-born baby could be faintly heard. His cries were interrupted by the clatter of feet on the stairs as the nanny brought up his two sisters to see him. Josephine was five and ran up ahead, while the nanny carried little Elsie who was just taking her first steps. Knocking on the door to their mother's room she brought them in to see their baby brother, John, who, it must be said, did not return their interest as he busily nursed at his mother's breast. It was August 17, 1897, and their mother, Caroline Kipling sat up in the bed, tired, but happy, having just given birth some hours before. "Now girls, be careful, John's feeding, but I'll let you see him properly when he finishes ... He's a hungry little guy." Her American accent still predominant, she smiled at them, relishing her family around her.

John, named after his grandfather, was only two years old when tragedy struck the family. They were on a visit to New York, when the father and both his daughters caught pneumonia. While Rudyard and Elsie lay sick in their hotel, Josephine was taken to the house of a friend, Julie De Forest, where she was looked after. But as the bleak weather continued outside, her condition continued to worsen and on March 7, 1899, with her mother by her bedside, she passed away.

They didn't tell Rudyard the news for several weeks afterward, as he was at death's door himself. The parents were stricken by the loss, and it is said that Rudyard never really got over the shock. Living at the Elms, their house in Rottingdean, reminded him too much of his daughter, and he became increasingly morose. In the end, they decided to move and bought a house in Burwash, where the family finally settled, and John began his schooling.

Though a healthy little lad, Jack—as he became known—suffered from nearsightedness and had to wear glasses. As a small boy, he enjoyed the country living, exploring the woods nearby and generally getting into scrapes as boys do. But he was doted on by loving parents, being the youngest of the two remaining children. When he finished primary school, he was sent to Wellington College, a co-educational day-boarding school in Berkshire. On the outbreak of war in August 1914, he was 16 years old. His father was a staunch Imperialist and tried to get his young son a commission as soon as he came of age, much to the strenuous objections of Caroline. She breathed a sigh of relief when John was refused by both the Navy and Army because of his nearsightedness.

Sadly, that was short lived. Blindly determined to get his boy off to war, Rudyard used his friendship with Field Marshal Frederick Roberts (Earl Roberts) to obtain a commission for John in the Irish Guards, and just before his 17th birthday he was commissioned as a second lieutenant into the 2nd Battalion Irish Guards. Kipling was urging his teenage son into something the boy was not ready for, and very much against the boy's and his mother's wishes. But following the reports of German outrages in Belgium and the sinking of the Lusitania, Kipling senior came to see the war as a crusade against evil and continued to push his boy into active service.

Following his training, Jack was sent to France in August of 1915 as part of the formation of the Guards Division. When the 2nd Guards were ordered to attack the Chalk Pit Wood, Kipling led his men along with another officer, 2nd Lieutenant Clifford, toward what remained of the wood near the mine head. Both officers were killed—though Clifford's body was later recovered. John Kipling was never found and to this day no one is sure where he may have been buried, if indeed there was anything left of him to bury.

His mother had deeply opposed her teenage son joining the army, and his loss put a severe strain on Kipling's marriage. They spent years searching around the area of Loos to find any evidence of his remains and Red Cross records to see if he had been taken prisoner.

All to no avail.

Shortly after his son went missing, Rudyard wrote a poem called "My Son Jack" which was not actually about his own son, but a young sailor—apparently the youngest death in the Battle of Jutland—but there is no doubt that he very much had his own boy in mind when he penned the verse:

"Have you any news of my boy Jack?
 Not this tide.
 When do you think he'll come back?
 Not with this wind blowing, and this tide.
 Has anyone else had word of him?
 Not this tide.
 For what is sunk will hardly swim,
 Not with this wind blowing, and this tide.

 Oh, dear, what comfort can I find?
 None this tide,
 Nor any tide,
 Except he did not shame his kind—
     Not even with that wind blowing, and that tide.

 Then hold your head up all the more,
 This tide,
 And every tide;
 Because he was the son you bore,
 And gave to that wind blowing and that tide!"

75th Field Company War Diary
September 29, 1915.

Visited advanced trenches meeting O/Cs 2nd and 3rd Coldstream Guards and decided that a certain length of 500 yards should be wired. Also that some material for a few dug-outs should be obtained. GOC Brigade ordered that 5 yard gaps should be left every 30 yards in the entanglement. Spent the night searching the neighbourhood for material which could not be collected till about 0500. Started an advanced store at Le Rutoire but had to postpone erecting the entanglement. No. 1 section employed repairing trench bridges from le Rutoire to Lonetree.

September 30, 1915.

Arrived bivouac on withdrawal of brigade from advanced trenches to billets (after relief in trenches.)—to L17 B 2.8. on map 36B. Arrived at bivouac at L17 B 2.8. Left with store and wired 1400 yards of front on far side of old German 1st line about 200 yards east of Lonetree, i.e. 800 yards northwards and 600 yards Southwards. Arrived back at bivouac 5 am on 2nd. One casualty—wounded.

October 1–3, 1915.

Close fighting was renewed in the Hohenzollern Redoubt, and all but Big Willie Trench was lost to the enemy. 12th (Eastern) Division relieves 1st and 2nd Guards Brigades in the area of the Chalk Pit. The Engineers are put to work on completing new trenches, roads and positions in preparation for the assault. Heavy enemy shelling causes many casualties among the working parties. Major-General Wing, OC 12th Division is among those killed. The renewal of the offensive is delayed until 6th October, to enable preparatory attacks on Fosse 8 and Hill 70 to take place. Following the day's loss of the trenches of Hohenzollern Redoubt, this area takes priority. The 12th and Guards Divisions are ordered to capture the Quarries and the Fosse 8 / Hohenzollern respectively, on 9th October.

Diary of Private Sidney Kemp
October 5, 1915.

We left Magingarbe to march back to the war. Terrific shelling was going on by both sides as we neared Vermelles again, for the main road passed through this village to go to Hulloch and Loos and Lens and further east. This is where the war really started for us … to the east of Vermelles … in that area what lay there not only shocked us but sickened us too, for the ground was literally covered by the bodies of Scottish soldiers laying in all positions, some facing the Germans, some to the left, some to the right.

These men were all dead and in their kilts. It looked terrible, for not only were they swelling to two or three times their proper size, but their faces and hands were black as coal, and the answer to that was gas. Not German gas as was used earlier at Ypres, but British gas, and these, the young Manhood of Scotland, had just rushed hell for leather into the gas they were supposed to have been following. Our second in command of B company, Captain Towse, begged to be allowed to take his company and bury these chaps. To put it mildly, I would say there were hundreds of the flower of Scotland, lying there dead, but we later on learned that two Scottish Divisions, the 9th and 15th were thrown into the battle, so those chaps like us in England who had all volunteered, were now thrown away, and hardly any German trenches captured. None of these Scottish soldiers was wearing a gas mask or respirator, whatever you call it, for it was impossible to go madly on to a bayonet charge wearing something that stopped your breathing. The mistake they made was to follow the gas and not try to travel into it. Still, that is that …"

75th Field Company War Diary
October 4, 1915.
Visited advanced trenches with Lt. Fraser and Lt. Bousfield. Dumped more sandbags and wiring material near front trenches.

Lt. Ure with No. 2 section sent to G5c8.6 to wire from there to G5C9.6 and thence to G5c9 ½.5; work could not be done as covering party had to be withdrawn on account of enemy fire; Lt. Ure R.E. missing—the presumption is that he accidentally walked into a German trench. But this is uncertain. One sapper wounded.

• • •

Lieutenant Henry Ure was not what one would call self-assured, unlike some of the other college lads he'd done officer training with. Whenever the training sergeant called for one of the cadets to lead a platoon, he'd shrank back, terrified at the idea of telling those other young men what to do, when he wasn't so sure what to do himself. Somehow, he'd graduated and been sent over to Ireland, where he'd joined the 75th Field Company, later than most of the others, and every exercise they carried out, he had gotten something wrong. The major told him not to worry so much, that's how we learned.

He was an only child and his mother had doted on him and was furious when he joined up; but he'd gone along anyway when all his classmates went to the recruiting office. Henry was in his third year of an engineering degree, and indeed it did seem a bit dull, compared with the exciting news coming in from France. Usually, the Major discreetly sent Sergeant Adams with him to help things along.

So here they were now, in the thick of it. The day before, he and Lieutenant Brindley had visited the new front-line trenches with Major Rolland; he had his map out and showed them where in

"No-Man's Land" the wiring should begin and end. There were three lots of coordinates: c8.6 to c9.6 and then to c9 ½.5.

Henry wrote them down in his notebook, and the major pointed out the remains of a small building where they needed to begin, at c8.6. The wiring had to be well away from the trenches; beyond grenade throwing distance but there was no way they could go out and put markers out, with German snipers watching every move. Rolland introduced them to the Guards sergeant, by the name of James, who would lead a covering party for them. There had been no wiring done there and "That," said Major Rolland, "would be a priority … or the Jerries will be through and on top of us before we know it."

So there he was, heading out with Number 2 section, without Sergeant Adams, who was with Number 1 section, four of them carrying the heavy rolls of wire. It was getting dark as they worked their way along the communication trench to the front line. By the time they arrived, it was pitch black, the area occasionally lit by German flares. They met with Sergeant James—Henry wasn't sure if this was his first name or last—and their covering party. The young lieutenant went ahead to pick out the spot where he remembered the landmark out on No-Man's Land was, and they clambered up out of the trench. Passing the coils of wire up, along with their cutting tools, posts and hammers, the sergeant asked him if he was sure it was the right place.

"I'm sure," Ure replied, though he felt anything but certain; he couldn't let the others sense his fear.

Just then, the guns had stopped, which was great, but he had to find the correct spot to start the wiring, close to the ruined building. He told the infantry and his sappers to lie flat and wait while he went to search for it.

Sam McLaughlin said to Beale: "I don't think he knows where he is."

"Quiet you lot," hissed the Sergeant.

"He did seem to be a bit unsure … I think you're right Sam. But he told us to wait here."

"I'm goin' out there, we need to get him back," said one of the sappers, John O'Boyle. "He doesn't know what he's fuckin' doin'…"

"No, don't!" they shouted … but Boyle stood up to a crouch.

The shock wave from the explosion arrived before they even heard it, catching O'Boyle, throwing him over the others right back into the trench.

"They know we're here!" shouted the Sergeant. "Get the fuck out … now!"

As they frantically rolled and crouched their way back to the trench, another explosion, to the left of the first and closer, rocked them, and with some help from that blast's shockwave, they tumbled headlong back into the trench and lay flat on the duckboards, faces in the mud, shaking.

• • •

Major Rolland sat at his table in the dugout that served as his home and headquarters. A candle played his shadow on the wall, flickering opposite the shadows of McLaughlin and Beale, who stood at ease.

"How is O'Boyle doing?" he asked, rubbing his forehead in shock and disbelief.

"He was brought to the CCS, sir," said McLaughlin. "Some shrapnel got him on his left side, but it's not too bad … the nurse sez he'd be OK."

"Tell me again what happened."

"Well … we all climbed up on the parapet," answered Beale, "and as we got the gear up, the Lieutenant said he was going to find a marker he knew, some building or other."

"Were you in the right place?" asked the Major, pointing to the remains of a small building on the map, but it would be near invisible in the dark.

"He said we were … but the Sergeant seemed a bit worried about that, 'n he was there when yez all were checkin' it out," replied McLauglin, looking at Beale for confirmation.

Beale nodded. "He was, well, askin' the lieutenant about that."

"And then," Beale continued, "O'Boyle decided he wuz goin' to find the lieutenant, and next thing, the mortar shells started comin'."

"It seems like they knew we were there," said McLaughlin.

"OK, lads," the major said tiredly. "There wasn't much else you could have done. We've asked the guards to send out a party to look for him if they can, but it's probably too dangerous." Then, peering in the dim light at the trench map on the table, he said, "It's possible he ran into the enemy trenches … *em* … he didn't have a great sense of direction, even in daylight, if I recall." He pointed with his finger at the area they were meant to work in. "OK, dismissed, go and get some sleep. There's nothing more we can do for now."

Lieutenant Ure was never found.

The Battle of Loos dragged on for another ten days, without much further gain.

CHAPTER 10

"Sister Susie"

"Sister Susie's sewing shirts for the soldiers
Sister Susie's sewing in the kitchen on a Singer,
There's miles and miles of flannel on the floor, and up the stairs,
And father says it's rotten getting mixed up with the cotton,
And sitting on the needles that she leaves upon the chairs..."

(Herman Darewski. "Sister Susie"—music-hall song 1914)[38]

ANNEQUIN, FRANCE
October 1915

Sheets of wind driven rain swept across the narrow streets, blending a lowering grey sky, grey stone buildings, and grey cobbled paving into a lifeless picture of bland cityscape. But at least the Engineers were billeted away from the front line, working on the trenches and various projects, but without the terrible urgency of three weeks ago, during the battle.

The lives of so many young men had been thrown away, with little result, except for the capture of Loos and Hill 70. This sad tale would be repeated over and over for the following three years. One

---

38 A Music Hall song popular in 1915, you can listen to Sister Susie here: https://www.youtube.com/watch?v=8IJHk6A6Yp0

outcome was the removal of General French, mainly at Haig's instigation, and largely as a result of the former's handling of the reserves. Had they been in place when needed, the outcome would have been different.

Vincent felt depressed by the heavy, leaden skies, which seemed to have become the norm the last few weeks. He was singing, or trying to sing, the complicated lyrics of "Sister Susie's Sewing Socks for Soldiers" to keep himself cheerful, with limited success, both in maintaining his good humor and in singing the song, which had become popular in the Estaminets on the nights they could get off. But at least he stayed dry in the workshop and was back on his lathe again. Meanwhile, his mates worked outside, getting a good soaking. The lathe and milling machines had been set up in a former stable in the town, and he was busy machining wheels for the trams they used on the light rail, running down to the trenches. They were housed in relatively comfortable billets in a camp just outside the town, a welcome change from the sodden conditions on the front line.

Finishing up the last job for the day, Vincent shut down his equipment and, donning his cape, walked from the shop to the mess, going inside to the welcoming warm fug, the smell of cabbage and corned beef reminding him how hungry he was. Work had finished for the day, and the evening was free. Waiting for John to return from Sailly-la-Bourse, which was two miles away, he sat down on a long bench by the tables. Finding a discarded two-week-old *Daily Mirror* that had come in the mail some time back, he opened it up—went straight to the football page. Then, having satisfied himself that Celtic FC were doing OK—at least two weeks ago, he went to the front page and glanced over it; it was all about the Lord Mayor of London's parade, which apparently was quite a spectacular affair, but of scant interest to him—he leafed through, onto page six, where he came across an article boldly headlined: **"The Heroic Englishwoman who Died for her Country at the Hands of the Germans."** It was dated "Brussels, October 15th, 1915."

The article described how the Germans had earlier arrested an English nurse, Edith Cavell, who had been hiding English, French, and Belgian escaped prisoners of war. She took care of them and provided food, then helped them make their way back to their own side. At her trial, the Germans accused her of espionage and subsequently found her guilty. She was sentenced to death by firing squad and executed on October the 12th.

Vincent was shocked that they would do such a thing—*she was a nurse for God's sake!* Then he thought the British would probably have done the same, but some doubt was there—*was she a spy?* She was working behind enemy lines and would have sent messages back with the escaping soldiers, and that could well be construed as espionage. She was a brave and selfless woman who treated wounded German and allied soldiers equally.

Reading the paper, Vincent felt little love for the enemy. The atrocities of the whole war sickened him, and he felt an uncontrollable longing for it all to be over so he could go home and be with his family. The experience of Loos still filled his dreams at night, and the stench of death lingered with him like an unwanted companion. War brought out facets in men that would have remained buried in peacetime, an amalgam of courage, humanity, brutality, and just pure unadulterated evil.

By that time other sappers were drifting into the mess, ending his ruminations; taking off their rain ponchos and rubbing their hands in anticipation of their evening chow, they sat around him and asked for the news.

He showed the paper to Alan O'Dowd, a bricklayer in civilian life. "Take a dekko[39] at this, Vincent said, and soon a group of them were animatedly discussing the atrocity, as they saw it. A few had heard of Edith, for her reputation in helping distressed Tommies had spread quickly. She was a courageous and big-hearted woman, who gave her life for her country and the men fighting for it. Most felt frustration at the idea of shooting a woman, and a nurse to boot. It was said she helped take care of German prisoners as much as her own side.

The conversation went on until the food was ready, then the paper was discarded as they jostled into line. Nurse Cavell was forgotten as plates were loaded and seats grabbed at the mess tables. The sappers' mess was formerly a café that had been requisitioned by the Army. It was bright and cheerful, still retaining the red and white checkered tablecloths, and brightly painted walls with oil lamps in sconces all round. It lifted the mood from the grey streets outside. A bunch of sappers, including John and Vincent, sat around the same long table. They knew they'd be moving again, and the talk revolved around the probable location of their new billets.

They'd been in Annequin for nearly two weeks, and in the evenings, they went to the local *estaminet*,[40] called *La Poule Rouge*.

"The Pule," as it became known to the sappers, was run by an elderly Frenchman, Jean-Claude, his wife, Sidonie, and adult daughter, Estelle. Annequin, being a coal mining town, had plenty of estaminets, still frequented by the miners, but the troops brought a lot more business. However, the reason The Pule had a draw like a powerful magnet was mainly Estelle, though it had to be said, the parents were a kindly couple who liked the English soldiers.

---

39 British slang for 'look.'

40 French pub.

Estelle, in her early twenties, was a pretty brunette, long curls falling down the back of a very attractive neck. A man could drown in the pools of those dark brown eyes; but the beautiful eyes saw only one sapper, the one with the red curly hair and green Irish eyes— John Kelly. For his part, the bold John was equally enamored with Estelle, and spent most evenings mooning over the bar at her as she served up the questionable French beer. She had a boyfriend, but he was safely—or maybe not so safely—out of the way with the French Army in Champagne. They hadn't heard from Jaques for quite a while and had begun to fear for his well-being. She and Jaques had known each other since school days, but it was generally reckoned from her remarks that she wasn't that keen on marrying him. So, John felt safe in pursuing his romance.

He'd progressed as far as persuading Estelle to go outside with him for a smoke. She was trying to teach him a few French words.

"*Je m'appelle*, Estelle," she said, and her accent melted him. It might have been a rough mining town accent, but it, to him, was soft and silky. She thought his Belfast accent was nice too—definitely not soft and silky, but nice. "*Vous Vous Appelez*, John,"[41] she said.

He was getting closer and trying to pluck up the nerve to kiss her when the door banged open emitting a cloud of cigarette smoke and a loud rendition of "Sister Susie's Sewing Shirts for Soldiers", as Vincent and his three comrades poured out, laughing, and then they saw the couple.

John went beetroot and pulled back.

"C'mon Romeo," Sam said, "we've got to get back by nine."

All he could do was take her hand and hold it for a second, then follow them.

---

41 "You call yourself John."

The next day he got back again to La Poule Rouge, and they got as far as a kiss and a cuddle behind the bar before he was sought out and dragged back to the camp.

"Don't fall in love over here," they had warned him. "It'll end in tears."

But John didn't listen.

• • •

"And should you knock at our street door,
  Ma whispers, 'Come inside.'
Then when you ask where Susie is,
She says with loving pride:
'Sister Susie's sewing shirts for soldiers,
Such skill at sewing shirts
Our shy young sister Susie shows.'"

• • •

75th Field Company War Diary
October 20, 1915.
Annequin. *Dumping stores from the Divisional store to Brigade (1st Guards) advanced dump at G10b7.8 (map 36c). Started a Battalion HQ dugout 16' below ground level – 16' x 8' with staircase at each end. Starting out new road from about G3c0.2 keeping south of Gordon Alley up to Hulluch Alley and then toward G4d5.0. Stores dumped at advanced dump (G10b7.8) up to about 25,000 sandbags and material for 1,000 yards of wire entanglement.*

October 23, 1915.

Stores taken to advanced dumps to replace wastage. "Aeroplane entan-glements" made for 150 yards of front and handed over to infantry. Batt. HQ dug-outs continued.

October 24, 1915.

Stores taken to advance dump to replace wastage. More timbering for deep dug-outs and six bomb shelters. "Aeroplane entanglements" made for 120 yards of front and handed over to infantry. Six bomb shelters made. Norton tube well completed - 31 ½ feet below ground level. Actual site in old British 2nd line support trench about 20 yards from Hulluch Alley (map reference about G10b6 ½ .9 ½). Second well started about G10 b 7.6 near Border Lane.

October 25, 1915.

Second Norton tube well completed in Border Lane. Lieut. Fraser engaged on scheme for improving lines of "in" and "out" traffic in communication trenches of 1st Guards Brigade area.

October 26, 1915.

Company marched to billets at Bas Rieux for period of rest.

• • •

"Some soldiers send epistles,
  Say they'd sooner sleep in thistles,
  Than the saucy, soft, short shirts
  for soldiers sister Susie sews."

• • •

On the 20th, the company began work on a new Battalion Headquarters dug out, sixteen feet underground, with separate entrances, one each end. They worked late into the night on this, carrying timber and cutting it to size. There were some tunnellers helping out with the excavation, digging with pickaxes and shovels, going deeper and deeper.

• • •

Vincent and Sam were bringing in pumps to keep the water down, and all the carpenters were going flat out putting in supports and walls around the dugout. On the 26th, when they were relieved, there were no complaints. They marched to Bas Rieux, a suburb of the town of Lillers, covered in mud but glad to get to the comparative safety of the town twenty miles behind the front line. This, of course, was where General French had his headquarters at Chateau Philiomel. But if they thought they'd be having a rest, that was dismissed fairly quickly. Orders were received to prepare a parade ground for the forthcoming royal visit of King George V.

At least this would be a diversion—they all wanted to see the King, and the news he would be reviewing the Guards came as a welcome surprise.

• • •

"Piles and piles and piles of shirts
   she sends out to the soldiers,
   And sailors won't be jealous when they see them, not at all,
   And when we say her stitching will set all the soldiers itching,
   She says our soldiers fight best
   when their back's against the wall."

• • •

75th Field Company War Diary
October 27, 1915.

Bas Rieux. Three sections employed preparing review ground for intended Royal Inspection of Guards Division at Haut Rieux.

October 28, 1915.
Three sections completed review ground.

October 28, 1915.
Daily Telegraph[42] *headline: King George V thrown from horse while reviewing the troops in France.*

"Readers today woke to the shocking news that King George V had had an accident whilst visiting the troops in France. A brief medical report announced that he was severely bruised after he fell from his horse when, excited by the cheers of the troops, it had reared up ... "

For a brief and gut-wrenching moment, England teetered on the edge of losing their Monarch. As the cheers died, one thousand faces, voices stilled in shock, stared as in slow motion the horse reared, the king slid off the saddle, his hat flying, arms flailing, dignity abandoned, and landed heavily on the ground. But the slow motion continued, as the horse itself lost balance and toppled over on the prostrate monarch. He was surely gone. The silence seemed to go on forever as the horse struggled on top of the regal legs, as generals leaped faster than they had done for years, an unbelieving knot of men gathered around King George, and extracted him from the panicked mare, feeling him for broken limbs, for consciousness.

Each thought, *Could it have been my fault?* But it was no one's fault. The horse had been trained to remain calm while loyal citizens shouted their fealty. But the roar of a Guards regiment was too much.

---

42 British newspaper *Daily Telegraph*, dated 30 October 1915.

Happily, the monarchy remained intact, with nothing more than very severe bruising and all-around embarrassment.

The King, after a short spell in hospital, returned home to a hero's welcome.

• • •

75th Field Company War Diary
October 29, 1915.
Halted in billets. Washing clothes etc. Major Rolland went to No. 6 CCS with Malaria.

• • •

Vincent and one of the other sappers, James Ball, were on their way to the workshops when CSM Pring called them over.

"Sapper McCann, yez can drive the lorry, can't yez?"

"Yessir, I can indeed" Vincent replied, his chest size increasing an inch, as it puffed out. He'd learned to drive the truck a while back, and he was immensely proud of the fact. Mostly only the drivers were able to handle the cantankerous vehicle, which, with its "double clutch," required the skills and dedication of a lion tamer.

Trucks were a relatively new innovation in 1915.

"Well then, we need you and Ball to take the major to the CCS in the town. He's in a bad way."

"What's happened Sarge?" Ball asked.

"He's down wi' the malaria again, and he's looking pretty poorly," Pring stated.

"So, we'll get a stretcher from the store, 'cause there's no ambulances available, they're all at the front." He continued, "But if we don't get 'im to the hospital quick like, he won't last."

The store was where all the "bits and pieces," including a couple of stretchers, were kept. By the time they'd brought the truck to the tent, the major was running a dangerously high fever, tossing from side to side and muttering in what sounded like Hindi. He was quite delirious. The three of them lifted him onto the stretcher, feeling his clothes wet with sweat.

"Go easy with 'im," said the CSM, the kindness and respect in his tone belying their liking of the major. "'Ere, let's get some blankets under the stretcher, it'll be a rough ride in the back 'ere."

With a grinding of gears, the truck took off up the rutted road, competing for space with vehicles and wagons going in both directions. Ball sat in the back with the major, Vincent driving as carefully as he could to avoid the potholes in the overused road, changing gear as gently as possible.

Casualty Clearing Station Number 6 was in an orphanage, and the yard outside was being used to take in the wounded soldiers. On arrival, they reported to an orderly, who came back with a tall, elegant looking woman, who had the uniform of a Matron in the Queen Alexandra Military Nursing Service.[43] Nurse Kate Luard was a strikingly handsome woman, with the red and blue cape on her shoulders, the nursing medal pinned to it. Her dark hair, showing a few streaks of grey, was tucked neatly under her cap, a straight "no-nonsense" nose and full generous lips triggered a memory in Vincent. He just stared, lost for words like a lovesick teenager. It wasn't the kind of love John Kelly felt for his Estella, but something much different, which he couldn't quite put his finger on.

Though not consciously aware of it, he still desperately missed his mother; he was, after all, only eight years old when she had died.

---

43 The full title of the service is: Queen Alexandra's Imperial Military Nursing Reserve Service (QAIMNRS).

Over the years, an image had evolved in his mind of what his mother was like. Gentle and caring, but firm and competent.

This woman in front of him characterized that image. He would have jumped off the top of the building if she'd told him to.

As they struggled with the sick officer into the ward, they witnessed the sometimes-grotesque injuries to the men lying on the beds. What they thought remarkable though, was the stoicism with which they bore the horrible wounds of the battlefield. What was equally striking was the kindness the matron showed them, regardless of rank. The other nursing sisters were the same, gently helping and working tirelessly. They placed the Major carefully on the bed, and as Vincent turned to thank the matron, he was totally tongue tied. Her direct gaze seemed to penetrate his soul. Somehow, this remarkable woman understood his need. Though she felt like folding him in an embrace, all Edith could do was touch him on the shoulder and smile her thanks for bringing the Major to his bed.

The two soldiers were very quiet on the way back to the camp. The image of the matron with her kind words would remain with Vincent, calm him in his troubled dreams, and fill an empty gap he never even realized was there.

• • •

"I forgot to tell you that our sister Susie's married,
And when she isn't sewing shirts,
She's sewing other things.
Then little sister Molly says,
"Oh, sister's bought a dolly,
She's making all the clothes for it,
With pretty bows and strings."

KATHLEEN EVELYN LUARD

A rail passenger traveling from Tilbury—a seaport on the River Thames—to London, on the 29th of June 1872 would witness a panorama of fields of golden wheat, heads blowing gently in the soft breeze, ripe for harvest. About a mile yonder they would see a church spire and spread around it, slate roofs reflecting the morning sunlight. They might possibly wonder what it is like to experience the slow life of the country town, the simplicity of the daily routine compared with the frantic bustle of London. That church spire and the slate roofs belonged to the small market town of Aveley, and the church was Saint Michael's.

Inside the church a man was on his knees praying, with tears running down his cheeks; tears of joy. The Reverend Bixby Luard had just finished putting up Sunday's hymns on the hymn board; Psalm 23, "The Lord is My Shepherd", and "All Praise to Thee, My God this Night." These were an appropriate expression of his feelings, for he was celebrating the birth of a baby daughter to his wife, Clara, this very day. It was indeed a miracle he thought, as he clasped his hands and gave thanks. Giving new life is always a miracle, but more so in those days when infant mortality was unacceptably high. Nevertheless, Clara had given birth to nine other children, all healthy; but one could never take anything for granted.

A week later, the Reverend Bixby and Clara, with some friends acting as witnesses, gathered around the baptismal font. They named the baby Kathleen Evelyn and sprinkled holy water on her in blessing, to which Kate, in response, opened her mouth and emptied her little lungs with a loud wail.

Kate, or Evie as she was known at home, grew up a happy little girl, always helpful; she was known for the compassion she showed to any person or animal who was suffering. And her delight, as three more siblings joined the family, was boundless. That made thirteen children all told. The father would tell anyone prepared to listen, that this was a special number, citing the twelve apostles and Jesus. Loneliness was never a problem in the busy Luard household. She was educated by her older brothers and sisters, long before she started attending the village school.

After completing her primary education, Kate attended Croydon High School for Girls. The three fruitful years she spent there were under the strict guidance of their headmistress, Dorinda Neligan, a lady ahead of her time and a prominent suffragette. Dorinda, whose last name proclaims her Irish heritage, was a woman of deep experience and understanding. She had served as a Red Cross nurse in the Franco-Prussian War, spoke several languages including fluent French, and without a doubt, had considerable influence on Kate's future life and choice of career.

Graduation opened up a world of opportunity to Kate; most girls being lucky to get a job as shop assistant or factory worker. With her prime education, she quickly found work as a private teacher and governess. Kate's sole ambition was to earn enough money to cover her training as a nurse, there never being any doubt in her mind that that was what she wanted to do. When she was ready, she applied and was accepted for nursing training at King's College Hospital, London.

The Second Boer War had been going on for a year when Kate decided that was where she was needed. In 1901, aged twenty-nine, she shipped out to South Africa, and served the next two years there, giving her experience she would never have gained working in ordinary hospitals. After returning home, she continued nursing and in 1911 she got the position of matron at the Maitland Sanatorium in Peppard, Henley-on-Thames.

She was still mourning the passing of her mentor, Dorinda Nelligan, who had died just three weeks earlier, when on 4 August 1914, Germany invaded Belgium. Kate was forty-two years old, when she enlisted in the Queen Alexandra's Imperial Military Nursing Service. She immediately began working on Ambulance trains and later at clearing stations, providing emergency care and evacuating the wounded soldiers. Her work always brought her close to the front, where she witnessed the appalling injuries suffered by the soldiers. She continued serving until demobilization on the 17th of November 1919.

In April 1915 she joined the No. 4 Field Ambulance, a mobile medical unit working on the front line pretreating the wounded before moving them to a casualty clearing station. While there she began keeping a daily journal of her work which she continued all through the war, and in it she referred to this period as her, "Life at the back of the front."

In mid-October that same year, Kate took charge of No. 6 Casualty Clearing Station at Lillers in France, where she was just getting things in order when Major Rolland was admitted.

She wrote two books, based on her letters home and diaries, and the second of these, "Unknown Warriors," commences at this time. In them she describes the horrendous injuries she witnessed while doing her work. Just a few days before Major Rolland was admitted, she wrote:

"Thursday October 21st; All last night a division was entraining at the station and rumbling unceasingly over the cobblestones past the house. A boy is lying smiling all day with his head, right hand and both legs wounded, and his left arm off. When asked 'Are you happy?' he said with a beam, 'Tryin' to be.' Today he is humming *'Sister Susie's sewing shirts for the soldiers.'* I happened to go into the Infant School this morning, just in time to see a delirious boy, with a bad head wound, with a large brain hernia, tear off all his dressings and throw a handful of his brains onto the floor. This is literally true, and he was talking all the time we re-dressed the hole in his head. Then we picked up the handful of brains, and the boy was quiet for a little while. He is very delirious and will not get better."

"Saturday October 30th: A boy came in at 6 pm with his right arm blown clean off in its sleeve at 2 pm. He was very collapsed when he came in, but revived a bit later. 'mustn't make a fuss about trifles,' he explained. 'We got to stick it.' What a trifle! He ran from the first to the second trench unaided. The boy who threw his brains on the floor, died yesterday."

Nurse Luard left the QAIMNS in 1919 to go home and look after her ailing father. She lived with her two sisters in a small village called Wickham Bishops, in Essex.

She died on August 16, 1962.

• • •

"Says Susie: 'Don't be silly,'
And she blushes and she sighs.
Then mother smiles and whispers,
with a twinkle in her eyes:
'Sister Susie's sewing shirts for soldiers,
Such skill at sewing shirts,
Our shy young sister shows!'"

NELLIE SPINDLER[44]

Just around the time Major Rolland was admitted to the CCS run by Kate Luard, another young woman, to her delight, was accepted into the Queen Alexandra's Imperial Military Nursing Service. Nellie Spindler's father George was, like Vincent's father, a police sergeant, who served in the town of Wakefield, where Nellie was born. As Nellie was celebrating her twentieth birthday, she realized her dream when, in 1911, the Wakefield City Fever Hospital accepted her for training. After twelve months there, she was taken in by the Leeds Township Infirmary and continued to work there until 1915, when she made her decision to join the Queen Alexandra's Military Nursing Service.

To join the Queen Alexandra's Nursing Service, a young lady had to be single or recently widowed and had to complete a three-year nursing training. She also had to be over 25.

Nellie was well qualified in all respects except one—she was only 24. However, due perhaps to a memory lapse, she gave her date of birth as 1889, instead of 1891, and no one saw fit to take it further.

---

44 Photograph from Wikimedia Commons, public domain. Source Russeltarr

After working as a nursing sister at the Whittington Military Hospital in Lichfield until 1917, Nellie was given the opportunity to serve abroad, and made the crossing to France. There she served at Number 2 General Hospital for a couple of months before being transferred to Number 44 Casualty Clearing Station, which was under the charge of Sister Kate Luard. Within a couple of months, they were transferred to Brandhoek near Ypres. They were to specialize in abdominal and chest injuries, and due to the urgency of these wounds, they were situated quite near the front. Brandhoek, with its ammunition dumps and railway connections, was a target for the German big guns, and frequently shells landed in the vicinity of the CCS.

On August 21, 1917, Casualty Clearing Station Number 44 was struck by a high explosive shell at 11 am wrecking one of the accommodation tents, seriously wounding Sister Spindler and four other nurses were concussed.

Sadly, Nellie died 20 minutes later in the arms of Sister Minnie Wood, the sister-in-charge.

Kate wrote afterwards:

"Bits came over everywhere, pitching at one's feet as we rushed to the scene. A group of stricken MOs were standing about and in one tent, the sister was dying. The piece went through her from back to front near her heart. She was only conscious for a few minutes and only lived 20 minutes. She was in bed asleep. It all made one feel sick."

Nellie was given a full military funeral and The Last Post was sounded over her grave, which is quite near the hospital at Lijssenthoek Military Cemetery. Her funeral was attended by General Sir Hubert Gough, C.O. of the Fifth Army, three other generals and the Director of Medical Services, the Surgeon General and over one hundred other officers.

The inscription on her grave reads: **"A noble type of good heroic womanhood"**

CHAPTER 11

RSM Elliot's Shiny Boots

When the sun is shining bright,
Dispelling all the dews of night,
With Sam Browne belt and buttons bright
Behold the Sergeant-Major![45]

BAS RIEUX, NORTHERN FRANCE
November 1, 1915

"We goin' for a drink tonight then, Vinnie?" asked John. "Maybe we'll be movin' soon 'n' we need to make the best of it. God knows where we're goin' to end up …"

"Aye, that's true," said Vincent. "Maybe just a wee one then." He smiled, knowing there'd be sore heads tomorrow.

Still, after the shenanigans of the last few weeks, they needed to let their hair down.

"Y … y … yez can c … c … count me in," said O'Boyle. He was still on light duties, which he hoped would continue indefinitely, but had developed a stutter after his experience with the shell explosion.

---

45 From the lyrics of "When the Sergeant Major's on Parade" 1925

They told him he was the first man to fly unaided a distance of twenty feet. But in truth, they worried about him, as they noticed his hands shaking as he worked in the shop.

"Well, I s'pose it'll be the Shanoir," said John, referring to Le Chat Noir. "Old Paulette does really good bangers 'n chips, and the beer's not bad."

"Right then, let's get cleaned up," McLaughlin said, picking up his plate. "It's All Hallows Day t'day y'know, we should be behavin' ourselves and sayin' our prayers."

"Uh … uh … I've su … su … said enough p … prayers at Loos," said O'Boyle.

"You'll be sayin' yer bleedin' prayers if Elliot catches you comin' home late," said Beale.

"Nah, he's bigger things t'do now, since he's been promoted to RSM." Sam grinned.

• • •

The racket in the estaminet rose to a higher pitch as a group of Irish Guards broke into a boisterous rendition of "Molly Malone".

Vincent leaned his chin on his hand, his elbow in a pool of beer on the bar-counter. He was expounding on the delicate taste of Bushmills whiskey to the Canadian sapper beside him, failing to notice the sapper was asleep on the counter. He explained carefully, for it was becoming difficult to pronounce some words, how Bushmills was made solely from single malt barley, whereas other distilleries used corn for their whiskey—a loud snore was the response. His eyes were half closed, and it was becoming somewhat difficult to stay upright on the stool.

A hard slap on the shoulder caught his attention and turning around he squinted at his good mate, John Kelly, and right beside him was ... John Kelly ...

How are there two John's ...?

One of the Johns shouted over the second chorus of the song: "Vinny, we're supposed to be back at eight o'clock, an' it's half-past nine now ..." followed by a loud and odorous belch. "Jaysus, the changer and bips ... b ... banger and chips were the best I've ever had," John stammered again. Vincent turned his bleary eyes on John, smiled warmly at his friend and fell off the stool into his arms. They struggled through the throng of soldiers, all shouting, laughing, and some crying, all trying to forget the horrors of Loos.

The six mates fell out the door and staggered their way back to the camp. Along with John, Vincent, McLaughlin, and O'Boyle, there was Billy Basson the horse driver, and Corporal Corcoran—known as Coco—all well saturated with the watery, but potent beer served by the bosomy Paulette. The walk in the freezing cold air did something to sober them up, and despite a brief pause on route to pee in the gutter, which ended up as a pissing contest, won by John who had an advantage of height, they arrived just before ten pm. As they weaved their way up to the camp gate giving an inharmonious rendition of "It's A Long Way to Tipperary," they saw to their horror, standing with arms akimbo, R.S.M Elliot.

Actually, Vincent could see two RSM Elliots. He also swore afterwards he saw smoke coming out his ears—probably just his breath in the freezing cold air; for he was breathing heavily.

"'Tenshun!" he shouted. "Where do you lot think yer goin' this time of night?" To which Sapper Kelly replied by leaning unsteadily towards the RSM, putting one hand gently on his shoulder for support and puking all over the speechless tyrant's puttees and boots. It didn't help either that Vincent was still standing there with a stupid smile on his face and humming, swaying like he was on the deck of a ship. Sam McLaughlin belched.

"OK," roared the affronted officer, "we'll see you lot at Major Rolland's tent 0800 sharp tomorrer and get the fuck out of here before I have you put in the brig." And to the smirking corporal Duggan in the sentry's hut, he growled, "Get some rags and wipe off these boots, ye piece of shit," righteous fury causing his eyes to bulge like red beacons of hellfire. He was back in martinet mode again.

Just after sunrise at 0800 sharp, six bodies turned up smartly dressed in full uniform, complete with throbbing headaches and mouths like, "the inside of a vulture's crotch," as Corcoran had colorfully put it. Captain Moreshead was behind the desk, standing in for Major Rolland, who was still sick, as R.S.M Elliot marched them in.

"Tenshun!"

Four pairs of heels snapped together.

"I understand you men were drunk and disorderly last night and got back two hours late?" asked Moreshead, himself nursing a severe hangover following the consumption of half a bottle of whiskey the night before. "I also understand that one of you—er—vomited on the RSM's boots." He stifled a smile, not expecting a reply. "OK. I know you've all been through a very difficult time, and I understand you have to unwind, but I'm afraid we must also maintain discipline. Seven days Field Punishment Number Two."

Four groans in unison, followed by rumblings of, " … Sir … "

And that was how Vincent found himself in handcuffs, thankful his own father couldn't see him.

Poor Kelly got the RSM's boots first though.

"Kelly!" the vengeful Sergeant shouted, eyeball to eyeball with the quaking sapper, "I want to be able to see myself in these fucking boots by the time you're finished with 'em, and if I can smell any of your fucking vomit on them, you'll be on latrine duty for a month."

"Musn't piss off the RSM," muttered Basson.

The next week was endured with quiet fortitude by the six friends. Every morning, rain or shine, and the same again in the evenings, they were marched around the parade ground for an hour with a full pack by the malevolent Corporal Duggan, who hadn't forgotten the indignity and humiliation of having to wipe the RSM's boots. Then they were put in a holding room and handcuffed for two hours, after which Duggan was supposed to release them. Most days, he "forgot" to free them by as much as an hour. "Sorry lads, got detained." He would grin, showing his yellowed broken teeth, breathing whiskey fumes as he bent over them to release the cuffs. Where he was getting the whiskey, they could only guess, for only the officers were allowed to have the precious liquor.

At the end of the week, they were released, and nothing more was said about the incident. When they returned to their hut, John sat down on his cot and started rummaging in the small locker they had for their personal belongings. He was going to write to his mother, who hadn't heard from him for a week now. But something else distracted him. Vincent, who came in just after, saw him on his knees, his rear sticking up in the air as he muttered incomprehensibly in his Short Strand brogue.

"What's up?" asked Vincent.

"Ach, I can't find me pocket watch," he said. "Me dada gave it to me before I left for over here."

"Are you sure it was in there?" one of the others asked.

"'Course I'm sure," he said as he got up, face red with anger. "It's fucking gone."

• • •

The 16 miles to Annequin ruled out any chance for John to continue his courtship of the lovely Estelle, even if he had a bike, there wouldn't be enough time between dinner and eight pm when they had to be back. They also knew RSM Elliot had his eye on them, and eight pm saw them smartly saluting the sentry at the gate. The RSM's boots never looked shinier. Three weeks passed, while they enjoyed the hospitality of Lillers, but they weren't allowed to forget there was a war on. Even though the Battle of Loos was officially over, there was fairly continuous and sporadic shelling by both sides, and ambulances drove through continuously, with their sad loads of crippled men, some physically, many mentally.

It was one of those rare, sunny but cold November days that came along every so often to brighten the gloom. Packs were being prepared, equipment put on the wagons, and all the general preparations for a move that they were getting quite used to by this time.

Beale was standing by his bed patting his pockets, rooting in his pack and muttering to himself.

Vincent walked up to him and asked, "What's the matter Andy? We need to get movin', or the Sarge'll be on our tail."

"I know, I know," Beale answered. "I thought I had two quid put away, but it's gone, can't find it anywhere".

"You're sure you didn't spend it?" Sam asked, standing beside Vincent.

"Yeh, I'm pretty sure, s'pose I'll just have to write it off."

"Coco was missing a cigarette case, too. A silver one his dad gave 'im," Sam remarked. The three looked at each other. "I think we'll need to make sure everythin' is locked up. We've a thief amongst us and I think I know who it is," Sam said. "C'mon, let's go."

• • •

They were well rested and the march, in the cool breeze, passed quickly, arriving at the new camp at three in the afternoon. They all got unpacked and the horses fed, before having their own meal.

Sergeant Adams came along and told number two section to get their heads down, as they'd be going out at eight pm to start some machine-gun emplacements. This had to be done at night, as they would be very visible. The others were able to get some rest before turning out the following day.

Laventie, which was also on the front line, was about twenty-five miles west of Lille. They remained here, working on the trenches and other projects such as building machine gun emplacements and dugouts in the trench system. There was ongoing sporadic fighting between the two front lines, and continuous damage to the structure of the trenches. Most of the work involved constructing dugouts and communications trenches and drainage, which became more important as the winter progressed.

On the 2nd of December they went for six days rest. Rest was a little misleading—they worked or drilled, but at least they were out of the front-line trenches and the horrible conditions that endured there.

75th Field Company War Diary
December 8, 1915.
Laventie. Took over northern section of front (Bond St. to Lonely Erith) from 76th Company R.E.

December 9, 1915.
Making Machine Gun emplacements. All sections employed reconnoitering water channels from the frontline to Rue Tillelloy and clearing them. 100 infantry to assist.

December 10, 1915.
All sections employed on drainage between Rue Tillelloi and firing line. 100 infantry to assist.

• • •

The weather was mixed, rain and sunshine taking turns to soak them and dry them out, so a man didn't know what to put on. It didn't matter anyway, because they were soaked in sweat, with the heavy work of lifting rail sections into place, despite the December cold. 1915 was coming to an end, and Christmas was approaching.

"The war should be over any day now, accordin' to what we been told when we signed up …" Basson said, laughing.

Vincent replied, "Aye, sure I've my bags packed and ready to go home." He laughed, too, and said, "We'll be doing our Christmas shopping in London, I suppose."

"Yes, and I've got me list ready," Basson said.

The two of them were bringing a cartload of rails up to the trenches, where the rest of the section were working on repairing the Decauville tracks. An earlier barrage had blown a train up, the smoke giving the German artillery a good target. The transportation had decided to move the train up during a fairly heavy fog, but it had cleared unexpectedly, and the second round had lifted it bodily and thrown it on its side. It's never good to second guess nature.

A bunch of the Guards infantry were filling in the shell holes and rebuilding the rail bed, under the supervision of corporal Duggan, who always seemed to manage to wrangle himself an easy number. Vincent noticed Duggan take out a cigarette from a rather nice-looking silver cigarette case, which he knew instinctively didn't belong to him.

• • •

From the 22nd to 26th, work continued with building machine gun emplacements, dugouts, and carrying out continuous repairs to the tracks. There was no rest on Christmas Day, though the mess did manage to get what looked like a turkey, with mashed potatoes and gravy—a rare treat.

But, still, the men worked through the day. This was probably because of the uproar over the previous year when the troops on both sides sang carols, fraternized and played football on No-Man's Land in some cases. The senior command gave strict orders that this was not to be repeated this year. They'd all heard the stories from some of the older hands, and from the newspapers what had happened a year ago.

THE CHRISTMAS TRUCE

In the lead up to Christmas 1914, there were several peace initiatives. The "Open Christmas Letter" was a public message for peace addressed "To the Women of Germany and Austria," signed by a group of 101 British women suffragettes at the end of 1914 as the first Christmas of World War I approached. Pope Benedict XV, on the 7th of December 1914, had begged for an official truce between the warring governments.

He asked, "that the guns may fall silent at least upon the night the angels sang." This attempt was officially rebuffed.

Nevertheless, a "Christmas Truce" was arranged in many places along the front, where the opposing troops themselves agreed on a cease-fire. In several cases the soldiers actually fraternized with those from the enemy trenches and exchanged chocolate and gifts. This was frowned upon by the senior officers, and the following year any truce was severely discouraged. They felt if the men on both sides were fraternizing, they wouldn't be able to fight each other.

However, not all the troops in the Laventie area obeyed the order not to fraternize with the enemy on this Christmas Day of 1915.

The following is from a diary kept by private Robert Keating,[46] who was with the Welsh Fusiliers in Laventie; they were fighting in the same trenches as the Guards:

"... 12 midnight came, Xmas day was now here. And the Allemans started shelling us very heavily until 1 am—I went to sleep after this.

Xmas Day, Dec. 25, 1915.

Had breakfast after which we shouted greetings to the Germans over the way. We shouted, "Come over"—they shouted, "Come over". We stood up and saw them walking on their parapets then one of the Jocks ran across and Gordon and I. The officer was shouting "come

---

46 Archives of the Royal Welsh Fusiliers Museum, Caernarfon, Wales. Lt. General Jonathon Riley, Chairman of Trustees.

back—come back". But we took no heed and went on. The Germans who turned out to be Wurtemburg reserves crowded round us and chatted about old England—one fellow we were talking to was born in Northampton and was longing for the day when he could return. They said the war would end in a few months in our favor and that they were absolutely fed up with the whole thing generally. Just as we were exchanging souvenirs the blooming artillery started and you should have seen us run. Heaps of fellows were caught in the barbed wire, but really, there was no danger to us as the shells were dropping on the German trenches. The reason why we rushed back was because our artillery firing on the Allemans might entice their snipers to fire on us. However, this was not so. Before leaving the Germans, one of their officers told one of ours that they would not fire another shot for two days, if we did the same and believe me or believe me not, on our part of the line not a single shot was fired until we were relieved by the Irish Guards on Sunday evening. Well, to revert, at 12 noon, I was told off for fatigue duty with about two dozen of the Scots. We had to go all the way back to the Headquarters and get a thousand sandbags. On the way back my load came undone so I was left behind and had to walk the whole length of the Southern Road in daylight which proved to be an advantage as I was able to jump over the shell holes instead of falling in them. On one occasion I kicked an old boot and to my surprise a foot fell out – I did not inspect it. Arriving back in the trench at 2.30 pm I dumped my load and joined a party who were burying a dead Scot on the "no man's land". We intended burying a lot of fellows but owing to our heavy artillery fire we had to abandon the attempt and return to the trenches.

The remainder of the day we spent shouting to the Germans, meanwhile the Brigadier General came round the trenches and told every fellow to shoot any German he saw. Notwithstanding this he told us all to keep well below the breastworks. Anyhow, no one took any notice of this order and carried on as usual. At 5 pm the rum was issued and somehow or other the Scots managed to get hold of a good supply and (consequently they were soon squiffy[47]).

Just as Gordon and I were tucking in under our shelter we were roused out by the Scots and dragged on to the top of the parapet where we found all the Welsh fellows gathered. Here we were, Welsh and Scots all clustered round the burning brazier which was placed on the outer parapet. The Germans were sending up starlights and singing – they stopped so we cheered them and we began singing Land of Hope and Glory and Men of Harlech et cetera – we stopped and they cheered us. So we went on till the early hours of the morning and the only thing that brought us down was one of our machine guns being turned on us. Fortunately, no one was killed. After this Gordon and I returned to our shelter and by the aid of a candle wrote letters..."

The Royal Welsh Fusiliers (Private Keating's battalion) were dug in near the village of Fauquissart, which was in the same area where the 75th were working. In fact, he mentioned above that they were relieved by the Irish Guards on Sunday evening.

75th Field Company War Diary
December 27, 1915.

Took over work on right sector on divisional front. (M24d to Sign Post Lane.) from 76th F.C.R.E. on 1st Guards Brigade relieving 2nd Guards Brigade along this line. Employed chiefly on drainage especially on right front which had been damaged by the recent rain. Gridding bottom of S. Tillelloy trench.

December 28, 1915.

Dug out a new drain from front line (between Sunken Road and Sign Post Lane) to Ebenezer Farm. Repairs to front line and draining the

---

47 Drunk

same. S. Tillelloy trench gridding completed and trench good for traffic. But work on reveting sides and clearing handed over to Pioneers.

December 29, 1915.

Drain from front line to Ebenezer Farm completed.

December 30, 1915.

Draining front line generally. Assisting infantry in repair to front line. Patrol (Lt. Bousfield and 3 sappers with infantry bombers) went out to report on state of wire in front of parapet from Ducks Bill to M29d69 and found it wanted considerable repairs.

December 31, 1915.

Draining front line and assisting infantry in repair to front line. Dugout for company H.Q. on right of Right Battalion fronts in Sunken Row commenced.

The trenches were awash.

CHAPTER 12

Dreams Are Best

"This is the song of the mud,
  The pale-yellow glistening mud
  that covers the hills like satin;
  The grey gleaming silvery mud
  that is spread like enamel over the valleys;
  The frothing, squirting, spurting, liquid mud
  that gurgles along the road beds;
  The thick elastic mud that is kneaded and pounded
  and squeezed under the hoofs of the horses;
  The invincible, inexhaustible mud of the war zone."

(Mary Borden. "The Song of the Mud")[48]

LAVENTIE, FRANCE
January 1, 1916

Unable to stop shivering, hunched in his greatcoat, with a wool scarf wrapped around his neck, he sat down on the wooden chair and got out the war diary. The only source of light in the unheated dugout was a candle on the wooden table. Major Rolland licked his pencil and began writing up the day's events.

---

48 https://www.poetryfoundation.org/poems *At the Somme: the song of the Mud.*

It was New Year's Eve 1915, and he was bone weary and psychically drained. The recent bout of malaria had taken the sap out of him, leaving him sallow and drawn, like, as his second in command cheerfully put it, "A starving horse."

Happy bloody New Year, he thought as he scribbled on the page for the last day of December.

How many more years would he have to record? And more importantly, would he live to record them?

The brief entry— *"Draining front line and assisting infantry in repair to front line. Dugout for company H.Q. on the right of Right Battalion fronts in Sunken Row."*—belied the exhausting work they had been doing over the last few days. The battle of Loos, and their terrifying introduction to the fighting, was behind them, and now the trench scuttlebutt had it that the Guards were moving north to the Ypres front, where there was intense fighting for control of the beleaguered town. Rolland shared his men's exhaustion, and in a way looked forward to the move north, as it would give them a break away from the front line.

Outside, the sappers were sloshing around in the dark, with the trench just lit with a couple of Tilley lamps, trying to get the pumps going to remove the accumulated rainwater. A miserable winter left them like wet rag dolls, left out and forgotten by their owner; near continuous rain and sleet filled the trenches beyond the Engineers' capacity to drain them. No matter how much clothing they wore, the bitter cold seeped to the very marrow of their bones.

Vincent and Sam McLoughlin were knee deep in freezing water, trying to get a blocked stirrup pump to work. It was a manual pump with a handle operated by two men. The two sappers had to open the pump up, where they found it was clogged with some cloth—probably the remains of some lost soldier's uniform. Having removed the offending rag, and cleaned the valve, they eventually got the cover back on, constantly having to fish for their tools in the mud.

"Happy New Year mate," Sam muttered to Vincent, tightening up the last nut on the casing.

"Same to you Sammy-boy," Vincent replied, then said, "I hope this next year will be the last of the war," even knowing all the while that wasn't going to happen.

The two stood up, easing their aching backs, and primed the pump, then gave the handle a try. It worked, thank God. The infantry could take over now. Working their way back along the trenches, they finally got back to the shop where they had temporarily set up their equipment. He and Sam had a coke fire going there, where they were able to warm up and make a cup of tea and get some rest, leaving those other poor buggers behind to keep emptying the trench.

It was an ongoing, and losing, struggle to keep the trenches dry, and the work had bedeviled them all winter. They were all wet and frozen, their gumboots waterlogged, and their socks sodden, without a chance to change anything. All this under constant enemy fire.

Men under stress find ways of coping. Vincent had developed a way of switching off and going back home in his head. A few lines he remembered from one of Robert Service's poems that really spoke to him, came to mind as he sat down with a steaming mug of tea and lit up a cigarette.

> "Yes, I'll smoke my cigarette,
>   Vestured in my garb of dreams,
>   And I'll borrow no regret;
>   All is gold that golden gleams.
>   So I'll charm my solitude,
>   With the faith that Life is blest,

Brave and noble, bright and good...
Oh, I think that dreams are best!"

(Robert Service. "Dreams Are Best")

That night, chin on hand, he drifted into the daydream; he opened the door of the bar on Agnes Street, near his home in Belfast and walked into the smoke-filled room. It was a Friday night after work, and he was getting together with some of the other apprentices from the yard. As he entered the warm fug, his mates called to him from over by the dartboard. There was a roaring fire in the grate, and they'd crowd around it with their pints, chatting, some playing darts.

Even just thinking about that fire warmed him up. He wasn't a heavy drinker but enjoyed a pint and the companionship once or twice a week, and a game of darts. Thinking about it, Vincent couldn't believe he had taken it so much for granted. Now he'd give anything to be able to grasp the brass handle and pull open the heavy wood door with the engraved glass windows, "Standard Bar and Lounge".

As a bleak watery sun rose above the German lines, on New Year's Day the 1st Guards Brigade sloshed their way through the communication trenches and relieved the 2nd Guards Brigade on the front line—the same trenches that Private Keating had manned. Sporadic fighting continued, though the intensity of the earlier battle had subsided, both sides having worn themselves out.

On the 8th they went into the reserve line and continued working on repairing the communication trenches. The fighting would continue here, but the Guards and their accompanying engineers were needed elsewhere.

LAVENTIE, FRANCE
January 14, 1916

Wrapped in a mixture of weariness and anticipation, the men of 75th Field Company were packing their kitbags and equipment for another move. Yesterday evening, as they got some hot food inside their empty stomachs, Sergeant Adams had come into the mess and told them the orders had come in and they were going to the front line in Flanders, Belgium. Most now had been tempered in the crucible of battle, having survived Loos and the misery of the trenches. It was plain, even to the dimmest, that the war was not going to end soon, and they were in it for the long haul. A sense of numbed resignation had settled in. Life revolved around letters and parcels coming from home, a few days of rest time, and even a change of location was something to break the monotony of the trenches.

The Guards were now moving further north towards Ypres, and the 75th Company was preparing to follow, with their wagon loads of equipment. This was a big operation for the Engineers; horses and limbers to get ready; machines disassembled and stowed on the wagons; farriers, shoeing smiths, sappers, cooks all bustling around, repairing damaged equipment, storing wire, pontoons, tools, and weapons for the long march. They hadn't been to the battered front in Belgium, but they knew the situation was as bad there as it had been in Loos.

The weather was bitterly cold, and their breath steamed up around them as they marched. There were thousands of troops and their equipment on the move, churning up the pavement on the already overused roadway. The glutinous mud was ubiquitous that winter; it stuck to their boots, where each step was an effort, like walking in a nightmare. Ruts in the road were covered in water, but the wagon wheels found them; then the wagon had to be extricated holding up the whole train of equipment behind. The horses were reluctant to go anywhere and needed constant coaxing. At night the men slept with their greatcoats on, but still shivered as the insidious cold found its way to their very bones. It was a long monotonous march, through small Belgian villages—many destroyed—the residents long gone after the initial German onslaught. They'd heard stories, some true and some not, where the German army had shot the civilians, accusing them of spying or sabotage. Even if they had a house left, the choice of flight with a few possessions was better than staying.

As Vincent marched along, once again coaxing Herbert and Horatio, the two cart horses drawing their equipment wagon, with Billy Basson on the other horse, he walked with Herbert's harness in his left hand. It gently brought him back to the summers when he was a boy in Tallanstown, walking with the horse drawing the hay-shifters[49] in the hazy summer sunlight. They would have spent the day helping the farmer load the dusty haycocks onto the smooth timbers of the hay-shifter. Then they headed off to the farm, to put the hay in storage. As the horse ambled along, most of the kids sat on the back of the wagon, but he liked to be on his own, walking in companionable silence with the tired old horse.

It was a different life, belonging to someone else, like he'd read it in a book somewhere. There was no continuity between the years before he joined the army and now. His father and family lived in that other place. The land he lived in now with his comrades was a lifeless sea of mud and misery, cold, forbidding and destroyed. Death and its smell were pervasive. Marching along the road to Eeke in Belgium, they passed troops coming in the opposite direction, ambulances carrying the wounded trying to get past, and on the side

---

49 Flat wagon used for transporting the "Hay-cock" from the field to the farm.

of the road lay broken and abandoned machinery—the detritus of war. Without the mental faculty to retreat into another life, he could not have survived. He was cold and miserable, feet blistered, wet and sore from the constant marching, the persistent rain running down his rain cape and dripping on his trousers; the only escape inside his head, where he sought solace in memories of a more pleasant time.

Though he was happy enough during his years as an apprentice in Harland's, his thoughts usually drifted to the days of his childhood in Tallanstown. In retrospect they had been a happy time, though the death of his mother still brought back a deep sadness. But with the resilience of youth, they got on with it. The memories were always around the river Glyde—fishing, occasionally catching a nice little trout, or just sitting on the bank with the summer sun warm on their backs, telling each other stories. It was said that the Salmon of Knowledge, which the legendary Fionn MacCumhaill tasted, was caught in that very stream, in a quiet pool just a half mile up from the bridge—their fishing pool.

The story, told and retold, spoke of ancient times, before the Celts arrived in Ireland. The fertile and heavily forested land was inhabited by a mysterious ancient race.

There was a hunter and warrior called Fionn MacCumhaill who was sent to live with a wise old poet called Finneces, as was the custom in those days. The poets, who were also accredited with great wisdom, would teach young men the ways of the warriors and how to survive in a land of magic and lore. Finneces knew that there was a salmon that lived in a magic pool, where hazelnuts fell from the nine trees of knowledge. Anyone who caught and ate the salmon would acquire "the knowledge of the world". After a long and arduous battle with the salmon, the bard managed to catch it with help from Fionn. He was too exhausted to cook it, so he asked the young warrior to cook it for him while he slept. Fionn had just finished cooking when he saw a blister on his skin where he'd burnt his thumb. Without thinking, he stuck it in his mouth to cool it off. When Finneces woke, he asked Fionn if he had eaten any of the salmon, and the boy truthfully replied no, but he had burned his thumb and had stuck that in his mouth. Finneces, realizing that the knowledge had been contained in the blister Fionn tried to burst and that Fionn had absorbed the knowledge, had little choice but to accept this.

Hopefully the two of them enjoyed the salmon afterwards. That was how Fionn, the future leader of the Fianna, a race of great warriors, acquired all the knowledge of the world.

The people of Tallanstown believed that the river where the salmon was caught was the Glyde,[50] and the magic pool it lived in was just up the river about half a mile; there were still old hazel trees enveloping the pool in their shade, grown from the seeds of even more ancient trees. The lads often fished here. Even if they caught nothing, it was quiet and out of sight of the grown-ups. For millennia, The Glyde had run through the place where his house was in the police barracks. Sometimes lower in the summer drought and fast and feisty in the winter—a symbol of permanence in an ever-changing world.

And Vincent had often wondered if any of the trout he caught in that magic pool could help him do his arithmetic any better. He wasn't worried about having all the knowledge of the world, but he'd have been happy if his schoolwork had become a little easier. He was good at it but learning fractions when he could have been out with his pals, was, to say the least, a pain in the neck.

---

50 The story comes from *The Boyhood Deeds of Fionn,* and it doesn't mention the river where the salmon was caught, but many say it was the *Glyde.* Who knows? It was a long time ago.

And he pondered on the seasons, each leaving its own impression permanently stamped in his mind. In February, as the frosts of winter got less frequent, there was the sharp smell of the manure "top dressing" as the farmers spread it over the meadows used for the long grass they would save and store. Spring was full of scent, with the smell of fresh growth, the green leaves appearing on the lime trees, wet and sparkling in the sun between cool April showers, or the salty tang of the sharp east wind blowing in from the Irish Sea.

As the days languidly stretched into longer evenings, growing warmer, white cotton boll clouds coming from nowhere and going nowhere, across a virgin blue sky, auguring the approach of summer.

Summer saw the fields of grass getting ready for harvesting into winter forage; during seemingly endless school holidays, helping the farmers with their scythes cutting it and building the haystacks. It was labor intensive, grueling work, with everyone—women, children, and old folks—all pitched in. After the sweet-smelling cut grass had dried to a golden yellow, it was gathered in piles called "haycocks", which were pulled up onto the "hayshifters"[51] and hauled to the haggard, the yard and barn where the crops were stored, with a bunch of kids sitting on the back. The long summer holiday from school passed in a blur of activity in the fields; games of skittles at the crossroads in the long evenings and the *cheili*[52] on weekends. In the summertime, the occasional visit from traveling players was a rare and wonderful treat always to be remembered. The troupe would set up a tent in the field behind the houses, with Vincent and his pals running around helping them, and perform there for a week. In a village starved for entertainment they had a rapturous audience.

---

51 Flat bed carts used for transporting the haycocks.

52 Irish dancing.

Before you knew it, autumn was easing in, with its shortening days and cool nights, rust red trees carpeting the paths with leaves and the first fire being lit, the sweet, pungent scent of wood and turf smoke. The year was blending gently into winter, and Halloween games and dressing up. Christmas, with carols and gifts, and on into the new year.

An apparently endless cycle, with its tragedies and highlights tucked in the years as they passed—all too quickly.

• • •

Herbert's hoof had gone down a mud-filled pothole and they stumbled to a halt.

Hang on …

• • •

Mostly though, Vincent had loved the autumn months: the river paths coated with leaves and the scents of damp earth and decay. Playing with his siblings and friends; coming indoors when the night was setting in, a hen's step earlier each day, to tea, fresh crisp soda bread and jam. Even the homework he had to do didn't seem as bad as he thought it was at the time. A necessary evil that interrupted the otherwise smooth harmony of his life.

Then came the end of his primary school, and his father had found a place for him in Hardinge Street Christian Brothers School, where he would continue his education but begin technical training as well…

• • •

Vincent was brought abruptly back to the present as they entered the small Belgian village of Eeke and then the work began, readying the camp. He supposed he'd had a better life than many and was grateful for the memories that brought him through the worst moments, reminding him that there would be an end to all of this, and a new beginning.

If he made it through, that is.

It was early afternoon as a wintry sun broke through the clouds and provided a modicum of warmth to the damp soldiers marching tiredly into the village. The rain had stopped a few hours ago, though the ground was still deep mud. There was plenty of time to get the tents set up, the animals tended to and most importantly some food in their bellies before dark. After the long march that morning they were starving.

75th Field Company War Diary
February 16, 1916.
Company remained in billets awaiting orders.

February 17, 1916.
Company moved to billets at K.12.0 and K.18 a & b. (Trench map ref.) Going via Steenvourde and turning into Belgium at K36d0.4.

February 18, 1916.
Inspection of all kit.

February 19, 1916.
Drill order parade, section drill. Sinking of well shaft for 2nd Grenadiers and completed today.

February 20, 1916.
Church of England parade (Sunday).

DEREK McCANN

February 21, 1916.
"P" type smoke helmets changed for "PH" pattern. Sections employed drilling, packing and unpacking pontoons and Weldon Trestles.

• • •

"You're not 'alf bad looking in that 'elmet," Billy Basson said to Vincent. "Maybe we c'ld go out on a date some night?"

"Sorry Billy, I'm already taken," Vincent said, his laugh muted through the smelly material of the PH smoke helmet. "Ask Sam, he's free."

Laughing and kidding about, they were trying on the new issue of helmets, which were supposed to be a big improvement on the "P" type, which had been issued in May 1915 after the Germans first used chlorine on French troops at Ypres. The effects were devastating, and even by the standards of a brutal war, were beyond savage. But the British used gas at Loos, and now it was yet another weapon in an increasingly barbarous war.

• • •

147

CLARA HABER
BERLIN, GERMANY
May 1, 1915

The deep orange disc of the setting sun was slipping below the roof-tops in the west, when, on a late summer evening an attractive young woman walked out into the back garden of her house. Her strawberry blonde hair was neatly coiffed to a neat bun on top. She stood a while, looking up at the indigo sky to the east, as if she were waiting for the first star to appear. Then, pointing the revolver in her hand, she shot it into the ground, leaving a neat hole in the soil. The bang echoed in the stillness, and, satisfied it worked properly, as her shocked husband rushed to the door, she raised it to her head and pulled the trigger a second time. She'd had enough of being married to a man whose purpose in life was to kill as many soldiers as possible, in the shortest time.

Clara Haber was a brilliant research chemist, and the fatal shot ended a promising career as one of the few women who had made it into the male dominated world of German scientific research.

Just over a week earlier, on April 22, as thousands of French and Algerian soldiers were eating their rations in the trenches northeast of the Belgian town of Ypres, they stood and watched, puzzled, as a green cloud approached them from the German front line. Their officers were shouting at them to prepare for attack, believing it was a German smoke screen. Frantically fixing bayonets, faces flushed with adrenalin, breathing hard, they noticed a strange pineapple, peppery smell, and stopped for a moment. As the noxious cloud flowed over the parapet of the trench, they began coughing, choking, and sucking in the poison as it lacerated their respiratory system. As they saw their comrades drooling froth and blood, it began to dawn on them; this was not smoke—it was gas. For most it was too late, and the chlorine gas had done its work. Within an hour, one thousand five hundred men had died an agonizing, writhing death, lying in the bottom of the trench, literally drowning in their own fluid.

FRITZ HABER

Fritz Haber, a German scientist engaged in helping the war effort, had developed chlorine gas for use on the battlefield. He lived with his wife and young son in Berlin and visited the front line to see his new weapon in use. Clara remained at home, agonizing over what her husband was engaged in, knowing the awful havoc the gas would wreak on thousands of soldiers. This, on top of the fact that for years now, Fritz's career was advancing to the detriment of her own brilliant research efforts, left her in a state of deep depression. Fritz returned home and a week later, was preparing to go to the Eastern Front, to supervise another attack with the gas. His wife, Clara vehemently against Fritz's activities to the end, wrote farewell letters to her friends and family, said goodbye to her son and committed suicide.[53]

After the attack, Canadian troops nearby, who had to respond, had a savvy medic, who told them to pee in a cloth and put it over their mouth. The ammonia neutralized the chlorine and allowed them to break through the gas and attack the Germans. But something better was needed. The allies well knew this would not be the last time gas would be used in this and future wars.

As an outcome of the research carried out, the "P" (or "Phenate") helmet, officially called the Tube Helmet, was introduced in July 1915. It featured two mica eyepieces and had an exhale valve fed from a metal tube, which the wearer held in his mouth. It gave the appearance of a space alien from one of H. G. Wells' novels. It had flannel layers of cloth dipped in sodium phenolate and glycerin and protected against chlorine and phosgene, but not against tear gas.

The "PH" (or "Phenate Hexamine") helmet replaced it in October 1915 and added Hexamethylenetetramine, which greatly improved its protection against phosgene and added protection against hydrocyanic acid.

This mask remained in service until the end of the war.

---

53 An excellent short film "Haber" was made of this story and can be found on Vimeo at https://www.haberfilm.com/

75th Field Company War Diary
February 22, 1916.

Sections employed as on 21st. 2nd Lt. Russell sent to C.E. XIVth Corps to obtain information about geological nature of ground near infantry camps west of Poperinghe, returning same day.

• • •

POPERINGHE, BELGIUM
October 4, 1914

As the women of the small Belgian market town of Poperinghe were preparing breakfast, they were distracted by the sound of many hooves, clopping along the worn cobbles of the Place de Ville. Rushing to the windows, they were in time to see a troop of German *Uhlans*,[54] on their stomping mounts, straight as the lances they carried, parading through the square. The invasion, to the astonishment of its denizens, had arrived in town. Children ran out, awestruck at this unexpected and uninvited show of military grandeur and power, running along-side the lancers, mothers screaming at them to come back.

Nothing much happened, no blood was let, and being unop-posed, the Germans left the people to go about their business, much to the relief of the citizenry.

Until October, when the town was entered from the opposite end by the French army, upon which the Uhlans decided to leave and fight another day. Many, many years later, those children, growing up and becoming grandparents, would regale their grandchildren about that day, October 4, 1914.

These sterling members of the Poperinghe community num-bered around 11,000 and though they may have suspected it on that memorable day, their lives were about to undergo a dramatic

---

54 German elite horse cavalry.

change. For Poperinghe was to become a military town, huge camps being set up outside the town, housing up to 200,000 British, French and Commonwealth soldiers at any one time. The train station was also a big advantage to the military, where ammunition, personnel and food could be shipped in, with the wounded being put on the outward-bound trains. The station and ammunition dumps also attracted the attention of the German artillery, which fortunately was just out of range, except for one mighty rail-borne howitzer—nicknamed "Percy"—which regularly lopped high explosive on the town. Nonetheless, the soldiers found "Pop", as they called it, a welcome refuge from the fighting.

CHAPTER 13

"Good-bye old man, goodbye"

Will ye go to Flanders, my Molly O?
Tae see the Bold Commanders, my Molly O?
Will ye see the bullets fly,
And the soldiers how they die,
And the ladies, how they cry, my Molly O.

POPERINGHE, BELGIUM
April 4, 1916

"Damn," Vincent swore as the shovel broke. He examined the sheared handle and decided he could fix it when they got back to the shop. There was a third shovel, and he put the broken one aside and resumed digging. Sam McLaughlin was happily digging away on a rose bed on the other side of the garden in the shade of a brick wall.

The two of them sang Percy French's *The Mountains of Mourne*, happy as the day was out.

"Oh Mary this London's a wonderful sight,

With people here workin' by day and by night…"

The three of them were clearing up brambles and weeds from the jungle that had taken over the garden. Andrew Beale was carting away all the cuttings and rubbish.

"We're diggin' up weeds and cuttin' the briars,
It makes a fine change from fightin' the wars …
Old Fritz can bomb us and give it his best,
I couldn't care less 'cause I'm havin' a rest …

Their day had taken a turn for the better earlier on when Vincent and Sam were working on a truck engine that they'd lifted out the night before. Captain Bulkeley, their new CO, walked in, with Corporal Duggan and a padre in tow. The latter was a relatively short, fair-haired man, peering shortsightedly through wire rimmed spectacles with an amiable grin that lit up his round, florid face. As they straightened, the captain introduced him as "Reverend Clayton", and they shook hands. No saluting with this man.

"You can just call me 'Tubby'," he said. "Everyone does," ignoring Captain Bulkeley's frown at this flouting of the Guards strict etiquette.

"The padre's going to need six men to help with his latest project." Bulkeley informed the two soldiers. "I'm sending five of you under Corporal Duggan with the padre for the next few days. I'll leave it to him to explain what he wants, but I expect you to do a good job."

With that he saluted the padre and left. Tubby Clayton just shrugged and told them what he needed.

"I'm with the 6th Division, and what we're trying to do is set up a place in Poperinghe where the soldiers and officers can have a bit of relaxation," he said. "We've managed to get a nice large town-house on Rue de l'Hôpital. It's close to the square, to use for the men when they come behind the lines for a rest period, and" he paused to clear his throat, "thanks to the Engineers, we've got it patched up and now we're furnishing it, and I want to get the garden right before the summer comes. It'll be a lovely place for the lads to relax in."

He beamed at them. "So, I'll need a few lads to work on the garden, and I also need some carpenters for the furniture." He paused, and his cheerful grin took them all in. "We've decided to call the place 'Talbot House,' after the brother of our senior chaplain. Sadly, Gilbert was killed last year at Hooge."

The sappers nodded, happily seeing an opportunity to work away from the watchful eye of the sergeant, and almost in the middle of the town as well. Manna from Heaven, in the form of this rotund little clergyman.

"Let's go then, what are we waiting for?"

They rounded up John Kelly and Andrew Beale, and the mechanic Willie O'Neill, who could fix anything he put his hands to, and headed off with the padre in the lead.

They worked hard in the garden, and at lunch Tubby brought them in and sat them around a large dining table made from tent floorboards, seated on chairs made from packing cases. He brought in a large bowl of stew with chunks of fresh baguette, and they laid into it hungrily. They ate better than they had for a long time. In the afternoon, Duggan disappeared with some muttered excuse, and the others carried on, delighted to get away from the workshops for a while, not missing Duggan's company one bit. They'd managed to scrounge a few garden seats, and some ornaments, and beavered away on the flower beds and grassed areas, stopping whenever they felt like it to relax on one of the seats to have a smoke. At six pm, they finished for the day and got cleaned up for a night on the town. Life was good.

This was to be the pattern for the next week.

On Sunday, the padre held a service and invited them all to join. He'd got hold of an old carpenter's bench, which he used as an altar, telling them, "Jesus was a carpenter, so was Joseph, so I think this is appropriate, don't you?" He laughed at his own witticism. But it was touching, really, to witness the enthusiasm of this jolly, enthusiastic individual, whom they had grown to respect. He was so proud of the Crucifix he'd bought after a lot of haggling with the woman who ran the shop across the road.

A week after they began working in the garden, they had to go back to the workshop, as the jobs there were piling up. The padre came out to thank them. They had cleared several of the rose beds and pulled out what seemed like a wagonload of wild blackberry and other brambles. The garden was beginning to take shape. Inside, the carpenters had done an enormous amount of work, and he was delighted. Things were getting done. Then, looking around to make sure no one was within earshot, he confided to them that some of the silverware that he'd gathered up for the dining room had disappeared.

Looking at them with a puzzled frown, he said, "I can't imagine anyone would take the silver, though it was real sterling silver and I suppose it would be worth something. But watch out, we've got a thief amongst us."

Vincent and Sam gave each other a knowing look, and Sam said, "Sorry to hear that, Reverend ..."—he couldn't get himself to call this good man Tubby—"... we do have an idea where it may be going, but we can't prove anything."

And so, the matter rested.

• • •

BELGIUM
October 17, 2019

It was a decidedly cool morning, but dry and good driving weather. Terry and I, having settled in on our canal barge, decided to have a look at Poperinghe and the surrounding area.

If you read anything about Flanders and the war, Poperinghe will come up somewhere. It was a railhead and depot for stores and ammunition, sufficiently close to the front to easily transport the matériel by wagon, but far enough behind the lines to allow the troops to use it as a rest area. Surrounding towns such as Brielen, Vlamertinghe, and Boezinghe were worth a visit too.

The gusty wind, an almost permanent feature of the flat Flanders countryside, blew out of the west, powering light cumulus clouds across an otherwise clear blue sky, their shadows flashing across the surrounding countryside. Driving southwest from Bruges, the fields we passed were green with ripening crops; the farmers were busy in their tractors spreading silage, taking for granted the peace that allowed them to carry on with their lives. It was a different picture in 1915.

Our first stop was a French military cemetery on the outskirts of the town, where many of the soldiers in the red pantaloons found their last resting place.

COLORS OF THE PANTALOONS

The French army traditionally wore light blue jackets and red trousers or pantaloons. In 19th Century warfare, with the limited range of musket fire, this was not too much of a problem, and provided a certain panache. But with the advanced weaponry used in the First World War, where the infantry used weapons with ranges of several hundred meters, the red trousers made the French soldiers easy targets. Even though there was considerable pressure to introduce a more concealing color, the conservatism of the military and the public wouldn't allow it. It wasn't until 1915, and partly due to a shortage of red dye, and a corresponding increase in dead soldiers, that the army switched to

"Horizon Blue". This color was supposed to make a soldier less visible while silhouetted against the horizon.

Sadly, many brave soldiers met their end because of the Red Pantaloons.

After paying our respects, we drove into the town centre, finding our way by trial and error. Nearing the Market Square—*Grot Markt*—we found a parking spot on *Gasthuisstraat* and got out to have a look around. As I stood on the cobbled pavement, massaging my stiff knees, I noticed a striking looking building on the other side.

The eye was caught initially by the beautiful wrought iron gates on the front entrance, but was quickly drawn upwards to the British, French, and Belgian flags hanging above. The three-story building had a clean white ornate façade dating it to the mid-19th century. A hotel perhaps? The hanging sign outside the front door said Talbot House.

Our curiosity aroused, we looked for an entrance as the front door was locked. Finding an entry on the side, we went in and to our delight discovered that the house with its lovely gardens was open to visitors. Apparently, it had been used for entertaining the troops who were on rest from the front line. This would be interesting. As we walked around the rooms, in the footsteps of the soldiers who came here, we learned its fascinating history. We felt a deep connection to Vincent here. The rooms contained the very same furniture and décor that was extant in 1915. While walking through, one sensed the spirits of those who had come here to enjoy the brief time off allowed them, and to forget the war. For many it was the last thing they ever enjoyed, and walking through the reception room, Terry felt a deep and inexplicable unease, a sense of some other presence, which lifted as she left the room.

• • •

POPERINGHE, BELGIUM
August 1914

Monsieur Coevoet-Camerlynck did very well from his brewing business, through good times and bad, thanks to the Belgians' passion for good beer. So much so in fact, he was able to afford a fine mansion close to the city square. Here, he and his family lived a comfortable life, until it began to come apart in August 1914, with the onset of war and the German invasion of his country. But he continued on, as the war didn't interrupt the consumption of beer.

However ...

One glorious spring day in 1915, while enjoying afternoon tea with his wife in the sitting room—he remembered it clearly for the rest of his days—he was just lifting his cup to sip the hot liquid, when an ear-splitting blast blew the door open, shattering plate glass windows and violently shaking the house. The whole ground seemed to rise up toward them, and amid clouds of dust and earth, they heard a continuing rumble as part of the roof gave way and collapsed. They were terrified. Covered in scalding tea, the monsieur stood shakily amid the broken china, and saw his wife crumble in a dead faint. They were both covered in blood, from shards of broken glass, and in deep shock. Madame recovered, and he helped her to a dust covered chair; he didn't bother to wipe the chair as Madame was equally covered in dust, and looking down at her, and realizing that but for the grace of God ... he proceeded to take inventory of the situation.

A large shell, no doubt a gift from "Percy", the giant German howitzer on Pilkem Ridge, had landed in the back garden. At that moment, the monsieur decided that he had had enough. This was the last straw on top of the general mayhem caused by quarter of a million foreign soldiers rampaging through his beloved town. Coevoet-Camerlynck decided that perhaps a prolonged holiday was in order. As a result of his rumination, he moved out with undignified haste, and brought his family to a safer residence in France. Nor was he alone, as many of the residents were leaving or had already left. But as the town's burghers left with their cartloads of possessions, refugees from worse-hit areas moved in, many of whom set up thriving businesses catering to the quarter of a million troops passing through. Without doubt, and Monsieur Coevoet-Camerlynk would agree, that, "one man's trouble is another's opportunity."

In addition, a few stalwart citizens who saw the possibilities and feared not the occasional stray shell, stayed on.

• • •

Serendipitously, an army chaplain was posted to Poperinghe.

Philip Clayton—known throughout his life as "Tubby"—was born in Australia in 1885. When he was two years old, his family moved back to London, where he spent his childhood and went to school. One of his friends at St. Paul's School was the author G. K. Chesterton. Those who knew both men claimed that Chesterton based his character Father Brown on Tubby.

After his ordination, he joined the army as a chaplain, and was posted to the Bedfordshire Regiment of the 16th Brigade, reporting to Neville Talbot, Senior Chaplain of the 6th Division. While he felt a certain fulfillment tending to the troops on the front line, his dream was to found a house behind the front, where men could attend services, enjoy recreation and spend the night if need be. There were numerous estimates of varying reputation, but Tubby felt the need to provide a more decent and encompassing alternative.

With the help of Col. R.S. May, Quartermaster of the 6th Division, he approached the town mayor. The latter introduced them to M. Coevoet-Camerlynck, who offered his large house on what was then known as Rue de l'Hôpital. One of the conditions was that they rebuild the roof and make the house watertight. Also, they had to remove a large, locked safe from the front room and store it in a secure place.

They accepted at once, and work began on restoring the house and removing the furniture—including the massive safe, which required the assistance of 16 soldiers and as many townspeople who could lend a hand. With the assistance of the Royal Engineers and a party from the Queen's Westminster Rifles, they carried out temporary repairs, pending more permanent work later.

The house had three floors; the ground floor consisted of reception rooms, which were to be used for recreational activities; outside was a conservatory, severely damaged by the shell blast. An elegant staircase painted in white and gold led up to the second floor which had four bedrooms. Above that, the third floor contained a nursery and three small bedrooms. From here a steep staircase led up to a huge loft covering the entire area of the house. This was to become the chapel. Tubby had found an old dilapidated but massive carpenter's bench which, after being cleaned, was installed in the chapel as an altar. Tubby, who often referred to Jesus as "the Carpenter's Son", felt this made a fitting structure for this purpose. It remains there on the top floor in the restored chapel to this day.

Across the road, there was a shop, run by a widow and her two children. The building had been partially wrecked by another shell hit, but that didn't deter Madame Coemans from continuing her bric-a-brac business. Her son Gerard became quite friendly with the padre, and with a good deal of haggling with the implacable Madame, he procured a crucifix, that, though she "deeply treasured it" she was willing to let go for the right price. This was hung behind the carpenter's bench. Tubby's dream had come true.

Being priests, Tubby and his boss, Reverend Neville Talbot, wanted to call it "Church House", but this went down like a lead balloon with Col. May, who had helped him acquire the building.

As soon as the colonel heard the suggestion, he scrapped it saying, "Church House? What? No, no, no, won't do at all—enough to choke anyone off. Why not Talbot House, after our chaplain, Neville Talbot?"

The latter, unwillingly agreed, but dedicated the house to his youngest brother, Gilbert, who had served as a lieutenant in the 7th Battalion, the Rifle Brigade. Gilbert had been killed a few months earlier at Hooge on the 30th of July of that year, 1915.

So it became "Talbot House". Later, Tubby shortened it to "TocH", using the signal corps' phonetic pronunciation 'Toc' for 'T'. The soldiers themselves provided the furniture, which included a large piano acquired who knows where, and no one asked. They improvised where necessary, such as a table made from two tent floorboards found in the garden, covering them with wallpaper, together with several chairs built from packing cases. There was no shortage of bits and pieces to use for men whose enthusiasm to get themselves a place to relax, engendered a spirit of innovation. Gerard's shop across the road supplied cups, saucers, and other small items. No doubt they were glad of the potential business the new establishment would bring.

The garden was large and peaceful, though terribly neglected. Tubby was all fired to put it to good use as a place of peaceful respite for trench-weary soldiers.

He wrote:

"It is a beautiful house with a lovely garden, full of standard roses, pergolas, wall-fruit and a chicken run. I'm going to get together a little batch of amateur gardeners to run the garden in spare time— it will be a peaceful relaxation, much appreciated and I'm anxious to have the place in apple-pie order. After the voluntary service last night, (held in a music hall), about forty men came round with me and went over the house, which was great fun and made them quite keen on it all. We have an inaugural Concert on Saturday night … Meanwhile, as I write, a stream of traffic, like that of Fleet Street passes slowly—staff cars, motor cyclists, lorries, wagons, horsemen, ambulances, soldiers of all sorts and descriptions, carts with furniture of refugees who can stand it no longer tied on precariously. I covet these chairs and tables greatly. Meanwhile, paper and books from time to time will be a real help. The men here are grateful for the simplest kindness shown to them personally: a cup of cocoa and a Belgian bun do not lack their reward."[55]

Sitting on a bench in the garden, one is absorbed in the blanket of tranquility that envelops it.

The outside noise recedes … and the bird's take over with their ongoing concert performance.

Warblers and Wagtails sing in the trees,

Berberis and Buddleia, humming with bees,

Stay a bit longer, stay and unwind,

Rest your tired body, rest your tired mind.

The garden is still there, and is beautifully kept, just as it was in 1915. Not satisfied with just relaxation and entertainment, Tubby

---

55 Chapman. P. *A Haven in Hell.*

also set up sleeping accommodation for exhausted soldiers travelling home from the front. He would provide them with supper, a good night's sleep, and a hearty breakfast in the morning, before putting them on the train. He even went so far as to supply them with carpet slippers when entering their room, which moved some of them to tears.

> Sit here tired soldier, sit down and eat,
> And after you'll go to your room, replete,
> Slippers and blankets, and sleep that will heal,
> Down in the morning, to another good meal.
>
> *(Derek McCann. "Respite")*

Gradually, decent furniture was found, and in addition, many paintings appeared on the walls, gifts from soldiers, no questions were asked. There are so many facets of this restful building that a whole book would be needed to describe them. But some things stick in the mind.

On the wall in the reception room, admired daily by the visitors and the shades of long dead soldiers mingling among them, hangs a beautiful painting commissioned by the Blue Cross Society in 1916, to raise money for the relief of suffering among war horses on the front lines and elsewhere. It was painted by F. Matana and entitled *Good-bye Old Man*. It depicts a soldier of the Field Artillery cradling his badly wounded horse's head in his arms while the limbers continue along the shell-pocked road.

The Soldiers Kiss
Only a dying horse! Pull off the gear,
And slip the needless bit from frothing jaws,
Drag it aside, there leave the roadway clear—
The battery thunders by with scarce a pause.

Prone by the shell-swept highway there it lies,
With quivering limbs, as fast the life-tide fails,
Dark films are closing o'er the faithful eyes
That mutely plead for aid where none avails.
Onward the battery rolls, but one there speeds,
Heedless of comrades' voice or bursting shell,
Back to the wounded friend who lonely bleeds
Beside the stony highway where it fell.
Only a dying horse! He swiftly kneels,
Lifts the limp head and hears the shivering sigh.
Kisses his friend, while down his cheek there steals
Sweet pity's tear: "Good-bye old man, goodbye".
No honours wait him, medal, badge or star,
Though scarce could war a kindlier deed unfold;
He bears within his breast, more precious far
Beyond the gilt of Kings, a heart of gold.

(Henry Chappel. "The Soldier's Kiss")

• • •

YPRES SALIENT
March 20, 1916

Looking out over a wasteland of blackened tree stumps and mud, wire and dead bodies, the men of the Guards division must have wondered if they hadn't "jumped from the frying pan into the fire".

It was March 20, and they were taking over a sector of the front line from the Menin Road to Wieltje.

Each brigade had two battalions in the front system and two in reserve. The forward battalions in the front line were relieved every four days. For the person who believes that time passes equally no matter the circumstances, try spending four days in a sopping, muddy front-line trench, in company with rats and lice; it could stretch out interminably.

165

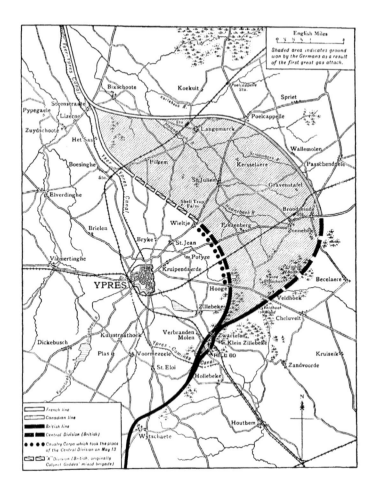

• • •

YPRES SALIENT
April 30, 1916

The Reverend Tubby Clayton wrote that, *"They dreaded the arrival of the Guards at Talbot House, but longed for their return."*

The men of the Guards, highly disciplined when on duty, also knew how to let their hair down. Now, unfortunately, they had to leave again and went back to what was incomparably the most unpleasant part of the whole British front. The holding of the Ypres salient at any time of the year was a task which made greater demands on the stamina and morale of the defending troops than did that of any other portion of the front, but in the cold and wet weather of the early spring of 1916 the conditions of life in this dismal and water-logged area, overlooked on three sides by the enemy's artillery, were even more deplorable than usual. The whole trench system was in a state of dilapidation and ruin.[56] Parts of the reserve line in front of the White Chateau were untenable in daytime and the communication trenches were so badly damaged by the enemy's artillery fire that it was impossible to use them—men had either to get out of them and walk across in full view of the enemy or to struggle along them up to their waists in water. In the front-line trenches, the parapets were very low and by no means bullet proof.

The Germans were very keen on taking Ypres, and as a result there was always an impending threat of attack. The Engineers were at first almost wholly engaged in the building of machine gun positions in ruined buildings in the old ramparts of the city, and on the front line between the town and the village of St. Jean and along the canal bank. They also dug some new trenches for local defense in the rear of the White Chateau, close to the village of Wieltje.

Vincent celebrated his twenty-second birthday in his new home in the ramparts of Ypres, the most contested town on the front line.

---

56 C. Headlam. *History of the Guards Division in the Great War 1915—1918.* Vol. 1. John Murray, London. 1924.

CHAPTER 14

The Road to Wipers[57]

"What's a salient? Asked private McBride,
  As they marched the road to Wipers,
  It's a bend in the front line, the sergeant replied,
  Where you're shot at by German snipers.
  They shoot us and bomb us from every which side,
  It's as safe as a nest of vipers.
  Don't worry my son, you'll be fine, he lied,
  Just follow us old three stripers."

(Derek McCann. "The Ypres Salient")

YPRES

April 30, 1916

Vincent was sitting on an old bench, salvaged from what used to be a park in the town, but was by then a mess of water-filled shell craters.

The bench, made of wrought iron, the black paint peeling, sat backed against the rampart wall where he and Willie O'Neill were working on the back axle of a truck that had broken. Vincent had spent most of yesterday working on a replacement, as there were no spares, and the other sections desperately needed the truck to bring

---

57 "Wipers" was British army slang for Ypres.

up supplies for the dugouts they were building. Willie was a young Kerryman, his round, guileless face made his mates think he was a bit slow, but he was in fact a gifted mechanic. He didn't say much, which suited Vincent's quiet temperament, and they enjoyed working together. Vincent had learned a good deal about motor vehicles over the past year and enjoyed the work, so he stayed on to help the mechanic fit the new axle.

As Willie sat down beside him, he offered him a Capstan and stuck one in his own mouth and lit up. They didn't say much, Willie being engrossed in a copy of the *"Wipers Times"* [58] he'd found, and Vincent lost in his own thoughts. All around them, the ruins of the once busy and beautiful city were a grim reminder of the fragility of human effort in wartime. Control of the town was essential to both sides, and it was probably the most fought over city in the whole war. So far, the allies held on by their fingernails, and the front line made a rounded detour to the north and along the hills to the west.

This was the Ypres Salient. These hills gave the Germans an excellent vantage for their artillery.

Vincent stared vacantly at a brazier the men had set up to make tea and cook a few rations. The flames were mesmerizing and brought memories back of the range at their house in Tallanstown. Their home was part of the police barracks where his father was the sergeant, and it was a tight fit for the whole family, but they managed. Many was the time though when he would go to stay with their Granny at Mansfieldstown, to relieve the pressure, especially during the summer when some of the cousins were visiting. Those visits were cherished, playing around the fields behind the house, where

---

58 A trench magazine run by a bunch of soldiers, in Ypres. *"Wipers Times"* is an excellent film telling the story of the magazine and the men who put it out. It can be seen on Amazon Prime.

they were spoiled by the granny, free from the restrictions of the family home. Leo, himself, and Wilfred were sent there most summer holidays and over Easter. The kitchen in the house was square, the middle of which was taken up with a large wooden table, worn smooth from years of heavy usage. All the food preparation was done there, and while the food was cooking on the large black range, they would clean the ancient planks of the table and put the oilcloth over it, setting the places around it. He could picture his grandmother, busily preparing the dough for the wonderful soda bread she cooked most days. The evening meal was a warm and cozy affair, with the oil lamps lit and raspberry jam spread on the soda-bread, hot, just off the griddle. The thought of it sent a warm glow through him.

His reverie was shattered by the voice of Lieutenant Briggs wanting to know when the lorry would be ready.

"Another couple of hours, sir," he said as he stood on the cigarette butt and got back under the truck.

75th Field Company War Diary
May 1, 1916.

Work in Ramparts (Ypres) on dugouts for Brigade Headquarters. Marking out of emergency road from Vlamertinghe to Canal bank being done by means of striped pickets. Hot water system at No. 4 Field Ambulance being fitted up. Ventilation of huts in "C" camp (A30c) carried on. Instruction in wiring to parties from 1st Brigade and Division cyclists. Stairways being fitted to infantry billet in Poperinghe.

May 2, 1916.

Same as 1st. 2 men employed with town Mayor (Ypres) repairing pump.

• • •

"McCann, come over here, I want you to meet someone."

Lieutenant Frazier was walking over to where Vincent and Willie were cleaning up after sending the lorry on its way. Their hands were greasy and hot water was a luxury they didn't have, so it was a tedious job to get the oil and grease off. Vincent wiped himself dry and, raising his head, saw standing alongside Lieutenant Frazer a tall, well-built man in his late sixties.

It was a warm day and he'd removed his hat to reveal a round head, closely cropped hair in what had become a fashionable style, as it was easy to keep tidy. He had a white beard and moustache in the style of King George V, with crinkled, humorous blue eyes. He was dressed in civilian clothes, which were rumpled and well worn, but his stature was that of a natural leader.

"I want you to meet the mayor of Ypres, Monsieur Colaert. He needs a couple of good men to help him get his pump working."

The man smiled at Vincent and Willie and shook their hands.

"I am needing some good mechanics to help with my, em … *pompe* … over in the Cloth Hall," he said in good, but accented English, decorated by a sprinkling of French—the common language between Belgians and British. "Can you please bring some, eh … *outils et équipement, s'il vous plaît?*"

The two men returned his greeting and, nodding, went over to where they had a tool cart, which they picked up and wheeled over to follow him. He led them through the streets, lined with rubble and the remnants of the once busy shops and cafés and across the square to where the remains of the Cloth Hall stood. It was a sorry mess of what once used to be such a fine building, and Vincent, looking at the mayor, saw a deep sadness descend on his seemingly habitually humorous face. They parked the cart as close as they could and went with him down to the cellar; the air outside was thick with dust and the smell of cordite from a recent barrage, and it was a relief to go down the steps into the cellar, and breathe the cool damp air, where the pump—a large manual machine—was sited. He was trying to keep the cellars dry, as they had survived the shelling and were being used to store food and provide shelter for the troops and remaining citizens. It was an old Deane & Beale pump that was often used in the trenches and had been scrounged from the Engineers by the mayor. They found the seals were worn and it leaked almost as much water as was pumped. The suction chamber was also clogged with debris. Willie went up to the cart where fortunately they had some packing from a previous job, and while he was gone, Vincent and the mayor chatted.

He learned that M. Colaert was born in Poperinghe and knew the town well. He had been mayor of Ypres since 1900 and his whole heart was given over to the town. He had been renovating the Cathedral and Cloth Hall when the German invasion had put a stop to all the work. His face turned red with the memory as he said to Vincent, "The *dikke nek geitenneukers*[59] took our money and kept three of us hostage until they left two days later."

He shook his head sadly and was visibly getting more excited. He asked Vincent where he was from. Glad to change the subject, in case the mayor had a heart attack, Vincent told him about Belfast. He was fascinated to learn about the Titanic when he learned Vincent worked at the shipyard. He showed the keen interest of a country-man, who knew nothing of ships, and Vincent was only too happy to tell him about the great liner. When O'Neill came down with the packing, they got to work, and M. Colaert took his jacket off, rolled up his sleeves and helped them. They removed the gland and wrapped it around inside with packing. The pump worked admirably when they finished and the few men with mayor René got working on it again.

---

59 Loosely translated as "the thick-necked goat-fuckers."

As the two sappers left, Colaert slipped a bottle of whiskey over to Vincent, who promptly put it inside his jacket. They would look forward to sampling that back at the billet that night.[60]

75th Field Company War Diary
May 5, 1916.
This evening No.s 1, 2, & 3 sections moved up into billets at 66 rue de Dixmuide, Ypres. No night work done.

Vincent and his section were busy, moving their gear to the new billets, just down from the Diksmuide Gate on the north side of the town. These houses were still relatively intact and most of the shelling had been concentrated on the south and center of the city.

On the 6th they were told to bring more wire to the stores dump at St. Jean and had loaded up five rolls of wire on the truck. Willie went round to the front and swung the starting handle. The job required muscle and a quick reflex as the cantankerous vehicle often backfired and the handle would fly around. Many a wrist had been broken this way. Vincent was in the driver seat, and they got the truck started and began to trundle their way out the St. Jean Road.

• • •

His uniform covered in mud, Sergeant Cronin stooped through the door of the captain's dugout, and saluted, blinking, as his eyes adjusted to the dingy interior.

"How are we doing, Sergeant," Bulkeley said.

---

60 When the war was over, the British wanted to keep the ruins of Ypres as a memorial. The people of the city, no doubt led by mayor Colaert, insisted it be rebuilt. This was at last agreed to, and with German reparations, the buildings, including the beautiful Cloth Hall and Cathedral, were rebuilt exactly as they had been before the war. Sadly the mayor didn't live to see the completion, as he died on October 3, 1927. He is buried in the old cemetery.

"Not too good sir," Cronin replied in his broad cockney accent. "Me'n the lads 'ave about a 'undred yards done, but we're not sure where we're supposed to put the gaps."

"Mm … " Bulkeley thoughtfully scratched his nose. "The CRE[61] sent coordinates, and I gave you a list of them."

"Well …" Cronin rubbed the back of his head in embarrassment, "I'm not that great wiv the map readin' and all that stuff, 'n wiv all the shell craters there, it's a bit difficult … like … " he trailed off.

"Oh fine, I know, it's hard to relate the map to the mess that's out there," the Captain said, smiling. "No problem. I've nothing on at the moment, let's go and have a look at the situation."

Relief flooded Cronin's face and they left the dugout as Bulkeley put on his jacket and helmet.

As they went out, they were joined by sappers driving three carts loaded with rolls of wire, on their way to the trenches. The small party stumbled their way along the road, pockmarked with craters. There were a couple of sappers with corporals Collingwood and Bailey, the party that had been sent back to get the wire. Up ahead, they could see the town of St. Jean, with the ruins of the church and the bare skeletal roofs of what was left of the buildings. The road, straight as a die, used to be lined with poplars; On a sunny early summer's day it would have been beautiful to the eye, now all that remained was burned stumps.

Captain Bulkeley, walking ahead a bit, turned around to Adams and said, "When you came in, I was just reading—"

But that was all he was able to get out when the shell hit.

Later, Sergeant Cronin told his superiors that they heard nothing, until this bang and a flash of light happened at the same time, no more than ten yards away. He came to, covered in earth and

61 Commander Royal Engineers.

entrails. He'd been protected from the blast by the horse he was walk-ing beside. The scene around him was utter devastation. Spitting out a lump of foul-tasting soft tissue that was in his mouth, he got to his knees, shaking off the dirt. Gradually as his hearing returned, he turned in the direction of continuous screaming. A few feet away, one of the horses had been penetrated by the shaft of the wagon, spilling his guts on the road. Cronin realized that was what he was covered in, and probably what he spat out. Suddenly his stomach erupted and emptied itself on the ground as he knelt, his head bent, as if in prayer.

One of the sappers, Jerry Gray, was stumbling around, dazed and suffering from acute shock. There was no sign of Captain Bulkeley. All the wagons had been hit, one overturned, with one wheel spinning quietly in the air. Only one horse was uninjured, and it was this horse that was neighing in a total panic, trying to break free of the harness. Its partner was torn open by a shell and dragged the unfortunate animal to the ground.

The German gunners, fortunately, had turned their attention on the sappers working on the trench, who had beaten a hasty retreat. Cronin checked himself first, and apart from being covered in a mess of offal and mud, he seemed unhurt. His head began to clear, and he looked for the others. He could hear moans and shouts for help and found one of the drivers first, who had been riding one of the horses. The terrified animal had gone berserk with fright and thrown him badly. His arm was broken, and he was covered in blood from a myriad of small cuts. Baily was under a roll of wire, pinning him to the ground, and Collingwood had been hit by shrapnel and both were bleeding badly, but he couldn't find the captain. Standing up and walking through the carnage, he eventually came across a body lying prone about 20 feet away. The captain's uniform was covered in blood, which seemed mostly around the stomach. He was unconscious. Cronin had seen abdominal wounds before and knew they had to get medical help quickly. He sent Sapper Gray to help get the wire off Baily and see how badly he was hurt.

Meantime, Vincent and Willie were weaving their way along the St. Jean Road, dodging shell holes. They saw the party with Captain Bulkeley about a half mile ahead where the shell landed.

"Jaysus, that doesn't look good," Willie said, as Vincent put down his foot on the accelerator.

"Let's get up there and see what we can do…"

They arrived to find Sergeant Cronin over by the Captain, who looked in a bad way.

"Let's get him on the lorry!" Cronin yelled—deafened by the explosion, he didn't realize he was shouting. "There's a few more and we need to get them to a dressing station quickly!"

Other soldiers had arrived on the scene and some of them started getting the rolls of wire off the truck, others were helping with the horses, shooting the badly injured ones and freeing the one horse that was still trapped in the harness.

They got boards from the damaged wagon and put the captain carefully on the makeshift stretcher, then struggled with him to the truck. He was still unconscious. They got the other wounded and the driver with the broken arm on as well, and Vincent and Willie set off back down the St. Julien Road to Number 4 Ambulance Station, which was about five miles away, just past Elverdinghe. Cronin stayed in the back with the captain, holding a jacket against the wound to stop the bleeding. Ypres was fairly easy to get through, as the roads had been kept cleared, and they made good progress. The medics got the captain off the truck as soon as they arrived and started to clean him up and get him ready for the trip to the Casualty Clearing Station. It would be touch and go.

Abdominal wounds were almost always fatal.

75th Field Company War Diary
May 6, 1916.

Sections getting settled into billets during the day. Night work done revetting and draining trenches in Canal Bank and Kaaie Salient. Owing to heavy shelling, parties for work at trench B10A near Wieltje and wiring between St. Jean and La Brique were not able to work. Capt. H.I. Bulkeley was wounded by shell splinter in the abdomen and evacuated to No. 10 CCS through No. 4 Field Ambulance. 2nd corporal Bailey, Lce. Corporal Collingwood and driver Goodganie were also hit as well as 5 horses, three of which were killed. These casualties all occurred on St. Jean Road on the Ypres side of St. Jean. Capt. Bulkeley was hit at St. Jean Cross Roads by the R.E. Dump.

2019

Wounds to the abdomen were bad news. Being hit by a red-hot piece of metal in the stomach always resulted in horrible injuries. I was curious to discover if Captain Bulkeley had survived. I hoped he had, as I felt, somehow, he was a decent man. The war diary made no further mention of him, so I began to poke through the records on the internet.

My search showed that he had joined the army in 1902 and was promoted Lieutenant in 1904. Not much else was found until he turned up as Commanding Officer of the 75th Field Company. After being wounded, he was taken to a field hospital and presumably taken back to England. He did in fact survive the wounds and returned to service. When, we don't know.

He remained in the Royal Engineers after the war. Bulkeley, who was thirty-two when he suffered the wound, remained on with the

Royal Engineers and rose to the rank of Lieutenant Colonel. Sadly, he came to an untimely death in Kashmir when he was the victim of a hit and run accident—though it apparently happened under somewhat mysterious circumstances. It was suspected that he was the victim of an assassination by Kashmiri rebels. At that time, Kashmir was being fought over by India and Pakistan, and Srinagar, where he was killed, was close to the front line. Due to heavy snow in this mountainous region, there was little fighting, but many skirmishes between patrols from both sides. It would appear that Col. Bulkeley got caught up in one of these.

Henry Ion Bulkeley is buried in a Church of England cemetery in Srinagar, Kashmir, far from his home village in Lanercost, Cumbria. He was sixty-three years old, having survived the First World War, as well as the Second, before he got caught up in yet another war in the remote hills of Kashmir.

> "In far flung fields, we die,
>   Our bodies buried,
>   Beneath the cold wet earth
>   Of a distant land,
>   Far from home.
>   Forget us not."
>
>   *(David Hollis. "In Far Flung Fields We Die")*[62]

75th Field Company War Diary
May 10, 1916.

On account of machine gun fire, no work done on B10A trench. Party worked on instead. Pickets of sawn timber in St. Jean – La Brique were mudded over. Work on Potijze Battn. HQ continued. St Jean battn. HQ additional entrance to cellar cut through outside wall. Machine

---

62 https://www.facebook.com/breadonthewaters/

Gun emplacement 8E carried on. Work on Canal Bank and Kaaie continued. Work on pipeline for Sally port water supply in Ypres.

May 11, 1916.

As on 10th. Parties for work on B10A were distributed and had commenced work when M.G. fire opened up on the trench. They were therefore withdrawn and worked on Pratt St. instead. Wiring from St. Jean to La Brique continued.

May 12, 1916.

As on 11th. Work on B10A done (Relief Right). Sallyport water supply completed. Machine Gun emplacement 8F (C27d5.4) carried on with. This concrete Machine Gun emplacement had not been completed since worked on by this company when last in this sector.

May 13, 1916.

At Wieltje work was carried on, though at first M.G. fire was heavy. Revetting and draining continued at Canal Bank and Kaaie. Machine Gun emplacement at 8F was continued. Wiring from St. Jean to Threadneedle St. finished off. Potijze Battn. HQ work on three galleries continued and each bay is sheeted as excavated. Sallyport, Ypres, tank was repaired. Work carried on in pipeline and tank outside.

May 15, 1916.

At Weiltje work interrupted by rifle fire. Party called in and work continued in Pratt St. Drains. Work on Machine Gun emplacement 8E and 8F continued. Work on Canal Bank and Kaaie continued. St. Jean – La Brique work carried on. Work in three galleries at Potijze continued. Additional tank put in at head of pipeline outside Sallyport. Holes in tank inside Ramparts stopped up.

May 17, 1916.

At Weiltje work continued on B10A. Work on Machine Gun emplacement at 8E and 8F continued. Work on Canal Bank and Kaaie continued. St. Jean – La Brique wire carried on. Work on 3 galleries at Polijze continued. Officers of 84th Fd. Coy. Shown around work.

*   **Capt. B.H. Fox RE** *arrived at 6 pm and took over command of company.*

May 19, 1916.

Company marched out of camp at 8am and arrived at new billets Winnezeele[63] *at 1.30 pm via Steenboorde.*

---

63 *Winnezeele is* about 5 miles *west of Poperinghe.*

CHAPTER 15

We Are the Dead

'E was killed so often sudden that 'e 'adn't time to die,
'E sorto jumped and came down wiv a thud.
Them corpsy-lookin' star shells kept a streamin' in the sky,
An' there he lay like nothin' in the mud ...

(Robert Service. "My Mate")

YPRES—YSER CANAL BANK, YPRES
June 27, 1916

"I think Beale is dead!" Sapper Rea yelled, pausing to catch his breath after his desperate sprint across No-Man's Land, "… and Adams is in a bad way, we need to get stretchers out there."

The urgency in his voice was unmistakable; as he sat down on the fire step, Major Fox could see the anguish on his face. His own heart was thumping with adrenalin, but he knew he had to remain calm in front of the others. Rea had literally rolled over the parapet, and landed in the trench, his helmet missing, and his uniform covered in mud. Two others had jumped in just behind him. It was still dark, and they were lucky to find their way back through the gap in the wire.

"They must've seen or heard us workin' and next thing this machine gun opens up, before we had a chance to get cover."

"But you were 2,000 yards from the German trenches," Major Fox said.

"It looked like they had a machine gun in a farmhouse a good bit out from the front, far as I could tell," one of the other sappers replied.

"Where exactly were you?" Fox asked. He knew they had gone out to check the condition of the wiring, and if possible, to do any quick repairs.

"We were 'bout 100 yards down the wiring, across from the trestle bridge over the canal and just had it all repaired, when it happened."

"OK, OK, you've got some contusions on your arm, probably from the wire. You need to watch for poisoning on those, so go and get them seen to at the CCS. Go on, we'll get the men back here."

It was still dark, and the Major thought they had a chance to get them out before daylight. They needed to move fast, though, otherwise, once the sun came up, there would be no possibility of doing it.

"Get some stretchers ready, and I'll order artillery fire on their trenches to keep them busy," Fox quietly ordered the sappers, who were getting ready to go out for their mates.

He took out the trench map from his jacket and, holding a lantern close, wrote down the coordinates just in front of the German trenches, opposite where he thought the wounded men were. No mean feat in a muddy trench, in the dark with just the feeble light of a lantern. But he knew the map well, and where to look. Nevertheless, he double checked the numbers, as given the wrong ones, the artillery could land their shells in No-Man's Land and potentially wipe out the men he was trying to extricate.

"Sapper Bean, take this message back to the Division dugout and give it to the artillery captain. I think his name is Effingham."

Thirty minutes later, as the men waited to go over the parapet, they saw flashes lighting the dark sky behind them, reflecting off the low cloud, as the artillery started up. Then the whine of the shells overhead, followed a second later by earth shaking explosions along the German trenches. Fox, gritting his teeth with tension, looked over the top and saw to his relief that the shells were landing around the German front line. There were five sappers and a sergeant, ready to go, with two stretchers. The Major gave the order and as they climbed cautiously over the parapet, he silently wished them Godspeed, as they made for the gap in the wire.

They had to cross the canal on one of the trestle bridges built earlier, and then ran doubled over to where the two men lay, five hundred yards on the other side of the bank, trapped in a shell hole, which was half full of water. Sapper Collins had remained with them, and if it wasn't for him, Adams would have drowned, as he was barely conscious, and kept slipping into the mud in the bottom of the shell hole. Collins also chased the rats away, trying to stop them feasting on the bodies. It took an hour altogether, and the first grey light of dawn was penetrating the heavy cloud cover when they scrambled back into their own trench. Andrew Beale was dead. Adams was badly wounded in the chest and losing blood. Thankfully, they were right beside the medical bunkers, and he was seen right away. It was a busy night for the 75th.

Andrew Beale was buried at the cemetery right by their company headquarters, later to be named after the smallholding across the road—Essex Farm. There was a mortuary there, set into the canal bank, and a couple of morticians on duty cleaned him up and put him in a coffin. The morning of the 28th, they brought the coffin to a freshly dug grave, and stood around while Major Fox said the funeral prayers.

As they listened, they pondered on their relationship with each other, and wondered how many other friends they would lose. Gone was that youthful sense of immortality they had come out with. As the company bugler played *The Last Post*, they lowered the coffin down and said goodbye to their friend.

Whoever had stolen his money earlier could keep it now. They were returning to their back billets today, and Andrew should have been with them. The gap at the mess table would soon be taken by a new arrival, and they would move on.

June had been a bad month, working under fire a lot of the time. They had marched from Winnezeele on the ninth and started work on the canal bank, making eighteen days on the front line, building dugouts, and repairing the trenches.

Thank God it was nearly over.

75th Field Company War Diary
June 27, 1916.

Bridge repaired also tramway which had been damaged by hostile shelling at (blank). Sections 2 and 4 moved to billets in Brielen from Canal Bank. Sections 3 moved up to Brielen relieving Section 1 which moved back to billets at A 28 Central. Lt. Bousfield laid out new dugouts for medical dressing stations at Willows. C 20 b 6.6. Lt. Fraser inspected sites for new Brigade HQ at C20 d 5.4. with 2nd Lt. Russell. Sgt. Adams wounded today, sapper Beale killed, buried in cemetery at C25 a 4.9.

• • •

Tubby clutched his forehead in mock horror.

"Dear Lord, the Guards have come back, Heaven help us," he said, and laughing with delight at seeing his friends again, welcomed Vincent, John, and with a little surprise, Corporal Duggan. He could tell by their faces that something had happened, and they told him about losing Andrew. Possibly one of Tubby's greatest assets was his empathy, and though he had to do this on a daily basis, it never got any easier.

"I'm so sorry lads," he said. "I remember Andrew, he was a good man. I'll dedicate a service for him on Sunday."

Vincent and John had asked the CO earlier on if they could help at Talbot House for a few days, while they were on rest time, and he had agreed. Then Ned Duggan came over and asked if he could go as well... Hiding their surprise, both had said "Yes," and the next morning, all three grabbed spades, pickaxes, and off they went.

Needless to say, the padre was delighted, and told them there hadn't been too much done since they were last here, due to the inclement weather.

Vincent thought about the trenches, the mud filled shell holes where a man could drown, as in fact several had, working in the slanting rain, and muttered, "Inclement indeed."

A pleasant routine was established by the end of the first day. The next morning, after working until ten o'clock, Vincent sat down on a bench, which had appeared since they were last here. He lit up a cigarette and had just taken a pull when Tubby came up and sat beside him.

After a bit of small talk, the priest leaned across, and said, "A strange thing happened today."

Vincent offered Tubby a cigarette, which was declined, and said, "Is that so?"

"Yes, when we were setting the tables for lunch, we discovered all our silver was accounted for. The missing stuff has returned."

Vincent couldn't think of much to say and just repeated, "Is that so?"

"Not only that," the priest went on, "but Corporal Duggan gave me a donation of two pounds, in sapper Beale's memory."

Vincent had to smile, and said, "My father used to say, 'Those who judge never understand, and those who understand, will never judge.'"

They looked at each other.

"Then let's not be the judge," said the priest.

• • •

They'd finished for the day and were putting their tools away. Both Vincent and Sam had been brooding on Andrew all day as they worked. He'd become a good friend, a bit older and a good deal wiser. Vincent had lost his mother when he was eight years old, and his older brother, Cecil, when he was still a baby, but that, painful as it was, had happened through illness. That he could grasp.

This ... this was what?

Just an argument between two countries. *What was it all about? What in the name of sweet Jesus was it all about?* They had seen countless dead bodies of fellow soldiers, some dead so long the bodies were blackened and bloated with gas. It was horrific, but this was the first time "one of them" had been killed. This brought it home, in a way nothing else could. Vincent and Sam must have realized they had been ruminating on the same thing, because they looked at each other, and could see the reflection of loss in each other's eyes, asking the same questions.

"Why?"

There was a pounding of boots on the stairs as John came down from where he'd been helping the padre put his chapel together up in the attic.

"What's up with yez?" he asked. Then, seeing the look on their faces, he realized.

He said nothing more, but put a hand on each of their shoulders, and they did the same, forming a small triangle of grief. As they stood there, heads bowed, Vincent felt a hand on his shoulder and looked around.

It was Duggan.

• • •

The Engineers had set up a workshop in the Brielen area, where Sam and Vincent were working on a Merryweather Valiant steam pump, which, if they ever got it going again, would be a great help in keeping the trenches dry. It had large wheels and was ideal for moving from point to point. But the camshaft was broken, and some of the valves had to be reseated.

As Vincent set his lathe to work on a new camshaft, Sam said to him, "Ye remember where we buried Andrew, in the Essex Farm cemetery?"

"Aye, indeed, I doubt I'll ever forget it."

"Well, see, the medical bunkers there, they go back to '15 when they were built," Sam said, sitting on a stool beside the lathe where Vincent worked, and lighting two cigarettes, passed one to him. "The fellow who wrote that poem, *In Flanders Fields* … d'ye remember that? *In Flanders Fields the Poppies Grow?*"

"I do, yes. I remember reading it in some magazine," Vincent replied.

"Well, he was stationed there. In fact, at those same bunkers. That's where he wrote it. I was just reading an article in Punch about him. He was an officer I think, with the Canadians, and a medic. Hang on a minute ..." and he walked over to the pump and picked up the magazine, brought it back and shuffled through the pages. "Here it is. 'Lieutenant-Colonel John McCrea wrote the poem *In Flanders Fields the Poppies Grow* while in charge of a medical station at Essex Farm near Ypres.' See?" said McLaughlin, pointing. "Look, I'll read it out for ye."

Vincent stopped the lathe, cleaned off the work, and the two of them sat down.

"In Flanders fields the poppies blow
Between the crosses, row on row,
That mark our place; and in the sky
The larks, still bravely singing, fly
Scarce heard amid the guns below."

After just the first verse, Vincent already had his head in his hands, hiding the tears that welled up as he thought of Andrew, lying alone in his grave. Sam continued stoically, though he appeared to be having problems with a runny nose.

"We are the Dead. Short days ago
We lived, felt dawn, saw sunset glow,
Loved and were loved, and now we lie
In Flanders fields.
Take up our quarrel with the foe:
To you from failing hands we throw
The torch: be yours to hold it high.
If ye break faith with us who die
We shall not sleep, though poppies grow
In Flanders fields."

A silence lay between the two soldiers as they contemplated their own loss.

"We'll take up the torch … for Andrew," Vincent said.

After a few minutes, Sam went on, reading bits from the magazine article. "It seems the doctor had lost a friend of his own—fella by the name of Helmer. A lieutenant in the Canadian army. This was the big battle last year, remember? At Ypres"

"That was when our honorable foe let off the chlorine gas, wasn't it?" asked Vincent.

"Yes, it was. Then we started doin' it at Loos," said Sam, "and now they're puttin' it in the shells."

"Ah well, we'll never solve the problems of the world. Are ye comin' over to Talbot House tonight? I hear the Welsh Guards have a few performers."

"Wouldn't mind," said Sam. "Now, if we don' get this bloody pump goin', we won't be goin' anywhere."

CHAPTER 16

The Epiphany of Ned Duggan

Once the homes of Lords and Earls,
Pale bosoms adorned with strings of pearls,
Powdered wigs, silk stockings and genteel gowns,
They were the elite of Dublin's town.
Then later they left for London's thrall,
In time the paper peeled off the wall,
Damp and mold replaced the sheen,
Rotting plaster where grandeur had been.
Now nineteen families lived in a house,
Where the titled few did once carouse,
In poverty they struggle day to day,
Their lives a tale of squalid decay.

(Derek McCann. "Henrietta Street")

HENRIETTA STREET, DUBLIN
1900

The boy sat hunched on the front doorstep and watched, as the police took his father away. He just stared, with a blank expression, not knowing what was going on. He didn't realize he'd never see his Dada again, because when Dada's jail sentence finished, which would be many years hence, Dada would just quietly vanish into the crowded streets of Dublin.

190

Dressed in a very old pair of wool trousers, that had seen three previous owners and much better days, a threadbare shirt and cap, his feet were bare. He hardly needed shoes; the soles of his feet were as hard as any leather. His mother, meanwhile, was upstairs, asleep on a chair, snoring, a tiny river of drool creeping from her mouth, running in a rivulet across the creases of her chin and onto an already stained floral dress. Beside the chair there was an empty gin bottle on the floor. Ned, for that was what he was called, after his daddy, decided, probably wisely enough, that he didn't want to waken his mother, and would wait on the steps till his older sister, Eithne came home. He was the second oldest of five children, all that was left out of nine pregnancies.

● ● ●

Their adventure had begun when Dada decided they would go to Dublin, where, he told them, there was plenty of work laboring, and they would settle. There was little point in remaining in Fermoy, where Ned was born, because dada found it difficult to get work anymore, due to his drinking habits and violent temper. Mama, who had given up caring long ago, went along with whatever he wanted. The three youngest, all girls, were left with Ned's aunt Rose, who, though she did not want any children, could see that their prospects living with her were infinitely better. After a few weeks, their bruises were hardly noticeable. The parents, with Eithne and Ned in tow, found temporary lodging in a room in Henrietta Street in Dublin, in a house where once the Eighth Earl of Thomond had lived in genteel luxury. Now it was a tenement, neglected and unadorned. The peeling paint, damp wallpaper covered in black patches of mildew, and rotting floorboards, all told a story of long neglect by the current landlord. They shared the building with eleven other families.

Ned's father, Ned Senior, could only find the occasional bit of work, loading wagons at Smithfield, or down the docks, but most of the wages he earned he drank—the cheap liquor only stoking his constantly smoldering temper. But the lack of work was to him, not really a problem; he supplemented his meagre income by the deft removal of goods from other people's premises, and the consequent sale thereof. He was developing skills in this area, becoming an accomplished cat burglar. However, there were things one did and other things one took care not to do, when one earned his occupation stealing stuff. One of these was "don't steal goods from a policeman's house." Ned Senior ignored this, primarily because he didn't know it was a policeman's house, and when the occupant of said house found his goods in a pawn shop, they were subsequently traced back to him. Hence the visit by the police to their room in Henrietta Street, and removal of same gentleman, witnessed by his young son.

Ned had no idea how his sister earned money, but she worked mostly at night, and at times seemed to be fairly flush, in that they occasionally had three meals in the day. Ned himself was developing some skills as a pickpocket, earning a few pence in O'Connell Street, which he gave to Eithne, who, these days managed the household, if a single room could be called such. Life stumbled on like this for a few months, then one day he got up and found his mother still sitting in the chair where he'd left her the night before. When he tried to wake her, she didn't respond, and when he shook her arm, it was stiff and cold.

He called his sister, who came over bleary-eyed, and she took one look and said, "Ned, your mother's gone."

"How d'ya mean 'she's gone'? She's sittin' right here."

"She's dead."

"…?"

Young Ned didn't know what to say or do. His mouth hung open, and then he just went back to what served as his bed and lay there.

Eithne called the priest, though they hadn't seen him for a long, long time. As he entered the room that served as their home, saw the peeling walls and torn furniture, he shook his head, and with his nose wrinkled in disgust at the stink in the room, he said a quick prayer over the dead mother.

He looked at Eithne then and said, "What's your name, girl?"

"Eithne … Father."

"When is your baby due?" He had noticed as soon as he came in, the swelling under the girl's thin shift. He'd seen it all before.

"… I … I don' know, Father," she said in a whisper.

Ned, listening to the conversation, couldn't understand what it was about. *Baby?* His sister was going to have a baby?

"I'll make arrangements to have your mother taken away, and then for you to be looked after." He sighed, knowing the conditions that he was condemning the girl to. "I can arrange for The Sisters of Charity to take you in."

"I'll be OK Father, I don't need any help …" Eithne muttered. "We're managing here. Mama didn't help out much anyway." But at the same time, knowing that she wouldn't be able to manage, she began to weep, suddenly and uncontrollably. Her life felt like a heavy blanket of suffering and responsibility, laid on her thin shoulders. Ned felt himself sobbing too, the filthy cover on his bed soaking up his tears.

"My child, the sisters will take care of you," he assured her. "I'll also make arrangements for your brother. He'll get an education and be looked after too."

The priest was desperate just to get back out in the fresh air, away from the utter, rock bottom desperation, and stink of unwashed human bodies, that pervaded the dingy little room.

• • •

And so it happened.

Ned never saw his sister again. She vanished into the laundry run by the nuns at number ten Henrietta Street, and he was taken in by the Coombe Ragged Day School and Boys Home, where he was given three meals a day, earned some money selling newspapers, and had a bed to sleep in every night. The newspaper money was supplemented by the occasional theft. Ned was a Socialist at heart, feeling that goods were really the property of the community, and he was ensuring that they were distributed properly. He would acquire them, sell them to the Pawn, who took care of the redistribution part. He took this responsibility seriously. He also learned an important rule, which his father had ignored.

Don't get caught.

Ned in fact, was good with his hands, both in picking pockets and in doing woodwork. He occasionally worked with some of the older boys who came back to do repairs at the school. Seeing this, the Warden got him an apprenticeship with a carpenter, James Collins, who himself, had attended the school. Ned was eleven at the time. The apprenticeship would eventually get him a good job, but there was no pay while he served his time. Ned got food and board at "The Home for Big Lads" on Townsend Street …

But a man had to have spending money.

• • •

Panting for breath, Ned threw the bag of silver plate he'd stolen from St. Catherine's Church into a bin, hoping to recover it later. He plunged out of the narrow alleyway into Hanbury Lane, turning left towards Meath Street. Looking back, he saw detective Callaghan coming out of the lane, windmilling his arms, trying to keep his balance. The policeman started after him, his long coat flapping behind him. Ned knew he could outrun the portly policeman, but they would soon be on his tail, as Callaghan had seen his face and Ned had made his acquaintance a while back. He ran into what he thought was a shop, hoping the copper didn't see him. Only when he was inside, did he realize it was a British Army recruiting office. There was a line of other lads waiting to sign up, and Ned inserted himself in between them, where he couldn't be seen from the door. The sergeant behind the desk smiled up at him. He'd seen Ned jump in the door, face red from his exertions. A few minutes later Callaghan looked in and asked if he'd seen a "little fuckin' rapscallion" go by.

The sergeant, summing up the situation, answered, "No, no one came in here sir, just these lads waitin' to sign up."

"You're in a hurry young man?" he asked to Ned. "Want to become a soldier then?"

Now, caught between the devil and the deep blue sea, and realizing a spell away from Dublin might be good for his health, Ned chose the latter.

"Eh, yeah, sure, I'd like to join up," he said as he saw Callaghan panting past the door, looking in again. The policeman never thought that Ned would be in an army recruiting office.

"Are you working now, son?"

"Um, yeah, I'm a carpenter," Ned replied, which was true enough as he'd just completed serving his time.

"Excellent. We could do with men like you in the Engineers, now how'd you fancy that?"

"Sure, that's fine," said Ned, considering his options.

After signing the attestation form, the sergeant told him to report tomorrow for a medical, and he walked out. Now all he had to do was lay low for that night, and maybe next, until he could get out of the city. As he walked up Meath Street, he passed a newsagent, and glanced at the day's papers on sale. He could see the shopkeeper was dealing with a difficult customer, and he just took one out of the rack and walked away. Later he went into a tea shop, feeling affluent, and ordered a cup of tea. Flipping through *The Independent*, he came to page five. The headline read **"Sarajevo Tragedy"** and under it, **"The Archduke Franz Ferdinand and Wife Shot"**. It went on to describe how an attempt to lob a bomb at the dignitary failed, but that later, the assassin had met the carriage carrying the Archduke again, and managed to shoot him and his wife, before being apprehended.

"Who the fuck is he?" Ned muttered to himself. "Looks a right ponce. Probably deserved it."

Being a fairly clement evening, he decided to sleep on a bench in Phoenix Park, just in case the police were watching his digs in Townsend Street.

• • •

As it turned out, Ned found that army life wasn't too bad. He was surprisingly fit, as all the running he did from the constabulary, and aggrieved shop keepers kept him in good physical trim. They'd sent him to Fermoy to join the training at Moore Park, in Kilworth. He joined a newly formed Royal Engineers unit, the 75th Field Company, and as they were just taking in recruits, he got a fairly quick promotion to second corporal. This suited him fine as he could get the best bed in the hut and some other privileges not to be ignored. Being in Fermoy, he was able to visit his aunt and sisters, after he made a few enquiries to find where they lived. They were the only family he had now, apart from his sister Eithne, whom he hadn't seen in years. He didn't even know if she was still alive.

• • •

Six months down the road, and Ned had settled himself into camp routine, when a bunch of Northern Irish recruits came in. As he lay on his bed, he could hear CSM Elliot give the poor bastards a hard time, and he smiled to himself. He reckoned he had gotten Elliot figured out, and *plamásed*[64] him every opportunity.

They'd all muddled along together over the next six months, and by the time they'd shipped out he had been promoted to corporal from second corporal. Being a carpenter, he worked a good bit with John Kelly, but the two didn't get along much, Kelly distrusting the "*gurrier*" from Dublin.

Then came shipment to France. That made for new opportunities, and Ned went into the liquor business. It was relatively easy to get local moonshine in the French towns, which Duggan, using his corporal status, managed to smuggle back into the camp. Selling it was a profitable venture, and Ned felt he was doing a service, helping the men drown out the reality of war. Despite the fact that this would merit harsh punishment, the profits were good, and when he got hold of the odd bottle of whiskey, he would give it to CSM Elliot, knowing the otherwise disciplined soldier had a weakness for the amber liquid. This was in fact, an important part of Duggan's arsenal, knowing other people's weaknesses, especially those in a position of

---

64 Plamásed; an Irish word for playing up to someone.

power. Ned's whole outlook on the war was that it wasn't such a bad thing, as long as he managed to stay out of harm's way.

• • •

The muddy, ravaged fields of Flanders caused many an epiphany for the men holding that front line, on both sides. And it was to be a turning point for Ned. When they arrived in Poperinghe it had been fairly easy, working at the padre's house. Ned had managed to filch some silver there which he was going to sell when they came back from the front and buy some Belgian liquor; business looked promising in this place.

But something happened, or at least, began to take root. As they worked in Talbot house, Tubby's kindness was infectious, and the whole atmosphere was somehow different. Ned, who had never experienced remorse for his actions, began to feel a bit bad about stealing the silver. But these tiny feelings were safely stowed in some nether region of his mind, as they went back to work on the front. But his policy of keeping out of harm's way was jeopardized, as virtually all their work was very much in harm's way. He began to take notice of how the others in his company looked out for each other, and the camaraderie, which he was rarely a part of. Since Loos, they had developed a harmony and rhythm that came with developing experience together.

Then came the day Beale was killed. They had been working on the trenches near the medical dugouts. Duggan's section had been resting and were just turning to for the day's work. It was still dark when the captain called him in and told him to lead a team across the canal to where the sappers were waiting for help.

When the artillery barrage started, they clambered over the parapet and ran for the trestle bridge. Duggan took the lead, and something changed in him. He felt clear headed, and his skills as a burglar lent him stealth, and a strange sixth sense, which allowed him to steer them through the breaks in the wire, and straight to where the captain told him the wounded men were. He felt exhilarated, empowered, with the same adrenalin flow that would boost him when breaking into a house. He seemed to work much better in the dark as well. The men behind him recognized the change too, and wordlessly crept over No-Man's Land behind him. When they got to the shell hole where Beale, Adams and Collins were holed up, they jumped into the cover and checked them out. Beale's lifeless body lay half in and half out of the mud at the bottom. Collins was holding Adams in his arms, trying to staunch the wound in his chest with his jacket. They got Adams on to a stretcher then Duggan and Collins lifted Beale's body out; Ned felt something he didn't recognize. Empathy. The shared distress at losing one of the team. Grief that he'd stolen money from this man a short while ago. This was all foreign to him as they worked their way back to the trenches on the canal bank.

The following day, they marched back to the rest billets. That night Ned didn't sleep much. His mind was in a turmoil, thinking about the day's events, and the alien feelings he experienced. When he did manage to drop off asleep, Andrew Beale was in his dreams; always there with his smile and as one of his friends. He woke the next morning, and as he was leaving the hut, he saw Vincent, John and Sam talking to the captain, requesting to go and work in Talbot House. Making a quick decision, he asked if he could go along too. He knew what he was going to do and making an excuse that he wanted to collect his toolkit, he went back into the hut, took the silver from its hiding place and put it in his tool bag.

Ned had made an important discovery, a lot more valuable than the silver in his toolkit. He had realized that if he wanted to survive the war, he could do it better by helping his comrades survive, and they, in return, would help him. He'd also discovered friendship, by observing others, because Ned had never had any friends during his life. That may seem difficult to believe, but his existence had been one of survival in the Dublin slums. He had learned to look out for himself.

He discovered that war opens a man's soul up, like a piece of shrapnel can open his body, exposing the inner contents. When it opened up, he could find the good and the bad in there. He had to figure out which is best for survival, for that's what it all comes down to.

Ned Duggan's life changed, and one would like to think for the better. Indeed, the lives of all the men changed. The lad who went out, would never return. If your son, or husband or father or brother came home, he was someone else. Maybe better, maybe worse.

The two pounds he had taken from Andrew Beale was still hidden in his kit. He brought it with him to Talbot House and gave it as a donation. That way, he felt he'd be returning it to Andrew.

CHAPTER 17

Wounded

There was something wrong about the room,
The smell; my God it stank.
There was an air of ghostly gloom,
The walls were wet and dank.

(Derek McCann. "The Abandoned Chateau")

CHATEAU DE TROIS TOURS
October 17, 2019

It had been a long time since I'd broken into any properties, having
earned an honest living for the past fifty plus years. But, on some
occasions, necessity demands, I suppose. Vincent's company had
spent a good deal of time working in the Chateau de Trois Tours,
near Brielen, a small quiet town about ten miles west of Ypres. This
place intrigued me.

As an inquisitive young lad, I had spent a lot of time mooching
around a similar building near where I lived. It had been the pala-
tial home of the Guinness Family, and later inherited by a Church of
Ireland Bishop, Benjamin Plunkett. During the Second World War,
it was burned down, but the ruins had been left, for me and my ilk
to explore. I remember the cellars, dank, mildewed walls, and old

shelving still intact. They had a particular fascination for me, and I found a small narrow tunnel, which I wriggled along, with a flashlight showing the way. It led into the large reception room. Some years later, the whole building collapsed, and I often wonder would anyone have ever found me if I'd been in that little tunnel when it happened?

Back to the present.

I knew from the company war diaries that they had been billeted in the town and had done extensive work rebuilding the cellars in the Chateau de Trois Tours. Terry and I, the indomitable research team for this literary project, had decided we were going to see the chateau, even if it took us all day to locate.

• • •

Earlier in the day, we had visited Sapper Beale's grave, in the Essex Farm Cemetery. This had brought his death home to us in a way the terse statement in the war diary would never have done. He was the first in the company to lose his life but sadly, wouldn't be the last. After that we decided to look for the Chateau. I knew it was nearby, but quite where I wasn't sure. While in the town of Brielen, a young man out walking his dog, told us how to find it. He described the tree lined road leading up to the gates and informed us they were locked. He also supplied the information that the place was for sale. Following his guidance, we arrived at two large iron padlocked gates. However, the fence was quite low, and easy to climb through. Doing just that, I found the driveway and walked up, and going round a bend, sure enough, there was the chateau. Indeed, what lay in front of me was a beautifully renovated building, though still with the towers. I wondered how much it was being sold for. But it was all closed up and I'm sure even if it was occupied, we could hardly have gone up there and said my father probably worked there one hundred and four years ago, could we come in and have a look around?

Apparently, it was used at various stages during the war as a headquarters and medical casualty clearing station. By the end of the war, it was a ruin above ground, but the cellars had been extensively refurbished by the 75th Field Company and others following in their footsteps. It must have made a fine target for the German artillery.

75th Field Company War Diary
June 28, 1916.

CRE approved of proposed site at Brigade dugouts at C 20 D 54. Work commenced laying out work that night. Medical dugouts carried on at Willows. During the day, Brigade HQ cellars were inspected with a view to their being strengthened. (Chateau Trois Tours B28 a 6.1.) Sections also employed strengthening Brielen billets during daytime.

• • •

CHATEAU DE TROIS TOURS
June 28, 1916

Coming out blinking into the bright daylight after inspecting the cellars, the captain had drawn up a work list to build walls, floors, and ceilings, in three of them, where they had been damaged. He'd told Vincent, who was between workshops, to check out a fourth cellar to see if it would be useful for storage and maybe a workshop for small jobs. Vincent was in there now with Duggan and Kelly, who were checking some shelving, and seeing how they could install a wood floor over the beaten earth that was the current flooring. The walls were damp and musty, the weak light from the lantern they had, absorbed by the gloom.

"Kelly, did you fart?" asked Duggan.

"No," John replied. "It smells more like a Dublin fart to me."

"No, on me fuckin' oath, I didn't," Ned said, as they both looked at Vincent, grinning.

"'Twasn't me. Anyway, that smell is more like something rotten, like a dead animal or something. Belfast farts aren't like that."

"Look, it's stronger over here," said John, and in the dim light of their lantern, they saw an opening about two feet square.

"That's some kind of tunnel," said Duggan.

"Aye, probably a service tunnel, for pipes and so on. Not in use now though," Vincent said. "But, by God, there's a terrible smell coming out of it."

"I'll have a look" said Kelly, leaning down and peering inside, "Sweet Jesus, there's a body in there."

They called the mortuary squad, who just happened to be working in Brielen setting up a morgue, and they came right over.

"Yez bunch 'f dingbats, wot's the matter 'ere," said the sergeant mortician.

Vincent nodded at the opening. "Well ... we think there's a body in there."

"Nah, yer kiddin', but mind you, it does smell a bit," the sergeant, whose nasal passages as well as his sensitivities had long been inured to the unpleasant smell of death, replied. "'Ere, gimme the lamp." He reached into the hole with the lantern. "Jaysus, yez'r right," he said, his voice muffled in the tunnel. "Gimme a piece of rope or sumpin.'"

They managed to find some rope, and the mortuary sergeant tied it off around the body's legs.

"Go easy, mind you," he called back. "If it's been there a while, we could pull the legs off. That wouldn't be nice."

They slowly pulled the thing out, all holding rags over their noses. Except the sergeant, of course, who was well used to the smell.

To their astonishment, the body of a German soldier was revealed. There was a good deal of dried and blackened blood on the chest.

"Well, blimey," said the sergeant. "Wot's 'e doin' 'ere?"

"Havin' a cup of tea, maybe ...?" remarked Duggan, with a smirk.

The sarge gave him a baleful look, and said, "I'll be back wiv some 'elp. Just leave him be." Then he left.

The conclusion reached, while they were waiting, was that the soldier must have been a prisoner who had escaped and been wounded, then crawled into the chateau to hide. But his wounds clearly got the better of him. It must've been that a shell landing nearby had caused a partial cave in of the small tunnel he was in, burying him.

• • •

75th Field Company War Diary
June 29, 1916.
Work on Chateau Trois Tours commenced but delayed owing on account for lack of timber. Work on medical dugouts at Willows and new Brigade HQ at C 20 and D 54 continued.

• • •

They had commandeered the truck and were going around Brielen picking up bits of timber from damaged buildings, and any other stuff they felt would be useful. The art of scavenging was another thing they were learning, but which Corporal Duggan proved particularly adept at.

It was a week before they could go back into the cellar, and they never went in alone. The smell had mostly been replaced with the dank, musty odor of a long unused subterranean chamber. By the time they had installed shelving and some machines and worktables, it was a new room, with the hole being covered up.

A week later, Vincent and a couple of others were making beams for the dugouts, when one of the carpenters asked, "Who's farted?"

Oh, no ... thought Vincent.

He saw a movement across the room, but when he looked over, there was nothing. Shrugging, he carried on, putting his jacket on, as it had gotten very cold suddenly. A few days later, they were in the cellar again working, when, once more, one of the lads wrinkled his nose... Vincent just smiled. The smell was getting familiar now. Then again something was in his peripheral vision, and he looked around. This time, an image of the German soldier was there, outlined against the dark walls of the cellar, looking at him. He was wearing a uniform, and he had a gas mask tied to his belt. His left hand rested on the gas mask. Again, the feeling of intense cold, worse than usual, was prevalent in the room.

When he found his voice, he said, "Do ye see him?" to John, who was hammering away nearby.

"What?" John asked, and as he looked in the direction Vincent was staring, he saw nothing, and when Vincent looked again, the specter was gone. But the image was burned on his memory, the serious young face, the uniform, and gas mask. Vincent felt it was trying earnestly to tell him something. For some reason, the gas mask made an impression on him. Vincent shook his head in frustration and carried on with his work.

The cellar next to the store was set up as an underground conference room, with walls and floors all made from timber garnered in Brielen and surrounding areas. The large table and chairs were from the chateau itself. The brigade commanders had a meeting in the room about two weeks later, on the twentieth of July. General Haig was visiting, and he sat at the head of the table. The agenda was the imminent transfer of the Guards Division to the Somme. The battle had begun on July 1 and was still in full flow. The losses had been appalling.

As the Guards officers sat around the table, Haig, his nose twitching, muttered, "Smells like a damn battlefield in here ... "

There was acute embarrassment around the table, until one of the aides mentioned about the visitation next door in the storeroom, and the peculiar odor that accompanied it.

Haig, being Scottish, was a firm believer in the other world, and said, "Well, we better get one of the chaplains in here to do something about it."

The next day, Father O'Byrne, a catholic priest with the Guards, said mass in the storeroom, and then, on the captain's orders, they barricaded it. Nothing more was heard from the disturbed spirit of the German soldier, much to the relief of the officers using the chateau as a headquarters.

• • •

JULY 1, 1916
7:28 am

One hundred miles to the south, near the tiny French village of La Boisselle, a series of massive convulsions shook the land as tons of high explosive were set off deep underground, announcing the beginning of the Battle of the Somme. Nearly 20,000 men died on just the first day of this three-month-long struggle to get a few miles closer to victory.

By mid-1916 the British controlled about sixty-seven of the eighty-seven miles of trenches that stretched from where the 75th Field Company was engaged at Boesinghe, near Ypres, in the north to the Somme near Curlu in France. Further to the east, the French armies controlled the front line as far as the French border with Switzerland. North of Ypres, the front was manned by French and Belgian troops. The armies had been in virtual stalemate regarding any movement since the German Army was pushed back to the Aisne River late in 1914.

The Allied Generals had decided the time was ripe for a major offensive against the Germans. This decision was made during discussions between the British and French at Chantilly, in December 1915. It was to be a combined offensive coordinating British, French, Italian and Russian armies, with the French and British contribution to be made along the area of the river Somme. However, at the end of February the Germans carried out their own attack on the city of

Verdun. This drew off most of the French troops, leaving the bulk of the assault on the Somme to the British Army.

By now, after a massive recruitment drive, the British army totaled just under 1.5 million men, under the command of General Sir Douglas Haig. Due to the massive attrition rate of experienced British regular troops, the bulk of Haig's army were raw recruits with little experience among them. This included Vincent's company, though they had been in action now for nearly two years.

The planned offensive began on the fateful morning of the first of July, with the French gaining a decisive victory over the Germans south of the Somme. However, the British attacks were unsuccessful and the casualties of 57,470 men was the worst in British army history. The Ulstermen of the 36th Division was successful in achieving their objectives, but at terrific cost, with over 5,500 men losing their lives, missing, and wounded. Four VCs were won by the 36th that day.

• • •

75th Field Company War Diary
July 1, 1916.
Work on HQ cellars at Trois tours continued B28 A 6.1.

July 2, 1916.
As on 1st: Gates and barbed wire fence on prisoner's camp at A23 c 1.9 completed. Merryweather pump at Elverdinghe inspected with a view to it's being used. Pump at Brigade HQ A 30 camp repaired.

July 3, 1916.
R.E. work on cellar dugouts at Trois Tours continued. Frames and roofing of all three completed, partitions and fittings being put up. Part of work on pump at Elverdinghe completed. Sections 3 & 4 returned

to billets at Brielen and continued work at night on new Brigade HQ dugouts. (C 20 b 6.7.)

July 4, 1916.

100 infantry employed putting up sandbag protection to dugouts in cellars at Trois Tours. R.E. work door hanging and making fittings continued. Shovels having been taken away, party for medical dugouts was employed carrying material. R.E. only employed on new Brigade H.Q. at junction of Coney Street and Boar Lane. Arrangements made for taking over work in Right Sector from 55th Field Company. New B 13 trench inspected C 22 C. Cross Country march from Trois Tours to C 25c8.5. Reconnoitered for wheeled traffic.

July 13, 1916.

Continued as above. Full infantry working parties but seriously interfered with owing to shell fire behind Cavan Trench.

July 14, 1916.

No work on Cavan Trench and its drainage owing to retaliation by our troops. Started to cut a new trench just East of where Boar Lane joins Stirling Lane – this being done by Lt. Briggs. R.E. Some work on Gowthorpe Lane as on 13th and new drain started to drain North line— into Turco Farm. Emergency pile bridges across Canal continued.

July 25, 1916.

Owing to reliefs, no infantry working party available. R.E. did a certain amount of work on a dugout for Right Battn. and in helping work on a Machine Gun emplacement near Mortalje. The emergency bridges were continued. Officers of the 9th Field Company R.E. was shown around the works by our officers and their NCOs. Half the section in Canal Bank back-to-back-billets at A28 Central.

• • •

"Sapper McCann, there's a paper in my pack," said the Sergeant. "It's only a few days old, an' they've all the news about the Battle of Jutland in it." He paused to yell for Madden, who'd gone outside for a pee, and continued. "Finish up that axle yer workin' on and Madden and me'll go 'n get more spare shafts at the dump."

He stomped outside, and Vincent could hear him shouting to Madden, "C'mon, Madden, get your arse up on the wagon, we're goin' to the dump!" and the sounds of the horse and wagon moving off.

He worked solidly for an hour, then stopped the lathe, stretched, yawned, and sat down on an ammunition box with the sergeant's paper. He groped in his top pocket and pulled out a pack of Gauloises, which he had decided to try, as there was a shortage of his own brand, Capstan. Tapping the pack as he read, he fished one of the fat, short cigarettes out and lit up, taking a deep pull, coughing on the strong Turkish tobacco.

Outside, thrushes were singing a concert in the warm July sunshine that you couldn't pay money to hear, though he was only half listening. They were working near Wieltje, just outside Ypres having turned an old barn into a workshop, repairing axles for the limbers and carts. Intermittent fighting was going on down to the South. The salient was always active. Every so often the artillery on one side or the other would start up, but these days they hardly noticed the noise, unless that is, it landed close by. He opened the paper, and started reading about the recent Battle of Jutland, where both sides took a pasting.

His reading was interrupted by a loud crash nearby, shaking the building and sending chunks of hay down from the loft above.

"Mother of God, that was a bit close," he muttered, looking around him. There was no follow up, so he began to relax and picked up the paper again. Jutland had been a major naval encounter, where both battle fleets faced off against each other, both suffering serious losses, both claiming victory. In truth, it was just a battle, lots of men died, and nothing was changed.

I've always wanted to be a sailor, he thought, gazing in front of him. *What the hell am I doing here?* Shaking his head, he took a pull on the cigarette and turned back to the paper.

With his back to the door of the barn, he didn't notice the wisps of green smoke drifting along the ground up towards the barn.

He didn't notice the birds had stopped singing.

Taking a final pull on the cigarette, he stubbed it out and stood up to get on with the job so as to have it done before Sarge came back. *Damn French cigarettes. They'd choke the Divil himself.* But the choking got worse, and his eyes were stinging. Turning to look out the door, he couldn't see the fields outside. There was a peppery smell, like pineapple.

It took a few seconds before the realization came to him that this was gas. It would kill in minutes. The stinging in his eyes forced them shut and now his skin was burning. He grabbed the gas mask slung on his belt and pulled it over his head. Those days, since he'd seen the grey soldier in the chateau cellar, he always kept his mask with him, in its bag on his belt. He knew that gas was heavier than air, and he needed to get up high. When they were setting up the barn, earlier, he noticed there was a large wooden ladder going up to the loft. But by now he could hardly see. Afterwards he could never remember how it happened, but somehow, he managed to find the steps and stumbled up onto the loft. He lay there, in a fetal position, gasping for air for what seemed like hours. The pain in his lungs was unbearable, as he tried to suck in air. The exposed skin on his hands burned, and his face too, where it was exposed before he got the mask on. Then he began to vomit. Time no longer mattered as everything went black.

Later, consciousness returned, but he was still in a torment, gasping for breath, half conscious, he heard a shout from below. Sergeant Buckley and John Madden had returned and were looking for him.

"Vinnie, where the fuck are ye?"

"Jayus man, we saw the gas from high up and came here as fast as we could."

"Vinnie … "

The Sergeant had come in with Madden, and they were looking around them. Something wet fell on the Sergeant's hand. He sniffed at it. Vomit. He looked up, and through the boards of the loft, he could see a shape and realized that Vincent had made it up there.

"He's up there," he said to Madden. "C'mon, let's get him down." The gas had cleared, but the barn still stank of chlorine.

Vincent, slowly regaining consciousness and hearing voices, crawled over, feeling his way to the edge of the loft. All he could do was croak. The men below heard the movement and rasping breathing and clambered up the ladder.

"Are yer alright mate?"

He couldn't answer but nodded weakly. They pulled the gas helmet off and managed to get his limp body down the steps and over to the cart, which hadn't been unloaded. Fresh air seeped into his tortured lungs, and his breathing improved slightly. That loft had saved him, getting up just high enough to keep out of the poisonous atmosphere below. The trip to the Ambulance Station passed in a haze—hallucinating, strange visions passing through his head, and the German soldier, standing with his gas mask, was there too. He could hear voices around him, and then passed out again.

The four sections had gone on rest routine and after spending three days in the field hospital, he was discharged and returned to the company. The doctor reminded him how lucky he'd been. His face was still sore and reddened, his lungs felt like he was breathing nails.

"It'll ease up after a while," he said. "You didn't get enough exposure to kill you, but I've no doubt your lungs will bother you in the future." Then, a word of warning: "Stay off the ciggies."

Vincent found out the company was already on the move and were now at billets at a place called Bamberque. When he got there, Sergeant Buckley gave him a warm welcome, and retold him what had happened. He was still very shaken and weak, so they put him on light duties.[65]

• • •

75th Field Company War Diary
July 26, 1916.
OC 9th Field Company (4th Division) took over old works in progress from their company and remaining men came back at night to back-billets at A 28 Central.

July 27, 1916.
Company marched out of billets at 12 noon and arrived at Bambecque via Popperinghe, Watau, and Herzeele by 4.30 pm.

July 28, 1916.
Company occupied sorting out gear and cleaning up generally. Interpreter Breton joined.

---

65 On July 25th, Vincent's army records show he was gassed. "Wounded, gas."

July 29, 1916.

Ditto. Lt. Russell R.E. with an interpreter left by train from Proven to do billeting in the new Somme area.

July 30, 1916.

Company with all its wagons left Bambercque and entrained at Proven, train leaving at 8.54 PM.

July 31, 1916.

Company detrained at St. Pol Station at 3.00 am and marched out at 5.30 am arriving at Bouque Maison at 11 am at 1st Guards Brigade billets in the same village.

• • •

After one month of fighting, with tens of thousands of casualties and dead, the Battle of the Somme was still being fought out.

The Guards were on their way to join in the fray.

CHAPTER 18

A Few Good Men

Some were for, many against,
A lot content to sit on the fence,
But a few good men made their voices heard,
Freedom was their magic word,
"We'll rule ourselves with dignity,"
Taken up by the shouts of Liberty.

(Derek McCann. "Irish Freedom")

September 9, 1916

"It's a damn shame," Vincent said. "They should've seen the war out first, then we could have worked with the government. Now that Padraig Pearce and his friends have been executed, there's no knowin' what'll happen."

"Yeah, but would they've negotiated? Once the war's over, it'd be back to business as usual, and they'd have the troops to put anythin' down," said John.

"Y'know, most of us joined so that we'd be treated fairly in this Home Rule business, 'n now it's all screwed up," said Dan Mullally, one of the sappers from Dublin.

"You *Jackeens*[66] would believe anytin' yer told," answered O'Sullivan from Kerry.

The argument, taking place as they rested in the new camp at Carnoy after the long march, was heated and set to go on late into the night. It was an argument that bounced back and forth in all the pubs of Ireland, over dinner tables and across church steps after mass. It had gone on for years now, but the Insurrection in Dublin a few months ago had changed the dynamic.

From the Irish Catholic point of view, Ireland was a country under occupation. From the English Protestant aspect, it was a colony, owing allegiance to the crown. The area surrounding the capital was known as the "Pale", and generally supportive of the crown, hence the nickname "Jackeens" by those "outside the Pale."

There were two basic schools of thought, in relation to the subject of British Rule. Ireland had been a British colony, since the Norman Invasion in 1172, for over seven hundred and forty years, usually rounded off to eight hundred years, the more the merrier so to speak. The moderates supported Home-Rule from Ireland while remaining in the United Kingdom of Great Britain and Ireland, while others, mostly Nationalist in their thinking, wanted total independence from Britain. Within the latter was the Irish Republican Brotherhood, later to become the IRA.

The moderate thinking was that if Irishmen fought with the British in the war against Germany, the British Government would be more inclined to allow Home Rule. A Home Rule bill had been passed by the British Parliament in 1914, but with the onset of hostilities this was postponed.

---

66 "Jackeen" was a derogatory term for those living in an area around Dublin, known as the Pale, and refers to the British flag, "The Union Jack".

But it wasn't so much the insurrection that changed the national thinking, but the execution of its leaders.[67] This had swayed a lot of people to the nationalist side and was to lead to the War of Independence following the Great War. Most of the men fighting in the latter were either Unionists from Northern Ireland or moderate nationalists.

The following is about two of the moderates.

• • •

75th Field Company War Diary
September 10, 1916.
Company moved into camp A.24.a South of Carnoy during the morning. 1st Guards Brigade all round Carnoy. In afternoon, reconnaissance of work to be done at T. 24. B. 6. Capt. Fox R.E. and 2nd Lt. Russell with NCOs. Timber carried up by night to East edge of Trones Wood by Lt. Fraser.

• • •

A day earlier, as Vincent's company was marching to their camp in Carnoy, an attack was being carried out to capture the village of Ginchy, which was crucial to the overall battle plan for an assault on the German trenches. Part of the attacking division was the Royal Irish Fusiliers, and leading "B" company was an Irish lawyer-turned-army officer, Lieutenant Tom Kettle. Behind him, Leading "A" company was another, younger Irishman by the name of Emmet Dalton. The latter would live on to make Irish history in both the War of Independence, and the subsequent civil war. The former would probably have played a prominent role in that same history,

---

67 Patrick Pearce, Eamonn Ceannt, Thomas Clarke, James Connelly, Sean MacDiarmada, Thomas MacDonagh, Joseph Mary Plunkett, and Roger Casement.

except for a German bullet, which found its way over a homemade breast plate Kettle was wearing.

These are their stories.

• • •

"Some of their splendid regiments had to endure ordeals that might justly have taxed to breaking point the capacity of the finest troops in the world … never in those terrible days did they fail me."

—*Field Marshal Ferdinand Foch, Supreme Commander Allied Forces 1918 referring to the Irish troops under his command.*

THOMAS MICHAEL KETTLE

On any given day in Dublin, thousands of office workers, shoppers, tourists, mothers with their children and students walk through Saint Stephen's Green in Dublin. They mostly enter through the grandiose Fusilier's Arch opposite Grafton Street, to enjoy one of Dublin's most beautiful central city parks. As they eat their lunch, chat, laze in the sun, listen to music, or feed the ducks in the central pond, few are aware of the simple plinth with a bronze bust on top, leafy shrubs surrounding it on three sides. This is the only memorial in the country to Thomas Michael Kettle, one of Ireland's most remarkable patriots, who, as is written on the bottom of the plinth, *"Died not for flag, nor King, nor Emperor, but for a dream, born in a herdsman's shed, and for the sacred scripture of the poor."*

Artane, now a densely populated suburb of Dublin, was in 1880, green fields and tilled farmland. And while the dream Tom Kettle died for was born in a "herdsman's shed," he himself was born in very comfortable circumstances to a wealthy farmer and politician, Andrew Kettle. He was the seventh child born in that home, and was followed by five more, leaving his busy mother little time for politics or otherwise, but looking after her growing brood. Andrew, on the other hand, was head, neck and heels in Irish politics and had a considerable influence on Tom's future.

Like a lot of Irish lads, he went to the Christian Brothers O'Connell School and then on to the Jesuits in the prestigious Clongowes Wood College in Co. Kildare, and finally University College Dublin, developing into a man of many accomplishments. He achieved distinction as an economist, journalist, barrister, writer, war poet and Home Rule politician. As a member of the Irish Parliamentary Party, he became MP for East Tyrone. In 1913 he joined the Irish Volunteers and then in 1914, he enlisted for service in the British Army. He was an old friend of James Joyce, as well as many other prominent Irish figures of the day. A gifted orator, using his talents well, he was admitted to the Irish Law Bar in 1903. In 1908 he became the first Professor of National Economics at University College Dublin.

There was a school of thought in Ireland, that on the outbreak of war in 1914, Irishmen joining the British army and fighting for the Crown, would positively influence the granting of Home Rule in Ireland after the war was over. Tom, belonging very much to this ideal, on the outbreak of war, insisted on forsaking a promising career to join the

British Army; even though he suffered from bad health, he was commissioned as a lieutenant, but was restricted to garrison service at home.

Not being at all satisfied with this, he persevered in his attempts to serve on the Western Front and eventually was admitted to the 9th Battalion of The Royal Dublin Fusiliers and was sent to France in the summer of 1916. Poor health saw him return to Dublin, but even though he was offered a permanent staff position there, he insisted on rejoining his battalion in France.

Of the conditions in France he wrote: "*The bombardment, destruction and bloodshed are beyond all imagination.*"

In this short sentence, he summed up the hopelessness and futility of that war.

Writing to his brother the night before the main attack on Ginchy, he said: "*I am calm and happy but desperately anxious to live ... The big guns are coughing and smacking their shells, which sound for all the world like overhead express trains at anything from 10 to 100 per minute on this sector; the men are grubbing and an odd one writing home. Somewhere the Choosers of the Slain are touching, as in our Norse story they used to touch, with invisible wands, those who are to die.*"

Tom Kettle didn't know whether that wand touched him or not, but he simply wanted to do his duty, survive the war, and go home. His numerous writings which survived him make this perfectly clear.

However, the following afternoon, at 4:45 pm, September 9, "B" company of the 9th Battalion of the Royal Dublin Fusiliers carried out an attack on the village of Ginchy. As he led his men across the field in front of the village, he was struck by a bullet, killing him instantly, notwithstanding that he wore a somewhat primitive bulletproof vest. He was 36 years old.

Tom's body was found and buried by the Welsh Guards, but afterwards, in the post battle chaos, the grave was never found. His name is etched on the monumental arched gateway for the missing of the Somme at Thiepval. His name is also inscribed on a plaque in the House of Commons, to the MPs who died in the war. In Ireland he was largely ignored after the war, except for the small bust in St. Stephen's Green, just opposite the Shelbourne Hotel.

As his good friend, G. K. Chesterton surmised, "Thomas Michael Kettle was perhaps the greatest example of that greatness of spirit which was so ill rewarded on both sides of the channel. He was a wit, a scholar, an orator, a man ambitious in all the arts of peace; and he fell fighting the barbarians because he was too good a European to use the barbarians against England, as England a hundred years before had used the barbarians against Ireland."

Tom wrote this lovely poem to his daughter just a few days before he died, in an effort to explain what he was doing over there.

Betty was just three years old.

To My Daughter Betty, The Gift of God
In wiser days, my darling rosebud, blown
To beauty proud as was your mother's prime,
In that desired, delayed, incredible time,
You'll ask why I abandoned you, my own,
And the dear heart that was your baby throne,
To dice with death. And oh! they'll give you rhyme
And reason: some will call the thing sublime,
And some decry it in a knowing tone.
So here, while the mad guns curse overhead,
And tired men sigh with mud for couch and floor,
Know that we fools, now with the foolish dead,
Died not for flag, nor King, nor Emperor,
But for a dream, born in a herdsman's shed,
And for the secret Scripture of the poor.

"Some of the flowers of Irish chivalry rest in the cemeteries that have been reserved in France and the French people will always have these reminders of the debt that France owes to Irish valour."

—*Engraved on a wooden cross on the Ginchy battlefield, a replica of which is to be seen in Glasnevin cemetery in Dublin.*

For 100 years, our history has told us that we can only have one set of heroes. You were either for the Easter Rising rebels or against. This binary approach is ahistorical and amounts to a false choice. The American writer F Scott Fitzgerald noted the test of intelligence is the "ability to hold two opposed ideas in mind at the same time and still retain the ability to function."

We can have two sets of heroes...

"Many more Irish men like Kettle died in the defense of the French Republic than died in the creation of our own. They died so that France might live."

—*Ronan McGreevy, Irish Times Journalist*

EMMET DALTON[68]

As Tom Kettle climbed out of the trench leading "B" company into the attack on Ginchy, a young, newly commissioned lieutenant by the name of Emmet Dalton was right behind him leading "A" company.

Emmet later recalled: "I was just behind Tom when he went over the top. He was in a bent position, and a bullet passed over a steel waistcoat that he wore and entered his heart. Well, he only lasted about one minute, and he had my crucifix in his hands."[69]

Emmet was born in the United States on the 4th of March 1898. He was called after the Irish patriot Robert Emmet whose birthday he shared. Like Tom Kettle, his father was an eminent Nationalist, separated from the Great Famine by only one generation and his mother Katherine was also of Irish descent.

---

68 Photo source Wikimedia Commons public domain. https://www.independent.ie/sport/golf/dalton-hell-hermitage-and-stars-of-the-silver-screen-30880123.html

69 Boyne, S. *Emmet Dalton: Somme Soldier, Irish General, Film Pioneer.* 2015 Merrion Press. Co. Kildare.

The family returned to Ireland in 1900, moving to Dublin, settling in a new house in Drumcondra, which at that time was on the outskirts of the city, surrounded by green fields. Emmet later went to the nearby Christian Brothers' O'Connell School. In 1912 he was sent away to the Cistercians at Roscrea College.[70] The following year, he helped his father who was a member of the fledgling Irish Volunteers, along with Tom Kettle.

In 1915, just seventeen years old, Emmet joined the British Army. He lied about his age, saying he was 18. The army posted him to the 7th Battalion, Royal Dublin Fusiliers and sent him to Victoria Barracks Cork and then to Kilworth Camp at Fermoy where he arrived six months after Vincent's 75th Field Company had left for France. On the 15th of July 1916, Emmet passed his military examinations and was given the rank of 2nd lieutenant with the 7th Battalion RDF, later being transferred to the 9th Battalion.

Thus, Emmet found himself behind Tom Kettle, leading his company into the attack on the village of Ginchy. Despite his tender years, he displayed great bravery and leadership in the battle, deploying machine-gun teams in key positions and staving off a counterattack by the Germans after occupying the village. They held out there for 24 hours before being relieved by the Welsh Guards. Only two officers walked out of the battle relatively unscathed, Dalton being one of them. For his actions on that day, he was awarded the Military Cross.

Emmet went on to serve in Salonica (where he contracted Malaria), Egypt, and Palestine. Later in the war he returned to France, instructing newly arrived American troops in the use of the Lewis gun. At the age of twenty-one, having survived the war he returned to Ireland, a hardened and decorated soldier, experienced in weaponry and battle conditions. For the next year he studied Engineering at the Royal College of

---

70 I would have gone there myself, after my mother sent me down to do a scholarship exam. Unfortunately, I failed miserably, beginning a series of exam failures throughout my life. Roscrea was not to be.(*DMC*)

Science.[71] But in late 1920, after his home was raided several times and both he and his father were arrested by the British, Emmet began training IRA volunteers, dropping out of his engineering studies.

He became known to "The Big Fellow," Michael Collins,[72] who was running the intelligence section of the IRA and gradually Michael began trusting him with more difficult assignments. One of these was the attempted rescue of General Sean MacEoin, who was imprisoned in Mountjoy Prison.

To accomplish this, they hijacked a British armored car and drove into the jail with Dalton and another IRA man, Joe Leonard, dressed as British army officers. The attempt ultimately failed due to the alarm being set off, but the men escaped in the armored car and subsequently hid from the British in the Stella Maris convent in Howth, North County Dublin.

After the Treaty was announced on 11 March 1921, Dalton traveled over to London with Michael Collins to take part in the talks with the British Government. As some readers will know, the terms of the Treaty[73] were not accepted by the Dail[74] President, Eamonn De Valera, resulting in a two year long civil war.

Towards the end of the war, when most of the country had been won over by the Free State, only the City of Cork and County Cork remained in IRA hands. Dalton led a seaborn force of four ships with 400 men to "invade" the county by sea. Two of the ships with Dalton in charge, landed their troops in Passage West, about 12 miles outside the city, and they proceeded to march towards Cork. The IRA sent troops out to meet them, and the two armies engaged at Mount Oval in

---

71   Later absorbed into University College Dublin as the Faculty of Science and Engineering.

72   Michael Collins was a larger-than-life figure in the Irish Republican Movement, and later became chairman of the Provisional Government of the Irish Free State. There is a very good movie, called "Michael Collins" starring Liam Neeson, which is worth seeing.

73   "Irish Free State with 26 counties and 6 counties remaining under British Rule."

74   Irish Parliament.

Rochestown. Here a fierce battle was fought, with many wounded and 20 men lost their lives.[75]

Not long after, Dalton was with Michael Collins when the latter visited Cork; while they were traveling through Bealnablath, the cavalcade was ambushed, and Collins was fatally wounded. He died with his head in Emmet Dalton's lap.

It was never known who carried out the ambush, and it was always assumed to be some members of the IRA who were on the run at that stage.[76]

---

75 It is noteworthy to the author as he lived there with his family in a house backing on the field where the battle took place. Many of the old iron gates into the fields around still had bullet holes in them.

76 In later years, Emmet Dalton founded the Ardmore Studios in Ireland, producing such films as *The Devil's Agent, Lies My Father Told Me*, and probably the best known film made at Ardmore, though not produced by Dalton, was *The Blue Max*.

CHAPTER 19

Little Willie and Big Willie

"See that little stream—we could walk to it in two minutes.
It took the British a month to walk to it—a whole empire walking very slowly, dying in front, and pushing forward behind.
And another empire walked very slowly backward a few inches a day, leaving the dead like a million bloody rugs. No Europeans will ever do that again in this generation. ... This western-front business couldn't be done again, not for a long time. The young men think they could do it, but they couldn't. They could fight the first Marne again but not this.
This took religion and years of plenty and tremendous sureties and the exact relation that existed between the classes.
... All my beautiful lovely safe world blew itself up here with a great gust of high explosive love."

(F. Scott FitzGerald. "Tender is the Night")

GINCHY, DEPARTMENT OF THE SOMME, NORTHERN FRANCE
September 9, 1916

The brain-jarring detonations of the artillery were constant and deafening with the shells zipping overhead to land on the German lines, clouds of black oily smoke and debris marking the line of German trenches. The enemy was taking terrible punishment; this was the prelude, the "softening up" dished out prior to any attack. This time, the goal was the small village of Ginchy, and the men tasked with this mission were the 9th Battalion of the Dublin Fusiliers.

The village had been previously captured by the 7th Division and then retaken by the Germans in a counterattack. What used to be a pleasant rural hamlet was reduced to a heap of rubble surrounded by muddy blasted fields, where the Germans had dug in. The British once more were making a determined attempt to regain it prior to a major offensive to be launched at the middle of the month.

The initial assault took part late in the day at 4:45 pm, to prevent the Germans staging a counterattack before night fell. The troops of the 7th Brigade of Royal Irish Rifles were caught under a heavy bombardment from the German artillery, forcing them to seek cover wherever they could, and to make matters worse, due to communications difficulties, the British Artillery also dropped rounds on them. Bombarded by the enemy and their own side, the battalion was decimated and had to be relieved by the Royal Irish Fusiliers and the Royal Dublin Fusiliers.

They managed to recapture Ginchy, but the loss of lives, like always in the Somme, was appalling.

• • •

75th Field Company War Diary
September 10, 1916.
Camp at A24a. Albert map. Scale 1/40,000. Company moved into camp A.24.a South of Carnoy during the morning. 1st Guards Brigade all round Carnoy. In afternoon, reconnaissance of work to be done at T. 24. B. 6. Capt. Fox R.E. and 2nd Lt. Russell with NCOs. Timber carried up by night to East edge of Trones Wood by Lt. Fraser.

September 11, 1916.

Work on Brigade battle dugouts carried out all day and night by Nos. 2 & 3 sections under 2nd. Lt. Crane and 2nd Lt. Russell respectively. Position of dugouts T24. B. 6 ½ .1. Lt. Briggs started work in evening on 3rd Brigade Battle dugouts at S23. C. 6.3. Wiring material carried up by night by Lt. Frazer to lines at T24. B. 6 ½ .1. just east of Trones Wood. Owing to heavy shell fire, work on dugouts at T24. B. 6 ½ .1. was stopped between the times of 5 and 9 pm.

September 12, 1916.

Lt. Briggs handed over dugouts at S23 c 6.3 to the 4th Coldstream Pioneers. Work on battle dugouts in T24. B. 6 ½ .1. continued as before. Lt. Fraser transferred all wiring material left near Trones Wood on the 11th to dumps along road from Waterlot Farm to Guillemont Road, parallel to trench running from S18 d 6.3 to T 9 a 1.6.

Author's comment: during the night of 12th[77]—13th the 3rd Guards Brigade was relieved by the 1st Guards Brigade (with 75th Field Company) and 2nd Guards Brigade (with 76th Field Company). These two brigades were preparing to carry out an attack on the Guidecourt—Lesboeufs—Morval line - marked on the map below. The green line is the trenches of the Guards, and the blue is their objective, about 3 km away. The 1st Guards were on the left of the green line.

September 13, 1916.

Work on dugouts continued by day and by night as on 12th. Lt. Briggs laid out lines of "assembly" for 1st Guards Brigade (by means of braids and pegs) to the NE of Waterlot Farm and Guillemont Rd. parallel to the trench running from S18d.6.3. to T9. A. 1.6. ("green line" Author)

---

77 Comments are based on Headlam. C. *The Guards Brigade in the Great War.*

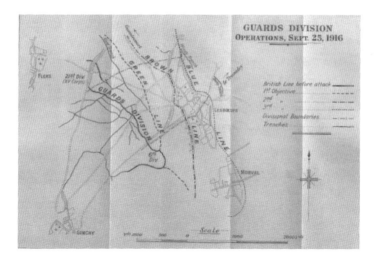

• • •

GUILLEMONT ROAD, NEAR DELVILLE WOOD
September 13, 1916

Sweat rolled down his face, stinging his eyes, as Vincent carried the heavy drum of wire, along with Sapper Dave Millar. Each had one end of a steel pipe going through the drum. It was dark, and stumbling through the shell holes and mud made the going almost impossible. When they got to Waterlot Farm and the Engineers' dump they put it down along with the others, and Lieutenant Fraser told the Sergeant to let them have a break for twenty minutes. There were ten of them, and they sat around in a group and took a drink from their canteens.

"What's happening sir?" one of them asked the Lieutenant.

With all the shelling and confusion, it was difficult to keep track of what was going on. Individual companies were given orders and followed their lieutenant wherever he went, hoping he knew what he was doing.

Vincent pulled on his cigarette; his hands cupped around it to stop any light showing.

Fraser rubbed his eyes, which were red and smarting from the cordite smoke that was drifting across the farm, and said, "The 1st and 2nd Guards are going in, two days from now. Our object is to get the assembly lines marked and get wire ready to bring up to the captured trenches."

He went on: "My information is that the 16th Irish have taken Ginchy and are holding it. The Guards have to move up about three kilometers from our trenches here … when we finish this, we'll help with marking out the assembly lines, with Briggs and his men."

He paused a moment as a shell screamed close overhead, landing with an ear-splitting explosion beyond them in what was left of Delville Wood, showering them with bits of tree and other debris.

Then, he continued: "We'll be moving up with the Guards to our battle positions shortly. I hope you can get a bit of rest there before the flares go up."

Like the rest, he looked exhausted, his face streaked with mud and sweat. They had been together close on two years now, through battles and marches, and had developed a respectful camaraderie, despite the rigid discipline expected of the Guards. They knew he was there for them, and they reciprocated.

As they rested, lines of stretcher bearers carried the wounded back, for the moment leaving the dead where they were. The rats, as usual, were the winners in the horrific game of war.

75th Field Company War Diary
September 14, 1916.

Dugout continued as on 13th and finished by the afternoon. Company, less all transport moved up into battle position in shell holes NE of Waterlot Farm and Guillemont Road about Square S24b (NE corner.) Got to their point by 11 pm. And took what shelter there was. Tool carts, pack animals and water cart under Lt. Fraser work brigade with carts of 55th and 76th Field Companies about point 300 ft. SW of Bernafay Wood.[78]

THE BRITISH SECRET WEAPON

By September 15th, when the second big push took place at Flers-Courcelette, the Somme offensive had been dragging on for two and a half months, with an excruciating death toll. Both sides were locked in behind a maze of trenches with the land between them a mass of tangled barbed wire. The shell pocked mud that used to be green fields and pleasant farming villages was now a death trap. The stench of dead bodies was overpowering, and men walking through the trenches were stepping on body parts buried in the mud. The British army had lost over 20,000 dead and 40,000 wounded on the first day of the Somme, and the toll just kept mounting. It looked like this nightmare would continue forever.

In 1915, the British started to develop a new weapon, based on years of research. It was a well-kept secret. To confuse enemy spies, it was called a *tank*, because it looked like a large steel water tank. The first prototype was called "Little Willie" and its clumsiness and inability to move well over rough ground left a lot to be desired. It's more successful second prototype was called, needless to say, "Big Willie." They had produced 50 of these monster machines, which were transported to France in high secrecy in the summer of 1915. They were called MkI and MkII and were made in two different types. The larger were equipped with two Hotchkiss 6 lb. guns in a recess on each side and two Hotchkiss machine guns. These were known as "Males." The other, lighter version was equipped with three machine guns. It was called the "Female".

---

78 This was to be known as the Battle of Flers—Courcelette, and there were a few "firsts" that the soldiers witnessed. One of these was the introduction of the tank for the first time.

General Haig had decided to use these mobile, armored, machine gun posts in the forthcoming battle, hoping it would provide the advantage he badly needed. The tanks were ordered to proceed to the battle lines between Ginchy and Flers-Courcelette. By the time they arrived at the front, only 32 vehicles made it, the rest broke down from mechanical failure or got bogged down in the mud.

The first tank to enter the field was a Male, under the command of Captain Mortimer. At 5:15 a.m. on the 15th of September, in platoons of two to three, the tanks were to penetrate enemy lines in its most powerful sections, covering advancing infantry. The tank approached German lines between Ginchy and Delville Wood. It destroyed a machine-gun nest that impeded British light infantry but was then knocked out by an artillery shell hitting the suspension.

At 5:30, other tanks entered combat. The highly claustrophobic conditions inside the tanks were insufferable. Their crews were subjected to suffocating fumes, the sound of cannon fire, and hammering of bullets against the armor deafened them. It was very cramped inside, with a spare oil tank, two small gas tanks, three water tanks, spare machine gun barrels, a spare machinegun, a cage with postal pigeons (who no doubt, added their protests to the general cacophony inside), a signal flag, and a set of signal lamps. Of course, there also had to be room for two days' worth of food and the crew's personal equipment.

The appearance of the tanks did have a critical psychological advantage, though.

The Germans were shocked by the appearance of tanks. When a German screamed, "Der Teufel kommt!"[79] in the first trenches, his words spread like wildfire. Through the tanks' observation slits, the crew could see many figures in feldgrau uniforms fleeing from their positions. The few brave men that attempted to open fire watched as their bullets bounced harmlessly off, and the machine thundered relentlessly towards them.

---

79 "The Devil is coming!"

The tanks advanced. Far from perfect, some fell into German trenches or got stuck in shell craters. Crews had to climb out to attempt to repair the tank. However, those MkIs that were spared this fate performed well.

For instance, the male D17 "Dinnaken" commanded by Lieutenant Hastie was the first to enter the village of Fleurs, slowly following running and hiding Germans. An airplane reconnaissance mission reported, "The tank is moving through the main street of Fleur, English soldiers are following it in good spirits."

Other tanks were of great help to the infantry, making holes in barbed wire and crushing machine gun nests. One MkI stopped above a German trench, cleared it with machine gun fire, and proceeded to move along the trench. With its help, approximately 300 enemy soldiers were captured. Ten tanks were knocked out during the attack for various reasons, seven more received superficial damage.

The night before was a long one, with the troops lying in whatever shelter they could get.

As one Guardsman put it:

"*There was no sleep that night of the 14th, what with the artillery blasting away at the enemy lines and the sheer nerves of waiting for the attack to begin. The noise was enough to obliterate your mind, and the smell of dead corpses was overpowering. As the men lay around with their packs for pillows, there was little talk. Some tried to sleep, but most just waited, awake, some writing letters home.*"

75th Field Company War Diary
September 15, 1916.

HQ and all dismounted sections at S24 b (3?) (NE corner). Battle[80] started at 6.20 am. 1st Guards Brigade advance NE direction and occupied German 2 lines of trenches T8a.0.6. to T8 d.1 ½ .8. and T2c.5.5. to T8 a 10.4. approximately. Elements penetrated further NE about T2 Central and took up a line; position very uncertain. At 8.30 am

---

80 Officially known as the Battle of Flers-Courcelette.

received orders to hold all sections to support 2nd Grenadier Guards about 1st objective T8 Central. At noon, Lt. Briggs with No. 1 section and his sapping platoon of 1st Irish Guards advanced but couldn't cross the ridge between Ginchy and Delville Wood owing to hostile barrage. I reported this to GOC 1st Guards Brigade at 12.45 pm. At 10.25 a.m. one NCO and 2 sappers reconnoitered for water for horses, returning with report in afternoon, which I passed in to C.R.E.

At 3.30 p.m. 2nd Lt. L.E. Crane R.E. went forward to reconnoiter and get in trench with 3rd Coldstream Guards supposed to be holding line about T2 Central. 2nd Lt. Crane got in trench as ordered but was slightly wounded in leg by shell on his return and went to hospital.

• • •

BRITISH TRENCHES, NORTHEAST OF DELVILLE WOOD
September 15, 1916

John Kelly looked at his pocket watch, the one that had been stolen, and had mysteriously been returned to his kit bag a couple of weeks ago. In the light of a flare, it showed 5:20 a.m., not yet daylight; dark layers of cloud threatened rain, the base lit by constant flashes of guns and flares. The men of Vincent's section were laying low in a large shell crater praying "lightning wouldn't strike twice" when Sapper Ennis pointed behind them and shouted over the noise.

"What in the name of Jaysus is that?"

Behind them, out of the morning haze, a large, metal, box-shaped machine, belching black exhaust fumes, was navigating its way over the shell holes, its tracks making easy work of it, though God help the poor devils inside who were having their guts shaken out. The two Hotchkiss six pounders mounted on each pontoon were blasting away at a machine-gun nest that had been holding the troops down for the last 30 minutes. Most of the shots were going wild with the unpredictable movement of the machine, but just after Ennis shouted one lucky shot got the nest with a loud explosion, sending mud and metal and large chunks of human remains into the air.

There was a brief silence. No machine-gun fire. Then, incredibly, a hunting horn[81] sounded and the Guards moved forward.

"I heard they're called a *tank*," Vincent shouted to the man beside him. "It's a new weapon. Weird looking thing. I'm glad it's on our side. It might win the war for us." He said this with a cynical smile.

Only minutes later, a German shell hit the tank at the base, literally stopping it in its tracks.

"Then again, maybe it won't," Vincent muttered wryly, trying to make himself as small as possible in the shell hole they were waiting in.

$$\bullet \ \bullet \ \bullet$$

75th Field Company War Diary
September 15, 1916 (continued).
At 7 pm orders from 1st Guards Brigade received to take rest of company to 3rd Coldstream supposed to be holding the line from T3 a. 9.0 to T3 a. 1.9. I started off to get there by daylight. The rest of the company under Lt. Briggs with 4 sapping platoons of Guards attached started at 8 pm to follow me. I eventually reached destination about 10.45 pm after a lot of misguiding by various troops I met on the way. The company log lists 3 & 4 sections became separated from the others owing to heavy shell fire, in which Lt. J. Russell was wounded. Lt. Bousfield reconnoitered forward and found that these sections had returned to camp when he got back, as they have been badly shelled. Nos. 1 & 2 sections under Lt. Briggs appear to have very nearly reached

---

81 This was Lieutenant-Colonel John Campbell, in command of 2nd Battalion Coldstream Guards, who used the hunting horn very effectively to rally the men in the attack.

3rd Coldstreams were again badly directed by advanced troops and eventually got back to 2nd Grenadiers Guards near T8 Central. They were preparing to help them with wire when a shell landed in the middle of the party wounding Lt. Heywood (Coldstream Guards) and a lot of sappers and Guards, also, scattering the wiring material. No work was done, and party retired to Camps. Reported all this to Brigade in early hours of morning.

[Signed]; *B.H. Fox, Capt. R.E.*

• • •

There was a lot of confusion in the "fog of battle".

The 1st Battalion Coldstream Guards moved forward too fast and came under the British "creeping barrage."[82] In the confusion caused by this mishap it lost its bearings amid the smoke, and moved forward in a northerly, instead of a north-easterly direction. This swing to the left by the Coldstream 1st Battalion resulted in a similar movement on the part of the two other battalions of the same regiment on the front of the 1st Guards Brigade. This caused a gap in the advance line of attack that led to an intermingling of units, officers, and men fighting their way forward in small groups. They were not able to pay much attention to what was happening on their flanks. The outcome was that the gap left between the Coldstreams moving to the left and the Brigade to the right allowed the Germans to hold on, forming a wedge between the brigades. Coming up behind, the 2nd Grenadiers, under Colonel 'Crawley' de Crespigny, thought they would be occupying positions already taken by the Coldstream Guards ahead of them. Instead, they found that part of the trenches being attacked remained in control of the Germans and they were

---

82 The British artillery had perfected the concept of firing just ahead of the advancing troops. Protecting them from enemy fire. It was known as a "Creeping barrage."

met by a barrage of machine gun and rifle fire. They did succeed in driving the enemy back and thus closed the breach in the line.

In the end, despite heavy losses, the Guards reached their objective.

The night was a wet and cold one, but they held on, pushing back numerous attempts by the enemy to retake its lost positions.

75th Field Company War Diary
September 16, 1916.

Battle continued. 3rd Guards Brigade replaced 1st Guards Brigade. HQ of latter going back to dugouts NE of Bernafay Wood. 75th Field Company attached for work to 3rd Guards Brigade. Orders received in morning from C.R.E. to wire in lines at night from T8 b.3.5. to T2 d.9.7 and make strong point about T8 b.3.9.

3rd Guards Brigade have received different orders i.e. to wire in front line and support its flanks. At 7 pm Brigade major agreed[83] with me after seeing C.R.E. 's orders that two sections should go to support troops holding line about T8 Central and 2 sections to get in trench with Battn. Commander of front-line troops. Nos. 3 & 4 sections under Lt. Bousfield R.E. with 2 sapping platoons proceeded at night to 3rd Coldstreams and wired in 500 feet of front from T2 a.1.1 ½. To T2 d.2.6. and 300 feet using our own wire and 200 feet of German wire which was lifted bodily up and transferred to the other side of the trenches about point T2 d.2.6. a strong point was made and wired all around. Nos. 1 & 2 sections under Lt. Briggs proceeded to HQ 4th Grenadier Guards at about T 7d 7.6 and after consultation with OC it was decided to work on the right flank infantry which was exposed. Guides took party to extreme bombing post (held by No. 3

---

83 Writing is very difficult to read in this section of the report. Sometimes transcripts may not make much sense. But I recorded it as accurately as possible. (DMC)

company, 4th Grenadier Guards about point T3 c.4.9. a strong point already marked with pins. 200 feet of wiring was erected around the head of this bombing post, from North to East and round along the right flank in direction N.West. A (double?) block was also made in their trench. Party then returned. All sections moved back to camp at Carnoy during the night of 16th/17th.

Casualties from 15th to 16th night; 2 officers wounded (2nd lt. Crane and 2nd lt. Russell), 2 NCOs and 8 sappers wounded, 2 sappers killed. 2 sappers missing, one horse killed.
September 17, 1916.

Camp near Carnoy A24.a. *Company at camp. 18th and 19th company remained at camp.*

• • •

The last two days had been like a nightmare. Reality became suspended and was replaced by a world of drifting smoke and explosions, bullets searching you out and the stench.

Oh, Dear Lord, the stench.

It was impossible to get used to it. The dull smell of decaying corpses, the sharp smell of cordite, excrement. Even the mud itself had a smell, sulfurous and cloying.

There was no green in this part of the world, just grey pimpled by the broken stumps of trees. Then the constant noise of shell blasts, screams of the wounded, shouts and commands and the rattle of machine guns. Any one of those thousands of *rat-tat-tats* could be sending a bullet to kill or dismember you. They were all filthy from the mud and blood and soaked by the incessant rain which had started on the second night and continued relentlessly.

Vincent and his comrades worked to exhaustion, digging new trenches, repairing the captured German ones and "turning them around",[84] putting up defensive wire in front of them in anticipation of the counterattacks which inevitably came back before they were ready. Even though they had special heavy gloves they were cut all over from the barbed wire. One of his mates said it was like the old Chinese torture, death by a thousand cuts. Vincent laughed at that—the odd joke, it kept them going. Dragging the rolls of wire over the trenches, laying it out and hammering the posts in. Often, this was done in darkness to escape the snipers. Somehow, they kept soldiering on.

Now the men were having a brief respite back at the camp at Carnoy. The noise of battle was still there, but it was separated from them. No bullets here. They could rest. They slept, they cleaned up as best they could, they talked about all the near misses they'd had and their comrades who weren't so lucky.

Sapper Millar and Sapper Rea were killed from a direct hit to where they were working. Two others were never seen again. The last memory anyone had of them was carrying a roll of wire to the forward bombing post, then they were lost in the smoke and rain. They were posted as missing.

Now, stationed at the rest billets, Vincent, like the others, was getting his bearings again, cleaning his uniform and equipment. Having a shave, he looked at himself in the mirror, hardly recognizing the face he saw. Large bags under his eyes and new lines around his mouth made him look years older. *Well, at least I'll be a clean-shaven old man*, he thought, and managed to smile at himself. He knew he'd be going back into battle again with his company but tried to put that out of his mind for the moment.

The sun had finally put in an appearance, and he was enjoying that, learning to live one day at a time, knowing it could be his last.

---

84 The captured German trenches were facing the British lines, they had to be "turned around" to face the German lines, which task was carried out by the engineers.

75th Field Company War Diary
September 20, 1916.
Company left camp at Carnoy at 2.30 pm and arrived at bivouac S 24 d (NE corner) by 5 pm, where they were joined by working platoons less platoon of 1st Battn. Irish Guards. 250 feet of communication trench dug same night from main trench T8 d.1 ½.8. backwards in SW direction. This was done by whole party. One sapper wounded.

September 21, 1916.
Working platoon of 1st Irish Guards arrived in morning. Whole of platoons dug assembly trench from T 2 d.9.4. to T 9 a.5.9. by night helped by 2nd Guards infantry and supervised by sappers. Lts. Briggs and Bousfield reconnoitered work in afternoon. Lt. Fraser took over charge of working parties. Sappers in dugouts for 9 o'c. R.E. stores carried up to advanced dump T 8 c. 7.5. by 2nd Lt. Marris.[85]

• • •

The group with Lieutenant Marris had worked their way towards the new supply dump being set up along the old German trenches captured a few days ago. Most of the supplies consisted of rolls of wire, which constantly had to be laid as new ground was gained. This was a hard-fought battle, ground gained foot by painful foot.

Freddy Bean and Sam McLaughlin had just reached the store, Vincent and John behind them, when Bean appeared to stumble, dropping his end of the pole holding the roll. He didn't get up and when they rolled him over, they saw blood seeping through his tunic, staining the mud red. A stray bullet had caught him in the chest. There was a lot of blood, and as they tried to bring him back,

---

85 This is the first mention of 2nd lt. Marris, who must have joined while the company was resting at the Carnoy camp. I think he was with 76th Field Company R.E.

he began convulsing, blood pouring out his mouth and nostrils. By the time they got him to the Ambulance Station, he was dead.

Five of their comrades were gone, and only one to bury. But even that had to wait. They trudged desolately back to where the wire was left and brought it to the storage area, turning around and going back for more.

• • •

75th Field Company War Diary
September 22, 1916.

Work in assembly trench started on 21st continued and completed to average depth of 5 feet under charge of Lt. Briggs. Assembly trenches for two Field Companies started and 200 feet dug by all spare sappers and working platoon men along line T8 c.6.6. to T8 c.9.3. 2nd Lt. Marris being in charge of the working party. This was shelled most of the night. More R.E. stores were carted up to dump at this place. 2nd Lt. Lawrie R.E. and 2nd Lt. Dunningham R.E. joined the company.

September 23, 1916.

Lt. Fraser with 100 Guards dig improved "assembly trench" from T2 d.9 ½.5. to T3 c.1 ½.2. and made (?) Lt. Bousfield with 4 working platoons dig an extension of assembly trench from T9 a.4.8. to Sunken Rd. at T9 a.6.7 distance 100 feet. 2nd Lt. Marris carried on with digging of Field Company's Battle Trenches as on 22nd. And more R.E. stores were carried to advance dump.

September 24, 1916.

At 6.30 pm Field Company and all attached working platoons moved up to its advanced battle trenches at T8c.8.7. After dumping kit, whole party of working platoons with one (active?) R.E. helped by 300 Guards infantry, dug a new communication trench from T8 b.2.2. to T9 a.1.7.

distance 600 feet approximately. This was completed with an average of 4 feet depth before dawn and joined up with Battalion assembly trenches.

• • •

Early on the 25th, the 1st and 3rd Brigades of the Guards were advancing on the village of Les Boeufs. Behind them, the sappers carried rolls of wire, and digging equipment forward, always ready to fortify the ground the Guards had gained. The brief rest seemed a long way in the past, as they trudged through the mud.

75th Field Company War Diary
September 25, 1916.

Lt. Bousfield with 2 men per section, accompanied OC support lines during the battle and just back, reported on work required.

Battle commenced at 12.35 pm and at 4 pm message received from Lt. Bousfield the village of Les Boeufs had been taken, so that company could come up for work.

Company, with all its working platoons, left for Les Boeufs at 4.30 pm by sections; Nos. 1 & 2 sections leading and Nos. 3 & 4 coming up a little later. These last two sections carried 20 extra shovels for the garrison by the order of GOC Brigade as they were short of tools. Capt. B.H. Fox R.E. with Lt. Bousfield inspected the ground and decided on positions of "Strong Points" before it was dark. No. 1 section (Lt. Briggs) made a strong point at N. 34 c.0.5. and obtained the help of 2nd Guards Company which joined up with its left flank to dig rifle pits and trenches protecting their "left flank", the situation was not quite clear. No. 2 section (Lt. Marris 76th Field Company) made a strong point at N 34 c.9.2. No. 3 section (Lt. Fraser) made a strong point at T 4 b.1.5. obtaining its work from some sections of 76th Field

Company. No. 4 section (Lt. Bousfield) made a strong point at T4 b.2.2. in the village and utilized old German wire. On completion of work, all sections returned to the original battle trenches. Two sections of the 76th Field Company reported for duty at Les Boeufs and were told by me to put in strong points on either flank on rear of village. These were made at T 3 b.7.3. and T 4 c.2.6.

September 26, 1916.

Whole company with working platoon fetching up more wiring material from Ginchy R.E. dump to Les Beoufs. Two working platoon parties salvaged Serpentine Trench and Trench T3a.7.2. to T3 d 3.2. At dusk, whole company with 2 working platoons wired in the whole of the 1st Brigade front from N34 c.6.5. to Sunken Road at T4 b.2.5. to T4 b.6.5. total amount 680 feet with double row trench wire with barbed wire over it and in between. Another 100 feet of wire was used to strengthen strong points.

Small party under NCO (2nd Cpl. Bridges R.E.) reconnoitered Les Boeufs for drinking water during the day. Water obtained from one well but bottle containing it broken by shell fire. Owing to continuation of heavy shell fire, this party was ordered to leave the village by the OC Garrison. After work that night, Field Company moved back to its old bivouacs at S 24 b. (NE Corner) the working platoons returning direct to their regiment near Carnoy. Capt. Jackson R.E. of 76th Field Company was taken around all work in progress and finished in Les Boeufs village by Capt. B.H. Fox R.E. Work handed over to 76th Field Company that night on completion of wiring.

September 27, 1916.

Camp near Carnoy. *Field Company moved to their old bivouacs near Carnoy at 2.30 pm. 1st Guards Brigade HQ at Carnoy.*

September 28, 1916.

At 5 pm company moved its bivouac to A23 d.1.3. owing to proximity to RA dump and enemy aircraft activities in bomb dropping of the previous night.

September 29, 1916.

No work done, company cleaning up generally.

September 30, 1916.

Morlancourt K9c3.8. *Transport under Lts. Fraser and Briggs left camp at 6.45 am to accompany transport of the 1st Guards Brigade on the march. Bivouac that night at Daours. Cyclists went with transport for unmounted portion of Field Company under Capt. B.H. Fox. Left camp at 2 pm for Morlancourt joining up with 1st Guards Brigade.*

• • •

The company remained in the Ginchy area through the end of 1916.

CHAPTER 20

"I Wore a Tunic, a Lousy Khaki Tunic…"

Khaki is the Hindi word for dust. The introduction of mechanized warfare meant that soldiers uniforms had to blend in more with the surrounding landscape. Prior to the introduction of Khaki, military clothing was incredibly brightly colored, making them easy targets for long range rifles and machine guns.

COMBLES, FRANCE
January 1917

The heaps of rubble, that used to be a small French farming town, became their new quarters. Their billets were in the few houses and barns that remained standing. Underneath the hillocks of shattered bricks lay buried the belongings of numerous lifetimes, and not a few bodies, judging by the smell. Some of these items had been salvaged to make life in the camp more comfortable —kettles, pots, the odd settee, and suchlike. But one had to be careful searching through the ruins because there were booby traps, unexploded shells, the decaying corpses, and all sorts of things that could ruin a man's day.

Some huts were also being built by the Engineers, and these were fairly clean and comfortable. The intense cold kept the smell of death in its place, until those days when the sun shone for a few hours, and then with the warmth, it crept out of its lair to invade the nostrils of the unwary. It had become a ubiquitous facet of the war, and most had ceased to notice. But like the tinnitus that they all suffered from because of the deafening orchestra of high explosive, one became aware of the smells every so often and then with the preoccupation of another task, it disappeared again. Such was life in the trenches. Along with smell and sound, their senses of touch and taste had become numbed, hands and feet so calloused they almost felt nothing through the thick skin, and military rations and field kitchens took care of destroying the latter.

But it wasn't just the physical senses that were forever altered, no, not by a long shot. The very sense of decency that they experienced in their nurturing years as a child had been destroyed. Maybe it was buried somewhere in the subconscious waiting to be retrieved at a later time, but it had to be put away because it had no place in the trenches of the Western Front.

The constant feel underfoot and sight of the shattered bodies of their comrades and the enemy (strange, they seemed strikingly similar in death, just the uniform was different), the relentless pursuit of death, the steady company of rats and crows waiting to consume the dead, the sheer battle with the futility of the whole thing they were experiencing, had altered their personality to a point where they were numb to any horror that would pop out of the dark void of war without warning. Probably the only human facet to survive this personality altering experience was the soldiers' sense of humor, which was all they had to carry them through the worst times. Many never did make it through. In fact, it is a surprising attribute to the human capability for survival that anyone came through this horror with a sense of normality.

Nonetheless, they all shared an experience that was unique to them alone. No person at home could possibly have any idea of what it was like here. A bond was created that held them together when the going was tough, developing a loyalty to each other that did somewhat alleviate the loss of sensitivity and humanness, the privilege of "other people" outside the war. The Irishmen felt too, that this shared suffering would diminish the difference between Protestant and Catholic that had been bred into them all at home. Men of both religions died alongside each other or survived together. Could that kinship be imported back to Ireland at the end of all this?

This tight-knit comradeship, the letters, and parcels from home, and sometimes prayer was what kept them all going.

The hope of a softening of acrimony between the Unionist and Nationalist causes was shared by another Irishman, William Redmond, who was serving with the 16th Irish Division. William was the younger brother of John Redmond, leader of the Irish Parliamentary Party, and was deeply committed to this ideal.

In December 1916 he told his good friend, the writer Arthur Conan Doyle, "It would be a fine memorial to the men who have died so splendidly if we could, over their graves, build up a bridge between the North and South. I have been thinking a lot about this lately in France—no one could help doing so when one finds that the two sections from Ireland are actually side by side holding the trenches!"

Willie Redmond was killed at the battle of Messines six months later.

• • •

Vincent had gone outside the small barn that was miraculously still standing and currently in use as a workshop. They'd been working hard making ladders for the trenches that were being rebuilt yet once again. He sat on a tree stump, gazing at the ground, forearms resting on his knees, a cigarette forgotten between his fingers, thinking about what the war had done to him, and how he was going to cope when it was all over. What would it be like going back into civilian life again? Because the last year and a half had just been continuous war, and he'd almost forgotten what it was like to come home from work, have a meal, and go out to the pub. But there were also other nagging thoughts inside his head.

The previous May, the British executed of the leaders of the 1916 rebellion in Dublin, creating a shock wave that ran through the Irish soldiers fighting on the front. Like many of his fellow countrymen, he thought the insurrection was a stupid and misguided move, taking advantage of Britain's preoccupation with the fighting on the front, trying to precipitate a move towards independence. Even though Vincent had lived and worked in Belfast, he had been brought up in County Louth, his father was from Cavan, and, most importantly, he was a Catholic. He saw himself as Irish first, and then as a British subject. The British had postponed the Home Rule Bill until after the end of the war, and those who had followed the lead of John Redmond felt that, in gratitude for the Irish contribution, Home Rule would be assuredly granted. But the execution of Pearse and his companions in the uprising had changed the Irish mindset dramatically. They were fellow Irishmen, who simply wanted to rule their own country. Now Vincent, as with others, found himself grappling with an uncomfortable dichotomy, fighting for a government and country that had treated his fellow countrymen so harshly.

Would they even be welcome if, and when they returned home? This feeling would fester inside him for the remainder of the war.

While on the Front, he knew he owed it to his comrades and unit to support them, and he'd keep going, but truthfully, he felt sick at heart with the whole damn thing.

In his pocket was a letter from his younger sister, Edith, telling him about the rebellion, and the Republicans who were still determined to claim Ireland for themselves. She wanted to join *Cumann na Mban*,[86] the women's branch of the Republican movement, and once he had urged her not to. But now? Things were different.

Suddenly his fingers burned, and he dropped the stub of the mostly unsmoked cigarette. Standing up, he stretched and stood on the stub. He went back inside, nodding to Sam, who was working with him, and they set to again with the ladders. The best thing was to just immerse oneself in work and worry about back home once you got there.

If he ever got there.

• • •

Good naturedly pushing and shoving each other, the men eagerly gathered around Corporal Moynihan who was sorting through the mail, deliberately taking his time, enjoying the anticipation:

"Heffernan!" he called out. "McInerney! Sullivan! Hewitt! ... McCann!"

Vincent reached forward for his letter, recognizing at once his father's writing. That was all the mail for him, so he went off to continue with the harness he was repairing. He would look at it after work when he had time.

---

86 Translated as "Women's Association" but understood as "Women's army."

Come five that evening, he sat down outside the workshop where there was enough light and lit up a cigarette. He savored the letter, as always, enjoying the news from home. His father's formal neat cursive script told him the local news—who had died, what his brothers and sisters were up to, and so on. At the end, he had a bit of bad news. Word had just come in of the sinking of the S.S. *Laurentic*. All his dad could tell him at this stage was that she had hit a mine off Fanad Head at the entrance to Lough Swilly, with a high loss of life.

Rubbing the stubble on his chin, Vincent drifted back to 1908 when he was a pupil at Hardinge Street School. His father brought him to see the launching of the *Laurentic* at Harland and Wolff Shipyard in the September of that year. It was a memorable day, late summer sunshine allowing them to leave their overcoats at home. Harland and Wolff was adorned with flags and all the gentry were there. They, of course, were confined to the public spaces, but he had a clear view of the slipway. Speeches were made, and the tension built up as the giant black hull sat, impossibly supported on a few blocks on the slipway.

Then finally, as the shipyard riggers knocked the last restraining blocks away and the launching triggers were released, the traditional bottle of champagne was broken on the bow and the big ship began to move, infinitesimally slowly at first, gradually gathering speed as gravity pulled it with invisible ropes to her natural habitat, in the waters of the river Lagan.[87]

Vincent watched in awe as the giant ship with her three propellers slipped into the water, to the cheers of the dockyard workers and onlookers, the large wave created washing the opposite shore.

---

87 You can watch the Titanic launch video on YouTube at https://www.youtube.com/watch?v=U2heZZ0aq1M

He knew then that he wanted to work in the yard helping build those leviathans, and his ultimate plan was to work in the engine-rooms of liners, sailing to foreign shores.

Laurentic sailed on its maiden voyage from Liverpool on April 29th, Vincent's 14th birthday, and he felt a deep attachment to this ship. A year later she became involved in the capture of the infamous Dr. Crippen[88] which he had followed avidly in the news.

Now the proud ship lay on the bed of Lough Swilly, with hundreds of lives lost; he felt his own heart go down with her.

The letter slipped from his fingers as he sat gazing into the distance, thinking about the *Laurentic*, the excitement he felt watching its launch, and the pride he felt in a ship like that coming from his hometown.

Not for the first time, he asked himself again: "Why?"

THE LAURENTIC'S FINAL DAYS[89]

The S.S. Laurentic, owned by White Star Line, the owners of the ill-fated Titanic, had been requisitioned as a troopship for Canadian soldiers destined for the Western Front, and later converted to an armed merchant cruiser, fitted with eight six-inch and two six-pounder guns. Her

---

88 See sidebar on the tragedy of the *SS Laurentic*.

89 Photo source is Wikimedia Commons, public domain. Anonymous source.

career had been spent initially ferrying troops from Canada to the Western Front and then after further conversion she spent her time patrolling as an armed cruiser in the Far East, Africa, and lastly off Halifax. In late November 1916, she departed for Liverpool, with cargo and passengers consisting of Royal Canadian Navy officers, seamen, and Royal Canadian Naval Volunteer Reserves.

As Mark Twain famously wrote in Pudd'nhead Wilson, "When ill luck begins, it does not come in sprinkles, but in showers."

Laurentic's bad luck began at 8:50, on the morning of December 1st, 1916, on a voyage from Halifax to Liverpool. Probably, it started earlier, perhaps the previous day. At any rate, it was discovered at 8:50 a.m., at which point it says in the morning entries of the ship's logbook:

"8.50 Discovered coal in No. 2 hold on fire"

"9.00 Started getting coal out"

Not something to be taken lightly, spontaneous ignition of a coal cargo could burn for days on end, quickly getting out of control; the heat damaging the ship's structure, the suffocating fumes blowing back over the accommodation. And worse, the powder locker was adjacent to the hold. The Laurentic was an armed merchantman.

There was a sense of urgency as the chief officer led a fire-fighting team into the hold to tackle the fire, by attempting to remove some of the coal and get to the seat of the blaze. The hatch covers were removed, and the derrick rigged to start removing the coal over the fire so that they could get underneath the coal surface.

As they fought the blaze, some of the men got trapped when the fire spread, cutting off their exit from the hold. Frantic signals were sent to their comrades working on deck. Hearing of this, the captain[90] left the bridge and came down to lead a second team into the smoke-filled hold. They did manage to get some of the men out and went back to get the others when a hatch beam across the hold opening, distorted by the

---

90 The ship was under naval control, and John Mathias, who was R.N.R. held the rank of Commander. But he was also captain of the ship, so is loosely referred to by that term as well. In the ship's log, his rank of Commander was used.

heat, fell, and struck Commander Mathias and several crew members. Another squad was organized and succeeded in getting the remainder of the men out, including Mathias, who was suffering from a fractured skull. He was immediately removed to the ship's hospital.

Meanwhile the crew got the fire under control with the chief officer, who was now in charge of the ship.

December the 3rd passed uneventfully, the captain had still not regained consciousness, and was under observation in the hospital by the ship's doctor. The prognosis was not good.

Then on the 4th of December, at 3:45 pm, the logbook contained this brief entry:

"3.45 Departed this life from fracture of skull, Commander John Mathias, RNR"

In that brief line in the logbook, the man who had been captain of the ship for the last four years, two of them under wartime conditions, passed away, two days before he was to be reunited with his wife and two daughters in Liverpool.

They arrived in Liverpool on Wednesday, December 6, 1916, at 8:45 pm. The ship remained at her berth in Birkenhead for over two weeks while cargo was discharged, and new cargo loaded. This included three days in dry-dock. On the 13th, her new master, Captain Reginald Norton joined and took over command. On the 23rd, a cargo of gold bullion was taken on board, which was intended to pay for war munitions from Canada and the United States.

She made one uneventful round trip to Halifax and back to Liverpool and then departed Liverpool again on the 23rd of January 1917, en route to Halifax.

That's when Lady Luck turned her back on the ship.

It started with something so small, no one could see it. A virus. Four of the complement had come down sick and were suspected of having typhus. Rather than risk the disease spreading through the ship, the captain decided to pull into the British naval base at Buncrana in Lough Swilly, Co. Donegal, in Ireland. They arrived at 7:45 am and anchored off the port. The four sick persons were put ashore, and the ship weighed anchor at 5:00 pm and departed, passing through the protective boom keeping enemy submarines out of the Lough. There had been warnings of a U-boat in the area and Captain Norton would have taken this seriously, but as it was blowing a gale and snowing heavily, he probably felt they could slip out into the Atlantic in the dark. What he didn't realize was that the submarine had been laying mines off the entrance to the Lough. About an hour after departure, the ship was passing Fanad Head when there was a loud explosion just under the foremast on the port side. The force of the explosion threw the captain off his feet, and as he scrambled to get up another explosion in the way of the engine room sealed the fate of the ship.

As water gushed into the machinery space, the generators stopped, and all the lighting went out. Without power, they were unable to work the pumps and water flooded the engine room. The ship began to list which made it difficult to launch the lifeboats. They did, however, manage to get some of them into the water, but those who made it into the boats faced extreme cold. The temperature was well below freezing. The survivors rowed towards the Fanad light, and some were rescued by local fishing trawlers. But sadly, by the time daylight came, many were found frozen to death in their lifeboats, with their hands still holding the oars.

Only 121 persons survived out of 475 souls on board. The last person to leave the ship was Captain Norton, who survived. Bodies of the dead continued to wash up on shore for weeks afterwards.

From an engineering point of view, the *Laurentic* was quite interesting. She had a sister ship, *Megantic*, also built by Harland and Wolff. The builders had powered the *Megantic* with two quadruple expansion steam engines powering two propellers, but the *Laurentic* was fitted with two triple expansion engines powering two outer propellers and a low-pressure steam turbine using the exhaust steam from the other two engines, powering a center propeller. They found that the arrangement on the *Laurentic* produced 20% more power and consumed

12–15% less coal. Consequently, this system was used to power the two next White Star Ships, the *Olympic* and *Titanic*.

The S.S. *Laurentic* also become well known when it became part of a murder story. In early 1910, Dr. Hawley Harvey Crippen murdered his wife, Cora. He buried her body under the coal in the cellar in their London home. Shortly after, his mistress Ethel Le Neve moved into his house and then neighbors and friends began to notice she was wearing possessions belonging to Crippen's wife. He had initially claimed his wife had gone to America to visit a sick relative and then he said that while she was there, she had died.

After some concerned friends of Cora went to the police, Chief Inspector Walter Dew from Scotland Yard visited Dr. Crippen, who told the inspector that in fact his wife was alive and had gone to live in America with another man, and he lied about her death to shield himself and his wife from scandal. Inspector Dew searched Hawley Crippen's house and found nothing. But Crippen panicked and he and his mistress left home and went to Antwerp. Inspector Dew went back to Crippen's house to make further inquiries, he found it was deserted, and he instigated another search. They found Cora's body parts in the coal cellar. A notice was put out for Dr. Crippen— ***"Wanted for Murder".***

Crippen and his mistress, meanwhile, boarded the Canadian Pacific Steamship Company's S.S. *Montrose* on the 20th of July 1910, and left for Canada. He started to grow a beard and she was disguised as his son, wearing boy's clothing.

Captain Henry Kendall of the Montrose became suspicious and sent a wireless message to his company relaying his concerns. This information was passed to Inspector Dew, and he boarded the *Laurentic* in Liverpool on the 23rd of July.

The *Laurentic* was much faster than the *Montrose* and arrived in Montreal dropping the detective off on the pilot boat. When the Montrose arrived in Rimouski on the 31st of July, Dew boarded the ship and arrested Dr. Crippen. The trial found the latter guilty and he was sentenced to death. He was executed on the 23rd of November, 1910.

The *Laurentic* and the invention of ship-board radio had played a major part in the solving of a famous murder case.[91]

75th Field Company War Diary
February 1–2, 1917.

Drying room work continued. Spray bath housework continued. Division canteen work continued. Division HQ; 2 carpenters on odd jobs. Company stables; old stables near dump being dismantled and new ones built on horse lines. (NB. A lot of the writing here is difficult to decipher. DMC.)

2nd line wire laid in dumps along proposed line on road along Ravine. The chalk excavated from hill is put on road and the excavation will be site for location of army hut. Work continued on dugouts at Priez Farm, but disturbed by heavy shell fire.

3rd much the same.

4th All ranks instructed in fitting new small box respirator and Company put through dugout containing tear gas. No helmets leaked.

• • •

First introduced in August 1916 and standard issue by the spring of 1917, the Small Box Respirator was the most advanced and practical anti-gas development used by British and Dominion forces in the First World War.

The respirator consisted of a face mask with glass eyepieces and was connected to a metal "small box" filter containing active charcoal and granules.

---

91 For the interested reader, there is an excellent book written by Eric Larson, telling the story of Marconi and the invention of radiotelegraphy. It culminates with the story of Dr. Crippen and his capture.

• • •

75th Field Company War Diary
March 15, 1917.
*News received at night of German retirement from in front of Division
– our troops occupied some of enemy's front line.*

March 16, 1917.
*Work stopped on all strong points owing to German retirement.
Repairs to Halewood Road. Cookhouse being made at Brig. HQ in
T 17 d. Duck-boards repaired. Heavy Trench Mortar Emplacement
worked on, revetting chiefly. 64' of duckboard track laid in U 13 d.
and U 14 c. after salving. New mule path taped out by 2nd Lt. Reid
and No. 1 section under heavy shell fire from our old front line at U
15 c.0.0. to Railway Station at Saillisel. (German R.E. dump) at U 15
c.8.6. Repairs to deep dugout at Sailly Church. 8 sappers reconnoitered
captured German deep dugouts. Repairs to duckwalk and Halewood
Road. Portion of Brigade H.Q. nearly finished.*

• • •

The following account is from Sister Luard, who was stationed
in a casualty hospital in nearby Warlencourt.

On **Sunday, April 22nd, 1917,** she wrote:

*"No one knows when we shall fill up again, but it can't be far off
with this din." The following day the wounded come flooding in—but
when there is a lull in the taking in, nursing and evacuating of the
wounded, Kate goes for a ramble in a nearby wood beside a stream to
revive herself both physically and mentally."*

Then, on **Monday, April 23rd:**

*"We have filled up twice. The men say our guns are so thick that
they're wheel to wheel; the earth-shaking noise this morning did its*

work; the wounded Germans tell me there are a great many dead. I've been looking after 100 stretcher cases in the tents to-night; they are all ready for evacuation."

Tuesday, April 24th:

"It has been a pretty sad day, 12 funerals, including four officers, all fine brave men. One mother wrote thanking me for writing to tell her about her son, but "it would relieve the news somewhat if she knew which son it was, as she has three sons in France." Two given-up boys whom no effort of yesterday or last night would revive - after more resuscitation are now bedded in one of the Acute Surgicals, each with a leg off and a fair chance of recovery. The others, with torn kidneys and spleens and brains, are no good, I'm afraid. The people who have been coming in all day are left-outs since Monday, starved, cold, and by some miracle still alive, but not much more. This last 300 has taken 16 hours to come in. It is piercingly cold again and looks like rain."

Finally, **Monday, April 30th:**

"We have had a whole week without snow or rain - lots of sun and blue sky. I went for a ramble yesterday to a darling narrow wood with a stream at the bottom, a quarter of an hour's walk from here. Two sets of shy, polite boys thrust their bunches of cowslips and daffodils into my hand. Also banks of blue periwinkles like ours and flowering palm; absolutely no leaves yet anywhere and it's May Day to-morrow. Very few left in the wards to-day, but what there are, nearly all tragedies."[92]

---

92 The diary extracts of Nursing Sister Kate Luard QAIMNSR during the second phase of the Battle of Arras from April 23rd to June 3rd 1917.

75th Field Company War Diary
Camp 16 Billon Map ref. F30a4.5 (Albert Map scale 1/40,000)
May 1, 1917.

Company training. Morning; Nos. 2 & 4 sections pontooning on River Somme at Bray. Nos. 1 & 3 sections instructed in bombs and throwing of live bombs.

May 2, 1917.

Whole company dug trenches for Brigade practice attack near camp 16

May 3, 1917.

Company training with ½ company pontooning on Somme as before.

May 4, 1917.

Orders received on night of 3rd to proceed to Havrincourt Wood to work under 20th Division. Company around Combles chalk pits at 4.30 pm, halting there for the night.

May 5, 1917.

Company (4 sections) reached bivouacs in Havrincourt Wood by 1230 pm. Transport remaining at P 8 c.8.4. near Bertincourt. Work consists of making 5 QPS for the 91st and 92 brigades of the RFA,[93] 20th division. All work inspected by section officers (No. 4 section) by night at Bilham Farm map reference Q 5 Central. (?) of a deep dugout and slits near wall of gateway.

May 6, 1917.

Work inspected in morning by officers and started at night. All consists of deep slits covered over with stout logs and earth. The map referenced being Q 1 b.4.0. – Q 1 d.3.6. – Q 8 b.7.1. and Q 9 a.3.4. Reference map

---

93 Royal Field Artillery. The CO was Lieutenant W.S. Oaten.

57 c SE. All night work to start on these locations. Sapper Hillis hit in leg by anti-aircraft shell splinter.

• • •

This time, Vincent volunteered to drive Sapper Hillis, who had his leg nearly torn off by the shell splinter, to the hospital, eighteen miles away in Warlencourt.

They got out the stretcher and put the groaning, half conscious man on it, and made him as comfortable as possible in the back of the truck; time was of the essence as he was losing a lot of blood, though they had put a tourniquet on his thigh. Vincent jumped in the driver's seat, and they headed off along the shell-pocked road.

To Vincent's delight, Sister Luard was there again when they brought Hillis in, and this time the ward wasn't so busy, and they had a chance to chat. While the others were taking care of his wounded mate, she brought him into the canteen, and they sat at a table with two mugs of sweet tea and talked.

She sensed his need to open up and, always ready to listen to the soldiers, she urged him to tell her about his family. He talked about his childhood in Tallanstown, and how he had lost his mother when he was eight years old. She realized that his mother was about her age, a little younger perhaps, and could see the desperate need in his eyes as he talked.

"You'll always miss her," she said. "Do you remember her at all?"

Vincent's memory was of a gentle but firm woman, who was always there for them all, who sang while she was working; but what she looked like had morphed into an image, based on the couple of photographs they'd kept of her—an image not unlike the sister sitting across the table from him. Talking to her felt like lifting a lead weight from his heart, and when his mates came looking for him, they found a happier, more light-hearted Vincent.

Vincent bid goodbye to Sister Luard, clambered into the truck with the others, and headed back to camp. Sapper Bellingham, who doubled as a medic, produced a canteen filled with French brandy, and soon the singing started as the truck zigged and zagged on its way.

Their favorite song was sung, to the tune of "*When You Wore a Tulip*" …

> "I wore a tunic, a lousy khaki tunic,
> And you wore your civvy clothes.
> We fought and bled at Loos
> While you were home on the booze
> The booze that no one here knows.
> Oh you were with the wenches
> While we fought in the trenches
> Facing an angry foe.
> Oh you were a-slacking
> While we were attacking
> The Gerry on the Menin Road…"

• • •

Work continued as above until 14th when they were marched out of the camp at Havrincourt Wood and headed to Clery Camp. The 15th was spent settling into camp and cleaning gear. The 16th, pontooning on the river Somme. On the 17th they marched out at 9:30 in the morning and returned to Billon Camp 16.

75th Field Company War Diary
May 18, 1917.
Sailly-le-Sac; Company marched out of Billon at 7.30 am following 76th Field Company R.E. and arrived at Sailly – Le – Sec on river Somme (East of Corbie) at 11.45 am. Men in billets.

May 19, 1917.
Cleaning up generally – men and horses. In London papers of 19th the following WO and NCO of the company were "Mentioned in Dispatches" (London Gazette of 15th May 1917) namely "Company Sergeant Major G. Pring No. 57096 and Farrier Sergeant T. Harrison No. 60668".

May 20, 1917.
(Sunday) No work done. About half the company were inoculated against Euteric[94] Fever.

May 21, 1917.
Men recovering from effects of inoculation – remainder washing wagons and general fatigues. 2nd Battn. Grenadier Guards marched into village.

May 22, 1917.
Pontooning and general training including bayonet fighting.

May 23, 1917.
Same as 22nd and more men inoculated.

May 24 to 30, 1917.
Made preparations to move again.

May 31, 1917.
Entrained at Edge Hill. Train started 3.06 pm for route for Cassel. All the company with its transport complete went in one train.

---

94 Typhus.

CHAPTER 21

Happy Birthday, Vinnie

"I don't know why," he said,
 we're not all dead,
 But we're not, and we should be glad,
"let's drink he said,"
 To the life we've led,
 And to the narrow escapes we've had.

(Derek McCann. "The Soldier's Toast")

ANNEQUIN
April 29, 1917

The incongruity of the scene failed to impress itself on them, as John and Vincent sat on an old and much-battered settee in a French living room, with an almost 360-degree view. This was because there were no walls, or roof, worth speaking of. The shell blast that caused this restructuring of the house had left the settee intact, sitting in the room among the debris.

As they sat there, John with his arm across the back of the settee, and Vincent with his feet on the wrecked remains of a bureau, gazed across the road at another bombed-out building. The only sound, the creaking of a broken joist hanging precariously over their heads, swinging back and forth in the breeze.

"I can't believe it," John said.

"Mm, it's hard to think we used to sit at the bar there, enjoyin' the beer, such as it was," Vincent replied. "I don't even know what the Jerries were trying to hit, they must've been drunk on too much schnapps."

But there it was, what was left of *La Poule Rouge*, "their" estaminet, when they'd been camped nearby. Now it was a heap of rubble, having suffered a direct hit.

They'd made inquiries and discovered that Jean Claude and Sidonie had been killed in the blast. To John's eternal relief, Estelle hadn't been there at the time. The old unshaven Frenchman whom they'd asked about it told them she had gone off to train as a nurse, to work with the French troops.

When they asked where, he just shrugged. *"Je'n sais pas... "*

The three of them—Vincent, John, and Ned Duggan—had wrangled a weekend pass, when John expressed a desire to go and see Annequin, and to see if Estelle was still there. Ned just happened to have a bottle of whiskey, which changed hands, and a pass was arranged. They had persuaded the beneficiary of the bottle to organize the truck for them too, as Ned wanted to see what he could pick up on the way. Just then, as they were reclining on the settee, mourning their old friends Jean-Claude and Sidonie, he was off scavenging around the town. The April sun shone down on them, warming them outside, but inside they felt cold. It was an early spring day, and the weather had been kinder, giving them a pleasant drive up north from where they were stationed. Though the Battle of the Somme had officially ended on November 18, last year, they were still stationed in the Somme sector. Still kept busy rebuilding and fortifying the new front line.

"Did ye see the news the other day, about the battle? They're calling it 'The Battle of the Somme', the last five months."

"Four months and three weeks," Vincent corrected him, instantly regretting his pedantic remark—he felt a bit tetchy these days.

"Well, whatever it was, d'ye know what we gained over that time?"

"I'm not sure … not much I think, but I know you're goin' to tell me anyway," said Vincent.

"They're sayin' nearly half-a-million casualties, over one-hundred-thousand British dead … just the British, mind you. The French were nearly as bad," said John, shaking his head sadly.

"And, what we gained was about six miles advance. Six, fuckin' miles."

"And are we any the better off for it?" asked Vincent. "No, it doesn't make a bloody bit of difference," he said, answering his own question. "Not a bloody bit …"

The two of them were sitting on the settee looking miserable when Duggan arrived outside the house with the truck, laden with scrap and booty. Some of the scrap was for the company to use for a new bath house being built, and then he had his own stuff. Among that were several bottles of a clear liquid, one of which he brought over to the two lads on the settee and joined them.

He produced three mugs, and said to John, "Sorry 'bout yer friends over there," nodding towards the destroyed estaminet. "At least the girl is OK?" he asked. Ned had so much loss in his life, he was pretty phlegmatic when it came to tragedy, but he could see that John was upset.

"Yeah," said John, "she'd left before it happened. But she's lost her mam and dad."

Lost for any other consoling words, Ned pulled off the cork with his teeth and poured. "OK, well, have a drop of this stuff, it's great," he said. "It'll put skin on your back like silk, as me mammy used to say." He handed John one of the mugs and Vincent the other and poured the moonshine into them. "Here's to the end of this fuckin' war ... y'know, I'm not sure I give a shit who wins at this stage. Anyway, here's to Estelle, wherever she is," he toasted. "'N when we get back home, I'll fix yez both up with a couple of nice Dublin girls I know."

"'N happy birthday Vinnie."

They drank another toast. It was Sunday, the 29th of April 1917—Vincent's twenty-third birthday.

The following day, Vincent walked outside the hut, and took off his jacket, and laid it neatly folded on a makeshift seat next to the wall. The strengthening April sun felt good on his arms as he sat down and took a letter from his brother Jim out of his pocket. The weather had been miserable, cold, and wet, turning the shell-blasted countryside around the camp into a grey, featureless swamp. But in the last few days the rain had eased up and the skies remained a deep blue that they hadn't seen for a long time. It was still cool in the mornings but in the sun, out of the wind he felt enveloped in its warmth.

The letter from Jim, in India, had arrived that morning, and in a characteristic exercise of self-discipline and delayed gratification, he'd held onto it until work had finished. Now, after washing up and changing into uniform, he sat down, pulled out a cigarette and lit up. With the mail he'd received a parcel from home with 200 cigarettes, socks, and some chocolate. He was delighted to get the Capstan, as he'd been existing on French Gauloises for the last few weeks and had never taken to the dark Turkish tobacco. Though it was better than nothing.

Jim, the eldest of the family, had left home eight years ago for India, where he'd buried himself in his missionary work with the Christian Brothers. The letter was full of enthusiastic descriptions of the country he'd adopted and the work he loved. Even though the heat in Calcutta where he'd been for the last year became intolerable at times, he'd adjusted remarkably well and immersed himself into his work.

The politics in India was something Jim took a keen interest in, knowing that in a primarily Hindu country, minority religions could come out of it badly, if things went belly up. He'd been telling Vincent about the Indian National Congress, and a lawyer called Gandhi who had recently returned from South Africa. His brother talked about this remarkable man, then in his forties, who lived simply, preached peace, but strove to help his fellow Indians achieve a better life. Though their doctrines were different, Jim could see he was a man of God, and admired and respected him.

The letter pointed out the similarities between India and Ireland's struggle for independence, the Indian National Congress and Gandhi's peaceful and cooperative approach. This also was the case with John Redmond's Parliamentary Party, but they had waned a lot in popularity since the executions the previous year. That was a mistake the British would come to regret. One thing became clear to Vincent, that when the war was over, there would be a lot of upheaval in the British Empire. He doubted anything would ever be the same again, as in the pre-war years.

Jim was of course greatly concerned about Vincent's safety, having recently seen news of the terrible death toll suffered by the British Army in the early days of the Somme fighting. Vincent smiled to himself as he thought about how Jim had taken over when their mother passed away; how he'd made sure they all got up for school on time, dressed properly, were fed and disciplined, and generally had been their father's mainstay in those grief-stricken years following her death.

Vincent realized that he still missed his mother terribly, but since he'd met Sister Kate Luard, he felt differently. At first, he couldn't understand what his attraction to her was, after all she was old enough to be his mother …

Until it had dawned on him that's exactly what it was. Sister Luard reminded him so much of his own mother, as he remembered her.

After reading the letter, Vincent absently picked a piece of tobacco off his lip and mused about Jim's enthusiasm for life. Leaning back against the warm side of the hut, he decided Jim was doing exactly what he wanted to do and that truly was a blessing. Vincent pondered what he would do when this mess he was in was over. He had wanted to go away to sea as a marine engineer, but that was something in the dim past. In fact, he realized he was just trying to escape life in Belfast; now he'd give anything to be back home. Funny how life changes you.

The only thing he was sure of was he wanted to get out of the army. But while he was there, he gave his best and did as ordered. He was that type of person, and it would never have occurred to him to do otherwise. But would any of them make it that far? Death was everywhere around them, and they'd already lost eight of their company, and a good few had narrow escapes. He'd had one himself with the gas. He was learning to shut his mind off that topic, as if he thought about it too much, he'd just get up and run and never stop. On to brighter things, as he got up to go to the mess tent.

The discussion at the mess table revolved around the latest big news: America had declared war on Germany.

"The Germans should throw their hat in right now," said one sapper, through mouthfuls of corned beef.

"Ach, ge'out of it, it'll be years before they get over here. We'll've beaten the shit out of them by then."

"The bleedin' Russkies'll have to give up soon, from what I'm hearin', 'n then Fritz'll be able to send all his troops to the front here," added another and somewhat better-read member of the discussion. "So don't get too cocksure there, it could change things here a lot."

Vincent had said nothing, listening to the back and forth of the debate.

"Truth is, none of it will happen before the next big push, now the weather's gettin' better," he said at last. "I heard rumors we'll be movin' soon."

That brought a silence for a bit, none of them wanting another repeat of the Somme. But it was in the air and made sense too. Neither side could stay sitting on their hands for long.

The past few months since the fighting had stopped had been miserable. Cold weather, snow and rain. Grey skies depressed them, and the mood was low among his mates. They'd been working solidly, rebuilding the trenches captured during the previous year's fighting, consolidating the camps set up behind the lines, and building rail tracks to transport the stores and ammunition constantly feeding the front line.

Vincent had spent a few days in hospital in February, when he got a metal shard in his eye. The doctors decided not to remove it, as it didn't affect his eyesight, and it remained with him, a constant reminder of the Somme, to the day he died.

A WAR TO END ALL WARS

April 6, 1917, was a day that proved to be a game changer in the titanic struggle being carried out around the globe. It truly became a World War when the final protagonist, The United States of America entered the fray. President Wilson had been working for the last two and a half years to keep the country out of the war, gaining strong support from the Irish Americans and German Americans among others. But several events tilted the scales, and entry into the war became inevitable. One of these was the sinking of the Lusitania, with a number of high-profile American passengers on board, and also the sinking of several other American flag ships during the German blockade of England.

American banks were profiting greatly, making huge loans to the Entente powers, for the purchase of munitions, raw materials, and food, transported across the Atlantic frequently on American flag vessels.

With the political upheaval in Russia, resulting in the latter opting out of the war, and credit dwindling for the Entente nations, Germany was looking towards a victory in Europe, using the free- up troops from the Eastern Front to support those in France and Belgium.

Germany also made a secret offer to help Mexico regain territories lost in the earlier war between the U.S.A. and Mexico, namely Texas, Arizona, and New Mexico, in an encoded telegram known as the *Zimmermann Telegram*, which was intercepted by British intelligence. Publication of that communique outraged Americans just as German submarines started sinking American merchant ships in the North Atlantic. Wilson then asked Congress for "a war to end all wars" that would "make the world safe for democracy", and Congress voted to declare war on Germany on April 6, 1917. U.S. troops began major combat operations on the Western Front under General John J. Pershing in the summer of 1918.

• • •

It was with some relief to be leaving the Somme when they got orders to move on the last day of May.

75th Field Company War Diary
May 31, 1917.
Entrained at Edge Hill. Train started 3.06 pm for route for Cassel. All the company with its transport complete went in one train.

June 1, 1917.
Company with transport complete detrained at Cassel at 4 am and marched to billets along road on the outskirts of La Cross I mile N.W. of Renescure. (Map Hazebruck 5A.)

June 12, 1917.
Company moved out of La Crosse at 7.45 am and marched with 2nd Guards Brigade to Wormhoudt area, arriving there about 2.30 pm. Men in billets.

June 13, 1917.
Company moved out of Wormhoudt area at 8.30 am and marched with 2nd Brigade to St. Jan–Le–Bezier area, arriving there at 1.30 pm. Men in Camp.

June 14, 1917.
Company moved out of St Jan-Le-Bezier area at 1.30 pm arriving at J camp International Corner[95] about 4 pm. Took on work from 76th Field Company in J camp and at St. Sixte.

---

95 "J" camp/International Corner was in Belgium, just north of Poperinghe.

June 15, 1917.

Erecting Nissen huts and general camp improvements at Corps HQ at St. Sixte. Fitting up "J" camp for Divisional HQ. 1 section on sand model of Corps front.

June 16, 1917.

Capt. Briggs rejoined the Company from leave.

June 17, 1917.

Erecting huts at camp HQ. Converting "J" camp for Divisional HQ. Working on sand model of Corps Front. Scale 1/50th.

June 18, 1917.

100 OR under Lt. Hardy, 3rd Coldstream Guards are attached to this Company for work and are employed on carting sand from railway to sand model. (60 men). Remainder at corps HQ.

• • •

They were back in Flanders, getting ready for the next "Big Push". The sand model of the front line was for planning the battle and this went on for the next month.

"In addition to the strenuous work in the forward area the actual training for the attack was continued. The troops who were to carry out the initial assault were given as much practical instruction as was possible in the details for the operation which lay before them.

A short length of a stream which ran through the wooded country in the divisional area was selected and converted under the superintendence of the CRE into an exact model of the Yser Canal, in the crossing of which the assault was constantly rehearsed. Close to Divisional Headquarters, a large sand model was erected of the whole of the area over which the XIV Corps was to operate. This model, which was laid out to scale and showed the enemy's positions together with the natural and artificial features of the country, proved most useful both to offi-cers and other ranks."

—Headlam, *The Guards Division in the Great War.*

The Ypres-Yser Canal was, in 1917, a wide, muddy ditch, in which a man could sink in the mud up to his armpits. It had been an effective barrier to both sides, since there was only a narrow stream passing along the center of the seventy-foot-wide trough. The Engineers prepared mats consisting of canvas with a backing of wire mesh and slats, which worked quite well for crossing the mud. In the event of considerable rain, petrol tin bridges were prepared too. These all were stored in nineteen special chambers dug into the sides of the canal, which could be broken through on the canal side and the bridges rolled out.

June was a busy month for Vincent and his company.

CHAPTER 22

Back to Flanders' Muddy Fields

"Mud, Mud, glorious mud
Nothing quite like it for cooling the blood!
So follow me, follow
Down to the hollow
And there let us wallow
In glorious mud"

(Flanders and Swann. "The Hippopotamus Song")

PASSCHENDAELE

"*Careful investigation of the records showed that in Flanders the weather broke early each August with the regularity of the Indian monsoon. Once the autumn rains set in, the difficulties would be greatly enhanced.*

The one major exception to the flatness [of the Flanders landscape] is the famous ridge, [east of Ypres] an arc of feeble hills and highlands, running from some miles north of Passchendaele, southward to Messines and then west towards Hazebrouck. Its average elevation is about 150 feet. Yet the German soldiers on these modest heights enjoyed a great military advantage not only in observation, but in the placement of guns and defensive fortifications.

Since early times, military offensives have failed in this mild seeming land because of a physical obstacle not apparent to the glance. For, in Flanders the ground is almost pure fine-grained clay, sometimes with a crusting of sand on top or a thin coating of loame. In certain places there is no topsoil at all: these clay fields, called "clyttes", exist at their worst north of Ypres in the vicinity of the Houthulst forest. Because of the impervious clay, the rain cannot escape and tends to stagnate over large areas. Unable to soak through, it forms swamps and ponds and sluggishly spreads toward one of the already swollen rivers or canals. The ground remains perpetually saturated. Water is reached at an average depth of eighteen inches and only the shallowest of puddly trenches can be dug by the troops, reinforced by sandbag parapets. When the topsoil dries during fair weather, it cracks open. The next rain floods the fissures. Then the clay blocks slide upon themselves, causing little landslides..."

—Army report to General Haig[96]

• • •

"There was not a sign of life of any sort. Not a tree, save for a few dead stumps which looked strange in the moonlight. Not a bird, not even a rat or a blade of grass. Nature was as dead as those Canadians whose bodies remained where they had fallen the previous autumn. Death was written large everywhere."

—Private R.A. Colwell

Sitting on top of the ridge, northeast of Ypres, lay the small town of Passchendaele. Its name became synonymous with bitter fighting, mud, shredded forests, death and destruction, only superseded by the

96 Charteris, J. (1929). Field Marshal Earl Haig. London: Cassell.

battle of the Somme a year earlier. The Battle of Passchendaele was only one of the many fought during the Third Battle of Ypres, in the struggle to dislodge the Germans from that ridge commanding the town and the salient surrounding it.

• • •

75th Field Company War Diary
June 1, 1917.
La Crosse (4.7 m east of Stoner). *Company with transport complete detrained at Cassel at 4 am and marched to billets along road on the LA of La Cross I mile N.W. of Renescure.*

• • •

"Gentlemen, I don't know whether we are going to make history tomorrow, but at any rate we shall change geography."
—General Sir Herbert Plumer (in a statement to the press, June 7 1917.)

General Plumer was referring to the planned explosion of 19 mines, set in tunnels deep under the earthen ridge of Messines.

• • •

The men in the tent slept like babies, oblivious to the constant crash of the British artillery as it hammered the German lines twenty miles to the east.

Without any warning, at 3:10 am, the ground shook violently beneath the beds, waking them better than any sergeant could. Tables fell over and belongings scattered across the floor.

Jumping out of bed, Vincent rushed to the entrance, which was facing to the east, thinking a shell had landed nearby. The overcast sky was already lighter as the early mid-summer dawn approached, reflecting the red glow from the massive explosions that partially demolished the Messines Ridge.

"Holy Jesus," said a voice beside him, as Bob Wright tumbled out of the tent to see what was happening. The ground continued to shake, as explosion after explosion threw up red flames, coloring the clouds of earth and debris rising to meet the cloud layer.

"Glad I'm not over there," Vincent replied.

Others joined them as they watched the spectacle taking place, their faces reflecting the red glow growing with every bone jarring blast.

During the short time they stood there, ten thousand German soldiers were wiped from the face of the Earth, becoming one with the mix of clods of earth and debris falling to the ground.

"That's the mines they dug under the Messines Ridge," said Lieutenant Lawrie, who had walked up to stand beside them.

"We heard they were tunnelling under the ridge; I think there were about twenty tunnels altogether."

"Now I wouldn't like that job," said one of the sappers. "Gives me the creeps just thinkin' of it."

The sappers slowly filed back into the tent, determined to make the best of the remaining hour before Reveille.

• • •

For Major William Redmond, brother of Irish Parliamentary Party leader, John Redmond, this was the beginning of the end of his life.

The attack on Messines Ridge, the overture to the larger battle which came to be known as the Third Battle of Ypres, or sometimes called the Battle of Passchendaele, was to be carried out by a combined force of Australians, New Zealanders, Irish Catholics with the

16th Division, and Northern Irish Protestants of the 36th Division, fighting shoulder to shoulder.

Willie, aged fifty-six, was one of the older officers on the front line. At about 4 am, as the smoke and dust began to clear from the mine explosions, the whistles blew, and he led his company over the top, running crouched in front of his men. A bullet caught him in the wrist, but he kept going on, adrenalin powering him, into the hail of machine gun fire coming from the defending Germans. A second bullet quickly hit him in the leg and then he went down. He lay there, urging the men on.

Then blackness.

But he wasn't to be alone. A private from the Ulster 36th Division found him and tried to get him back to safety. John Meeke was himself wounded while tending to Willie, but helped carry him back to the trenches, where he was transferred to the field hospital. Willie died from his wounds that afternoon.

The inscription on his grave tells the story:

"Near this spot on the morning of 7th June 1917, Major Willie Redmond MP, 6th Royal Irish Regiment, 16th (Irish) Division, was wounded during the opening attack of the Battle of Messines. He was found by Private John Meeke, 11th Royal Inniskilling Fusiliers, 36th (Ulster Division), who tried to carry him to safety until he was wounded himself. Meeke remained with him until further soldiers from the 36th Division arrived. Redmond was evacuated to the Dressing Station at Dranouter where he died of his wounds. He was 56. His body was taken to the convent chapel in Loker and he was buried in the convent grounds. His grave remains in the same place to this day. John Meeke was awarded the Military Medal for his gallant action. Willie Redmond had joined up following the passage of the Home Rule Bill in the House of Commons and the call for volunteers by his brother John Redmond

MP, *the leader of the Irish Parliamentary Party. He urged others to do the same with the words "Don't go but come with me."*

Willie Redmond believed to his dying breath that the shared experience of fighting alongside each other for a common cause would bring Protestant and Catholic Irishmen together and agree to settle their differences amicably.

He was a friend of Sir Arthur Conan Doyle, and told him in a letter:

"It would be a fine memorial to the men who have died so splendidly if we could, over their graves, build up a bridge between North and South. I have been thinking a lot about this lately in France—no one could help doing so when one finds that the two sections from Ireland are actually side by side holding the trenches!"

Willie was given leave earlier in 1917 and during that time, gave his last speech to the House of Parliament, of which he was a member, being MP for East Clare:

"In the name of God, we here who are about to die, perhaps, ask you to do that which largely induced us to leave our homes; to do that which our mothers and fathers taught us to long for; to do that which is all we desire; make our country happy and contented, and enable us, when we meet the Canadians and the Australians and the New Zealanders side by side in the common cause and the common field, to say to them: 'Our country, just as yours, has self-government within the Empire.'"[97]

Willie was conscious enough to realize that the man bringing him back to the trenches was a Northern Irish Protestant.

---

97 https://en.wikipedia.org/wiki/Willie_Redmond

THE FLANDERS OFFENSIVE

The Allies were planning an attack in the Flanders sector, the above mentioned Third Battle of Ypres, and it was intended the Guards Division would take part in it. So, on arriving in the Boesinghe sector, they underwent extensive training and tactical exercises in open warfare, together with steady drill and the infantry was given as much practical teaching as was possible in the art of attacking established enemy positions.

On the 10th of June, their Commander, Major General Feilding held a divisional conference at which he outlined the role which the Guards would be called upon to fill in the coming battle. He explained that the division would be on the left of the XIV Corps, which was to be the northern corps of the Fifth Army, and that its task would be to capture the enemy's defensive positions east and north-east of Boesinghe.

The plan was for General Gough's 5th Army to strike eastward from Ypres and to take possession of the Passchendaele Ridge.

The initial attack was to be carried out by the 2nd and 3rd Guards Brigades and the 1st Guards (the brigade the 75th F.C.R.E. was with) should be employed to exploit their success. Two days later the 2nd Guards moved up to the front and relieved a brigade of the 38th Division, which was holding a line east of Boesinghe. The 1st Guards moved forward also and went into bivouacs in the woods west of Woesten and divisional HQ was established in "J" camp near International Corner, west of the Poperinghe Canal.

This sector in which the Guards and their engineering companies found themselves was situated along the bend of the Yser Canal, north and southeast of the village of Boesinghe, the canal itself forming the dividing barrier between the two hostile trench systems.

On the other side of the canal were the German Trenches. The canal itself was mostly thick mud, with a narrow stream in the middle. It was uncrossable, which is why the lines ended up on either side. The land behind the German trenches was flat as far as the Houthulst Forest to the north. It was studded with farmhouses which had been fortified by the Germans. There was higher ground which they commanded which stretched North of Ypres ending at the village of Pilkem. This is the land the Guards had to capture and cross to push the Germans back. The enemy commanded a view of all the preparations for the attack and shelled them mercilessly.

The Engineers with the pioneer battalions had to build roads and railways, repair trenches and then find a means of crossing the canal. They had to build dumps for their equipment, which would have to be transported across the canal when the German trenches had been taken. Nineteen chambers were built into the canal bank to store the equipment for bridging the canal. The chambers were designed such that they could be broken open onto the canal and the bridges built across directly. All under the noses of the Germans, who constantly harassed them with sniper, machine gun and artillery fire.

The troops were constantly training for the attack and to assist with this, a short length of stream was turned into a model of the canal, to rehearse the crossing. This model showed the disposition of the enemy trenches and natural and artificial features of the land on the other side of the canal.

The most critical problem was the crossing of the canal, which as mentioned above, was mostly thick mud into which a man would sink up to his waist. It was crucial that the crossing be made as rapidly and precisely as possible. To achieve this, mats about 3 feet wide, were designed made from strong canvas, backed with wire netting on one side and small wooden slats. The length of the mats was a little more than the canal width, and when rolled up could be easily carried to the site and rolled out across the mud. Ropes were used to guide the soldiers across when the mat sank below the water. The only problem was when it rained, the water got deeper and then it would be more difficult to cross by this means. To back up the mats, light single file bridges made of wooden piers with a foundation of petrol tins and joined together by trench grids, were also constructed by the Engineers, and carefully stored in the chambers under the canal bank mentioned above.

This operation would clearly be very dependent on the companies of engineers to work together with the infantry, efficiently, all the time under heavy fire.

The following war diaries tell their own story.

75th Field Company War Diary
June 18, 1917.

Ditto. 100 OR[98] under Lt. Hardy, 3rd Coldstream Guards are attached to this Company for work and are employed on carting sand from railway to sand model. (60 men). Remainder at corps HQ.

A conference was held at divisional HQ, laying out the plan of attack. This involved the 2nd and 3rd Guards brigades crossing the Yser canal and forcing a path in a north-east direction. The 1st Guards were to exploit the successes made by the 2nd and 3rd and make a crossing of a stream called the Steenbeek.

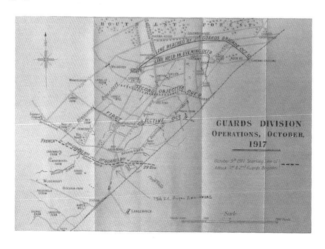

GUARDS DIVISION
OPERATIONS, OCTOBER.
1917

---

98 "Ordinary Ranks".

July 1, 1917.

Decouck Farm (Sheet 28B 13 a.8.8.) *No.1 section making battn. HQ at Boesinghe Chateau. No. 2 section advanced dressing station in cellars in Boesinghe Main Street. No. 3 section Guards and supervising work done by support Battn. on communication trenches forward of X line. No. 4 section making Battn. HQ in Chasseur Farm and sapping platoon under No. 4 section on Cardiff St. new trench.*

July 2, 1917.

Same as on 1st except No. 2 section finished advanced dressing station and are employed on repair of Bridge St. between X and Y lines and Hunter St. Sgt. Corby of sapping platoon wounded at duty. Sapper Blackburn wounded at duty.

July 3, 1917.

Same as 2nd. Cpl. Clapp and Spr. Thomas took part in a raid on enemy front line at railway crossing with object of getting information about Yper – Lee. Cpl. Clapp wounded at duty. Sapper Thomas missing. The party did not reach Yper – Lee.

July 4, 1917.

Same as 3rd. No. 3 section take on repair of Clarges St. Driver Childs wounded to hospital. Lt. Hardy of sapping platoon wounded at duty.

July 5, 1917.

No. 2 section finished Bridges St. Start camouflaging of Hunter St and Boesinghe Main St. Remainder as on 4th.

July 6, 1917.

No. 2 repairing brick culvert under Boesinghe Main St. takes on upkeep of trench tramway system. 4 breaks mended – remainder same as 5th. Spr. Waddington wounded at duty.

July 7, 1917.

Same as 6th. Railway mended in 5 places. L/cpl. Ezard wounded at duty. Sapper Luvick evacuated sick.

July 8, 1917.

Same as 7th. Also No. 1 section start Heavy Trench Mortar Emplacement in railway embankment at front line with working parties from trench mortar battery. Spr. Turner wounded. Pte. Hickey of sapping platoon wounded. Spr. R. Wright wounded.

July 9, 1917.

Canada Farm (28NW A17b8.8) *Company moved to bivouac at Canada Farm owing to heavy shell fire on old billet and to the presence of too many 6"? in the immediate vicinity. No. 1 section TM emplacement in Railway Embankment at B 121 b.4.4. heavy shell fire hindered work on dugouts at Boesinghe Chateau. No. 2 section mended railway in 3 places and overhauled tracks and line generally. Camouflaged Boesinghe High Street and repaired Bridge St. No. 3 section worked on communication trenches supervising support Battn. No. 4 section dugouts in Chasseur Farm constructing new portion of Bridge St. communication trench from Y to S lines.*

July 10, 1917.

Same as on 9th. Chasseur Farm finished.

July 11, 1917.

Same as on 10th. No. 4 section all now completely on Bridge St. L. Cpl. Bailey 3rd Coldstream Guards attached, wounded at duty.

July 12, 1917.

Same as 11th. No. 2 section make Battn. HQ for assembly for the attack. Spr. Hunter wounded at duty.

July 13, 1917.

Company relieved by 55th and 76th Field Company R.E. front now organized as a two-brigade front for assault. Company march back to "J" camp. Cpl. Jacobs wounded at duty.

July 14, 1917.

"J" Camp (B8b3.4) Making notice boards. 2 Lt. Crane showed Tunneling officer where bank of canal required blowing up for bridging. 2 Lt. Reid oversaw position for artillery bridge across street rear at Elverdinghe St. No. 4 section look over work on dressing station at Old Mill, Elverdinghe. No. 3 section repairing trench railway. 1 NCO and 5 men on upkeep of sand model.

July 15, 1917.

All tracks reconnoitered to X line. Overhauled pontoon equipment. Blew up trees for gunners as they masked batteries. Continued work on Old Mill. Made up petrol tin bridges for infantry in file and bridge over stream on tracking.[99]

July 16, 1917.

Work on tracks, trench tramway, notice boards, petrol tin bridges, Old Mill.

• • •

The preliminary to the upcoming attack on the German lines was an artillery barrage to "soften up" the German troops and cut the wire defenses on the German side. They also wanted to destroy as many of the farmhouses and blockhouses being used as defensive positions by the enemy. This barrage began on July 16th, using heavy artillery, 4.5-inch howitzers and trench mortars. Inevitably the

---

99 Tracking was the mats for crossing the canal, referred to in a previous chapter.

German artillery began to retaliate, mostly aimed at the British guns, but also any troop movements on the west side of the canal. They also shelled the back areas behind the front line with gas, and for the first time, the Germans used Mustard Gas.

CHAPTER 23

A Fateful Day

For ever since then, if a war they would wage,
Behold us a-shinin' on history's page—
First page for Her Majesty's Royal Engineers,
With the rank and pay of a Sapper!

(Rudyard Kipling. "The Sapper")

NEAR BOESINGHE
July 31, 1917

Low grey clouds had been dominating the sky since before noon, getting thicker by the hour, and around four in the afternoon, rain started coming down in sheets across the tortured landscape.

From there the weather went downhill. It poured, soaking the men and turning the canal into a river. Thankfully the pontoon bridges held because the board walkways across the canal were becoming submerged; soldiers navigating them couldn't see where they were going, and to walk off one in the center meant sinking in the mud and possibly drowning. The infantry had already crossed the canal and were slowly pushing forward through the maze of cut wire, shell holes and tree stumps that comprised No-Man's Land. No matter which side of the front you were on, it was becoming increasingly impossible to move. In the shell holes, men were sinking up to their waist in liquid mud. If they strayed off what was left of the road, they could literally drown. For the British, supplies had to be kept coming or they'd soon run out of ammunition and their advantage lost.

• • •

Thigh deep in the muddy water in the canal, the sappers of 75th Company were struggling with the heavy, waterlogged hemp rope, pulling it across the water and up and around the pulley system they'd rigged on a sheerlegs built on the canal bank, matching the one on the Boesinghe side. Stores of ammunition were being laid on the duckboards ready for transport across the canal as soon as the pulley system was set up.

As Vincent helped pull the rope across, he glanced at the growing heaps of shells and bullets, and said to Noel Byrne, who stood behind him, "If a shell hits that lot we'll all be taking flight lessons!"

Byrne laughed and said, "Let's get as far across the canal as we can then ... "

• • •

At Red Crossroads in No-Man's Land, about 800 yards to the east from where Vincent's section was working at the canal bank, a group of soldiers from the Royal Inniskilling Fusiliers was laying down planks across the road, to make a surface over the mud so that the carts could make their way.

There were six of them: L/Cpl Francis Ledwidge, L/Sgt. John Harte, Privates Henry Evans, Frank Mattingly, Robert Sharman, and Henry Newman.

They were all Irish, and one of them, Frank Ledwidge, had been an up-and-coming poet before joining the Inniskillings. He still wrote poetry any chance he got, and his work, and depiction of the wartime conditions on the front, found a willing audience in Ireland.

Newman had gone off to fetch an urn of tea to bring back to his mates laying the timbers. It was hard grueling work, their hands cut and full of wood splinters. The rain was coming down in torrents, soaking them through. The work had kept them warm initially, though it was cold in the rain and a chill had set in. When Newman returned, they gladly huddled down in a shell crater with their hands warming around the tin mugs. The muddy water leaking through their puttees and soaking their feet had ceased to bother them—they were beyond feeling. Nor did they pay much attention to the shell fire which had become background noise, was continuous, and mostly directed at their own artillery on the other side of the canal.

• • •

On the ridge near Zonnebeke, the Germans had built a major defensive position called Mittelriegel, and this is where *Oberleutnant* Alberich Babler found himself commanding a German 150 mm sFH '13 howitzer.

They'd had a pasting the day before with gas shells from the British artillery and were still recovering from it. Two of the gunners had been gassed when their masks leaked and had been replaced with new conscripts who didn't know their arse from their elbow. One of them, *Kanonier* Achen, had stood too close to the shield when the gun fired this morning, which, despite the hydro-spring recoil system, still kicked like a mule. Achen had been thrown back, his collarbone broken, and knocked the gun layer *Unteroffizier* Eberhardt on his back, the latter losing his glasses in the mud. When the shortsighted gun layer got up, cursing the unfortunate young conscript, who was screaming in pain, he stumbled around looking for his glasses, and stood on them, cracking the lens.

They had just received orders to fire on a ropeway being erected across the Ypres-Yser Canal and Babler shouted to the gun layer to line up on the men working on the canal bank. Eberhardt peered into the telescopic sight and made an adjustment to the elevation control of the powerful gun, while the team loaded the heavy 42 Kg high-explosive shell into the breach. He was shivering uncontrollably with a mixture of fatigue, hunger, and discomfort in the rain, which had started an hour ago and didn't look like it was letting up. His hands were cold and numb from the wet and tiredness. They had been in action now for over 12 hours, and he hadn't eaten anything since morning.

"*Bis genau einen grad!*" he shouted to Babler—"up exactly one degree"—and when Babler nodded, Eberhardt spun the wheel with his numb fingers, peering through the broken lens of his spectacles.

Rain poured over the lens and made it even more difficult to see, but he set the gun, not caring much at this stage, he felt so miserable. Were one to inspect the gradations on the gun setting, it would be observed that it was only forty-one degrees fifty minutes instead of forty-two degrees.

"Fire!"

The huge gun recoiled with a deafening explosion.

Fifteen seconds later, the gun and its crew disintegrated as a British shell scored a direct hit.

• • •

While Eberhardt was sighting the German artillery piece, across on the other side of the canal at a forward observation post, a British spotter was shouting urgently into his field telephone to a battery commander, Lieutenant Dalzell, to target a German Howitzer that he saw lining up on the canal bank. He'd guessed they were going to try and take out the ropeway now being constructed by the Engineers to carry ammunition across the ditch. Both sides were aware of the critical importance of getting munitions across to the advancing infantry, who would be left sitting without being able to fight if it didn't arrive on time. The construction of temporary infrastructure was of vital importance in this respect.

Dalzell raised his binoculars to spot the German gun, and instructed his gun layer, Corporal Todd, to line up on it. Todd could see the figures around the gun through his scope and made a traverse adjustment for the fifteen mile an hour east wind, then carefully, very carefully, adjusted the elevation, until he was sure they would hit the target. Todd was an experienced gun layer and knew that gun in particular, which tended to need five minutes of arc added to the telescope reading.

Just as he was about to give the fire order, he saw the German Howitzer fire, cursed himself for his tardiness, and gave the fire order. He managed a smile as he saw the direct hit on the German gun.

• • •

Down in the shell hole at Red Crossroads, Lance-Corporal Ledwidge lifted the mug to his lips, savoring the taste of the bitter, strong, hot tea. It was the last thing he ever did. The shell from Babler's gun exploded about six feet away, throwing up a cloud of mud, water, and pieces of wood and human bodies. A group of their fellow fusiliers nearby dived into the mud to protect themselves and when one of them looked up, he saw a shower of debris and mud crashing down around them.

A tin mug splashed down about ten feet away, and then it all stopped and there was a comparative silence for a few seconds, that seemed like hours.

• • •

Noel and Vincent instinctively ducked as the shell struck and then looked over at the location.

"I think they're trying to target us," Noel said. "Jaysus, let's get this fucking thing finished and get the hell out've here."

Noel looked at Vincent's blue eyes, which were scanning the distance where the gun was.

He smiled and said, "Ye needn't worry Noel. Not just yet anyway." Vincent nodded towards the black oily mushroom of the exploding British shell, and what looked like a gun barrel cartwheeling upwards.

When it settled, what remained of *Oberlieutnant* Babler and *Unteroffizier* Eberhardt lay in a bloody heap with their comrades and the tangled wreckage of the howitzer.

But for a small extra twist on the elevation wheel of the howitzer, only 10 minutes of arc, Francis and his comrades might have lived on and drank the rest of their tea, carrying on mending the road. His poetry would have continued to delight and charm us, his mother might have greeted her son coming home from the war. The twist of a freezing cold hand was all it took.

It wasn't just the men who died, but also beauty that died with them; and hope. For what is the point of hope when men behave like this?

> He shall not hear the bittern cry
> In the wild sky where he is lain,
> Nor voices of the sweeter birds,
> Above the wailing of the rain.
>
> *(Francis Ledwidge. "Lament for Thomas McDonagh")*

FRANCIS LEDWIDGE,[100] IRISH NATIONALIST AND WAR POET

In the tiny village of Janeville on the main road from Dublin to Belfast, just a mile from Slane Castle, a family welcomed the latest addition; a baby boy, matted dark hair covering the soft skin of his scalp, tiny arms flailing in readiness to take on the world. It was the 19th of August 1887.

---

100 Photo courtesy of Wikimedia Commons public domain. Unknown contributor.

Away to the East a solar eclipse was taking place, but that was far from the mind of Patrick Ledwidge, the baby's father. They lived in a small cottage which housed seven other children with the parents and trying to feed this large family was a constant headache for Patrick. He worked hard as a farm laborer and brought home what he could get on the farm, the rest was a juggle to feed those hungry stomachs. His own stomach rumbled as he sat with his wife Anne while she nursed the little baby in her arms. The midwife had left, after pronouncing baby and mother healthy and Patrick was getting ready to leave for work, a bowl of porridge filling his growling stomach. The neighbors were helping with the children, as always in this small community, and just as he went out, Janie McCauley arrived at the door with a large dish of stew and bustled inside to organize the kids for school.

They named the baby Francis, and he was the second to last in a family of nine children. Life was hard in the little house, but they all pulled together, and Patrick and Anne did everything they could to make sure the kids got a good education to get them out of this poverty rut and make something of their lives.

When Francis was only five years old, tragedy struck the Ledwidge household. In 1892, his father was taken ill, and died shortly afterwards, just three months after Francis' youngest brother, Joseph was born. Anne was now left with nine children and no income. The older ones all had to find jobs and in this way the family kept together and struggled on.

Francis was going to the local national school, where he studied under an old Fenian, Thomas Madden, and was popular with the other children, but like Vincent McCann, born 7 years later and just sixteen miles from Francis' home, he tended to enjoy his own company.

Old Madden used to call him "The boy who knew too much" due to his scholastic ability. However, studious as he was, he wasn't beyond giving Mr. Madden a bit of lip. He was a good-looking boy and developed into a fine well-built young man.

Because of the family circumstances, he had to leave school when he was thirteen and worked at various laboring jobs in the local farms and on the roads. But like Vincent too, he kept up his reading and continued his self-education.

Francis was a handsome young man, strong as an ox from his years as a laborer, with a sensuous face and brown eyes that captured the heart of many a young lass. From quite early in his life he became a keen poet, writing whenever he had a chance in cheap copy books. When he was fourteen, he began having his poems published in the Drogheda Independent, one of the earliest being "Behind a Closed Eye".[101]

I walk the old, frequented ways

That wind around the tangled braes,

I live again the sunny days

'Ere I the city knew.

While working as a road laborer, he sent a copy book of his poems to Lord Dunsany,[102] a prolific author and soldier, who, when he received Frank's poetry,[103] immediately recognized another fellow poet. Dunsany, well known in Dublin and London literary circles, started his own literary career with a few poems. He was well connected and later introduced Frank to W.B. Yeats, who he became friendly with.

Dunsany continued to support Ledwidge with money and literary advice, letting him have access to Dunsany Castle's library, where he met the Irish writer, Katherine Tynan. From here came Frank's first collection of poems, "Songs of the Fields", which found great acceptance in Irish literary circles.

Always a keen nationalist, Frank, with his brother Joseph, founded a branch of the Irish Volunteers in Slane town.

As a young teenager, growing up in Janeville, he fell in love with a neighbor, Ellie Vaughey, with a passion that is the special domain of teenagers. Sadly, Ellie didn't return his love and the two drifted apart,

---

101 You can listen to a beautiful musical rendition by Anuna at https://anuna.bandcamp.com/album/behind-the-closed-eye

102 Edward Plunkett, 18th Baron of Dunsany—a relative of Randolph Plunkett, 14th Baron Louth, who lived at Louth Hall, Tallanstown.

103 As he grew older, he became known as Frank, rather than Francis.

though Frank always maintained his feelings for her. But growing up, he shifted his attentions to Elizabeth—or Lizzy—Healy, who lived in the nearby village of Wilkinstown.

He loved that little hamlet and the surrounding countryside, and wrote to Lizzie's brother-in-law, that, "I could have stayed down in Wilkinstown forever, it is so infinitely peaceful ... I think of you in the lap of the quiet bog. You don't know how fortunate you are. I would easily swap twenty years of my life with whatever powers shape our destiny for a home like yours ..."

The pair went out together and met often at dances at Slane and Ardee, though Frank was conscious of his working-class background and compared himself unfavorably to her family, who were teachers. While they were together one day, Lizzy asked him shyly if he'd write her a poem. This resulted in the lovely poem "To Eilish of the Fair Hair"—Eilish being the Gaelic for "Elizabeth".

> I'd make my heart a harp to play for you
> Love songs within the evening dim of day,
> Were it not dumb with ache and with mildew
> Of sorrow withered like a flower away.
> It hears so many calls from homeland places,
> So many sighs from all it will remember,
> From the pale roads and woodlands where your face is
> Like laughing sunlight running thro' December.

At the outbreak of World War I in August 1914, and on account of Ireland's involvement in the war, the Irish Volunteers split into two factions: the National Volunteers who supported John Redmond's appeal to join Irish regiments in support of the Allied cause, and those who did not. Frank was originally of the latter party; nevertheless, he enlisted on October 24, 1914 in Lord Dunsany's regiment, joining the 5th Battalion Royal Inniskilling Fusiliers, part of the 10th (Irish) Division. Lord Dunsany had offered him a stipend to support him if he stayed out of the war. Ledwidge himself wrote, quite forcefully, that he could not stand aside while others sought to defend Ireland's freedom.

Army life suited Frank well. He was fit and able to take care of himself. It didn't take long before he was promoted to lance corporal.

In 1915, he saw action at Suvla Bay in the Dardanelles, where he suffered severe rheumatism. Having survived huge losses sustained by his company in the Battle of Gallipoli, he became ill after a back injury on a tough mountain journey in Serbia, a locale which inspired several of his poems.

The news of the Easter Rising seriously upset Frank, for like Redmond, he believed the sacrifice he and other Irishmen were making would lead the country toward Home Rule. But when he overstayed his home leave, and also got drunk while in uniform in May 1916, he was court martialed. He gained and lost stripes over a period in Derry, and then, after returning to the front, was once more promoted to lance corporal in January 1917, when posted to the Western Front, joining 1st Battalion, Royal Inniskilling Fusiliers, part of 29th Division.

Frank continued to write his beautiful poetry, despite the strain of combat. Perhaps that was what kept him sane. Unfortunately, the conditions of the battlefield being what they were, he lost much work. He sent much of his output to Lord Dunsany, himself moving on war assignments, as well as to readers among his family, friends, and literary contacts.

On July 31, 1917, a group from Ledwidge's battalion of the Royal Inniskilling Fusiliers were road laying in preparation for an assault during the Third Battle of Ypres near the village of Boezinge, northwest of Ieper (Ypres). While Ledwidge was drinking tea in a mud hole with his comrades, a shell exploded alongside, killing the poet and five others. A chaplain who knew him, Father Devas, arrived soon after, and recorded: "Ledwidge killed, blown to bits."

CHAPTER 24

Passchendaele

We lay down their sidings an' help 'em entrain,
An' we sweep up their mess through the bloomin' campaign,
In the style of Her Majesty's Royal Engineers,
With the rank and pay of a Sapper!

(Rudyard Kipling. "The Sapper")

YPRES-YSER CANAL
August 1, 1917

"Soaking hopeless rain, holding up the advance. Everything is a swamp and a pond, and tents leaking and dropping. Water in some of the wards is half-way up the legs of the beds.

11.30 p.m. Just finished my last round. Soaking rain all day still going on, complete hold-up of British Army. Absolute silence of our guns and only an occasional reminder from Fritz. The abdominals coming in are very bad to-day—both Boche and British. We are to take Chests and Femurs too as soon as No.44 and the Austr. C.C.S.'s [Casualty Clearing Stations] open which are alongside. It is getting very ghastly; the men look so appalling when they are brought in, and so many die."

—Sister Luard's Diary, August 1, 1917

• • •

"The enemy has been driven from the whole of his front system, on a front of eight miles, and the British and French troops were firmly established in or beyond the German second line on a front of seven miles."
—General Gough, C-in-C Fifth Army, BEF, August 1, 1917

• • •

"The Corps Commander thanks every officer and man in the XIV Corps, for their splendid efforts today. Royal Engineers, the Field and Heavy Artillery share the chief honors of an advance of two and a half miles. The Labor Companies and all sorts of transport drivers deserve the fullest recognition also, for the way they have stuck to their job, under harassing fire."
—Lieutenant-General, Frederick Lambart, 10th Earl of Cavan

• • •

BRANDHOEK

"6:00 p.m. This has been a very bad day. Big shells coming over about 10 a.m. - one burst between one of our wards and the Sisters' Quarters of No.44 C.C.S. and killed a Night Sister[104] asleep in her tent and knocked out three others with concussion and shell shock. This went on all day. The Australians' Q.M. Stores, the Cemetery, the Field Ambulance alongside, the Church Army Hut, all got hit."
—Sister Luard's Diary, August 22, 1917
"The rain began last evening and is still going on; an inch fell in 8 hours during the night. The ground is already absolutely water-logged—every little trench inches deep, shell-holes and every attempt

---

104 This was Sister Nellie Spindler, mentioned in Chapter 10.

at bigger trenches feet deep. And thousands of men are waiting in the positions and will drown if they lie down to sleep. Three of the men we have in will die to-night, and there's a brave Jock boy who's had a leg off and is to lose an arm and an eye to-morrow who said, 'If you write to Mother, make it as gentle as you can, as she lost my brother in April, died o'wounds.'"

—Sister Luard's Diary, August 27, 1917

75th Field Company War Diary
August 26, 1917.
Handed over work to 76th Field Company R.E. and took over work in line from 510th /29th Division. Company moved to billets at Lunaville Farm in evening.

September 1, 1917.
Flanders. Belgium. *Improving German blockhouses in forward lines. Camouflaging line through Abriwood so as to hide movement behind and gun flashes. Railway maintenance to Steenbeek. Duckboard tracks to R.E. dump.*

September 2, 1917.
Same as 1st. started new railway track on East Bank of Steenbeck to join main Decauville railway.

• • •

"The weather has not cleared up enough yet for Active Operations. Last night some rather nasty shelling was going on and had been all day and lots of casualties were brought in; 6 died here, besides those killed in the Camps."

—Sister Luard's Diary, September 2, 1917

"Crowds of letters from mothers and wives who've only just heard from the W.O. [War Office] and had no letter from me, are pouring in, and have to be answered. I've managed to write 200 so far, but there are 466.

2.30 a.m. The bomb fell and blew one of our Night Orderlies' sleeping tents out of existence. They'd all have been wiped out if they'd been in bed, but they were all on Night Duty."

—Sister Luard's Diary, September 3, 1917

"Got to bed in my clothes, at 4 a.m., up at 7.30. Brilliant morning; Archie racket in full blast. This acre of front so far bears a charmed life, but how long can this last? Shells and bombs shave us on all sides.

Orders have come for the final evacuation of the Hospital—site considered too 'unhealthy'. We close down to-day, evacuate the patients still here, and disperse the personnel. I stay till the last patient is fit to be moved, probably to-morrow, or next day—then probably Leave for 14 days! But don't count on it, as you never know."

—Sister Luard's Diary, September 4, 1917

75th Field Company War Diary
September 9, 1917.

Company shelled out of Lunaville billets and moved to Elverdinghe defences.

One sentence.

The record in the 75th Field Company War Diary on September 9, 1917 says nothing of Captain Briggs having to sit down a day later, after they'd evacuated the farm and trudged to Elverdinghe, to write to the families of Sappers Duignan and Locher.

Poor Locher, he'd had a hard time, because of his German surname. But he swore his ancestors had come to England generations ago. "What's in a name?" he'd argue.

One sentence says very little about the grief of a mother or a wife, opening the captain's letter when they came in the mail. Expecting some news from the front, they would open a letter saying a soldier—their soldier—died bravely.

• • •

The collection of farm buildings had made excellent billets, if one didn't mind sharing it with the fleas, rats, and other inhabitants. They'd arrived there on the first of August, a bright sunny day, small cotton wool clouds scudding before a brisk westerly wind. The fields had been untended for over a year after the family, fed up with the constant shelling, had finally given up the ghost and went to live with relatives further south.

Vincent wandered through the rooms, the wallpaper peeling off the walls, and mold and mildew taking over. There was a dresser in the kitchen, and a framed photograph had been left on it, showing the husband and wife, and their teenage daughter and son, smiling into the camera, not knowing the horrors that lay ahead. He was fascinated, wondering what their life had been like, imagining the mother looking after the two siblings—clucking, scolding, cooking, sewing, all the homely activities he missed so badly.

There had been little of that in his own home since his mother had died. Every day he looked at that picture and longed for the one thing he knew he could never have again.

Mother.

The sheds and outbuildings had been set up with rough but usable beds and mess tables. Life was tolerable, but like all things, especially in wartime, it never lasts.

Vincent and the other sappers in his section had been working down in the farmhouse cellars when the bombardment started.

Luckily, there were no direct hits on the house itself, but when they crawled out of the cellars, the building had been partly destroyed by the blasts nearby, walls down and wooden beams dangling, ready to brain anyone walking underneath. The dresser in the kitchen had fallen over and the family photograph lay in the rubble. There was dust and smoke everywhere, no fresh air to breathe. The scene was chaotic as they emerged, running over broken furniture and rubble; Vincent's boot landed on the picture, smashing the glass and frame, the iron studs in his boot tearing the family picture apart.

The building in front of them was burning hard, belching black, stinking smoke. There had been hay stored there, and two sappers, James Duignan and Henry Locher, had been in there clearing it. Their blackened bodies were dragged out later after the fire had been extinguished. Captain Briggs had ordered an immediate evacuation, leaving most of their equipment behind. Another barn, where section two had been resting, had collapsed, and the men had to be dug out from beneath the wreckage of the building. All day they ran the truck between the wrecked farm and the ambulance station.

As he helped carry a sapper with a badly fractured femur out of the building, Vincent couldn't help wondering how long this could go on for before it was he who became the next person blown to pieces.

Life on the front line helped one learn to live day to day and make no plans. The only wish was to come out of it all alive.

• • •

The general British advance, which had been resumed on the 20th of September, was continued on the 26th of September and again on the 4th of October. Steady progress was being made and the German defense was weakening. The British troops had now reached the important line of high ground which stretches from Reutel and the spur of hilly country north of Poelcappelle to Broodseinde.

Although admittedly it was getting late in the season, the British Commander-in-Chief hoped that, if the weather remained fine, he would still be able to strike northward and to carry out the operations in the coastal area which had been one of the main objects of the offensive. He decided to renew the advance on the 9th of October with the intention of gaining possession of the remainder of the ridge between Passchendaele and Poelcappelle.

The Guards division would once again be used in this effort. Their objective was to advance across the Broembeek River and then to push forward to the southern edge of Houthulst Forest, working in conjunction with the 29th Division astride the Ypres-Staden Railway Line on the right and the French on the left.

75th Field Company War Diary
October 7–8, 1917.

Work on Captain's Farm for Brigade HQ. Formation of battle dump of bridges and mats etc. for crossing Broembeek. Maintenance and control of tramway.

October 9, 1917.

Division attacked and reached all objectives to edge of Houthoulst Forest.[105] 1 section taped Hunter St. forward to front positions and put tape on white pickets. 1 section maintenance of trench tramway to Wijdendrift. 2 sections and 2 platoons attached infantry proceeded at 2 pm to wire strong points. Could not wire in daylight owing to sniping, so lay in shell holes till dusk. Were caught in heavy barrage and

---

105 Headlam. C. *The Guards Division in the Great War.* pp 270-275.

lost heavily. Wire disorganized being short of men and material was scattered. Party had to return.[106]

• • •

The 1st and 2nd Guards met with relatively little opposition, with the Germans either retreating or surrendering, the initial artillery barrage by the British taking them completely by surprise. However, on the extreme right of the 1st Battalion Irish Guards was the Newfoundland Regiment, who were not able to advance as rapidly as the Irishmen, and consequently, the Irish were subject to a good deal of machine-gun fire on their right.

The carrying forward of the lines of communication to the new front over an area of marsh and water-logged shell holes exposed to the enemy's artillery and machine-gun fire was, as usual in the Ypres Offensive of 1917, a task which tested the capacity and the endurance of the R.E. and Pioneers. On the 9th of October, the 75th and 76th Field Companies, and the 4th Battalion Coldstream Guards (Pioneers) emerged from their trying ordeal. Two sections from each Field Company with infantry carriers followed close behind the attacking brigades with the materials necessary for wiring the new line. But the difficulties of the carriers were so great, especially in the flooded area round the Broembeek, where they also came under heavy artillery fire, that it was found impossible to lay out more than about 200 yds of wire on the left front south of Faidherbe crossroads.

The important work of taping out the track leading to the new front line was carried out more successfully, for, within half an hour after the capture of the final objectives, the RE had laid tapes to Egypt House and Louvois Farm. This was done under the direct observation of the enemy snipers. They also proceeded with the laying of

---

106 Some of this is not very clear as to meaning—copied verbatim. DMC

duckboard tracks and with the carrying forward of the trench tramway which was essential for carrying ammunition and other supplies forward and for bringing the wounded back to the casualty clearing stations.

THE MYSTERY OF CELTIC WOOD

About a mile or two away to the southeast, while the Guards were attacking Houthulst Forest, at 5:20 a.m. on October 9, another attack took place by an Australian battalion which ended in one of the war's many unsolved mysteries.

This refers to the apparent disappearance without trace of thirty-seven men of the tenth Battalion of the 1st Australian Division during a diversionary attack on German positions in Celtic Wood, near Passchendaele, during the Battle of Poelcappelle (October 9, 1917). These were operating on the right flank of the Guards Division two miles to the southeast during the same push against the Germans.

Official Army reports of the action state that investigations failed to account for the fate of thirty-seven of men of the 10th Battalion. No trace of the men—no ID-tags, no possessions, nothing—was found. German records contain no mention of the attack. Rumors persist that the men had simply walked into a mist and disappeared. Some investigators attribute the lack of record of the missing to confusion, misreporting and clerical error.

The 10th Battalion of the 1st Australian Division was known as the "Terrible 10th", a name given for the fighting spirit displayed in the trenches of the Western Front. Two of its members had been awarded the Victoria Cross during the Gallipoli Campaign, where they led the Australian forces in the initial landing and later defense of ANZAC Cove.[107]

---

107 https://en.wikipedia.org/wiki/ANZAC_Cove

The 10th Battalion were given orders to carry out a diversionary attack on an area known as Celtic Wood, just outside Zonnebeek. The plan was for a couple of platoons to charge the woods, blow up German dugouts and retire on a flare signal, to mislead Germans that the attack was part of the main advance. At 5:20 a.m. on October 9, the barrage began and fifty-one men of the 10th Battalion under the command of twenty-two-year-old Lieutenant Frank Scott advanced.

To this day, no one knows what really happened, though there were investigations carried out, using the testimony of eyewitness accounts.

10th Battalion commander Lieutenant-Colonel Maurice Wilder-Neligan wrote in his report of the action, "...a desperate hand encounter followed, in which heavy casualties were inflicted upon the enemy...I am only able to account for 14 unwounded members of the party."

Official army records list 37 men who took part in the attack as missing.

To shield the attack, an artillery barrage was called to pulverize the wood before the soldiers went forward. Unfortunately, the barrage was light and scattered when they advanced across the 180 meters separating Celtic Wood from the Australian trenches. The terrain to be crossed consisted of tree stumps, bomb craters meters wide and due to heavy rain over the preceding days, mud that in some places was knee-deep. Compounding this, the 10th Battalion had raided Celtic Wood twice the previous week, leading the Germans to reinforce the position and install more machine-guns. Lieutenant Scott ordered a frontal attack on the German trench, while he led a group around the flank to attack from behind. Despite being outnumbered, Scott and his men, showing characteristic bravado, were successful, and the German troops began a retreat as soon as they were fired on from the rear.

German reinforcements quickly arrived and engaged the Australians in hand-to-hand combat, pushing them back while at the same time German artillery opened fire, barraging No Man's Land, making a retreat impossible. Within a short time, all the officers were dead or wounded and Sergeant William Cole, who tried to fire the flare signaling the withdrawal, was killed as he was firing the flare and the survivors were left to find their own way back.

Celtic Wood has lingered as the greatest mystery of Australia's Great War. It is the nation's wartime equivalent of "Picnic at Hanging Rock", only soldiers instead of schoolgirls disappeared.

But rather than vanishing into the mist, it is most likely they vanished into the "fog of war."

75th Field Company War Diary
October 10–11, 1917.
Repair of Hunter St. track. Maintenance of railway. Extension of railway from Wijdendrift Rd. forward to Broembeck. Reconnaissance of roads and shelters in captured areas.

• • •

While they were laying wire along the newly captured German trenches, Vincent paused to look up at an aircraft flying low above them. It must have been only about 300 feet above, and he could clearly see the black German cross on the wings and fuselage.

Aircraft were fascinating to watch, and he wondered what the plane was up to—surveying the troop formations or dropping bombs?

Then as it neared the area of Houthulst Forest—if you could call the collection of tree stumps in a sea of mud a forest—a volley of shots rang out from a battalion of Grenadier Guards working their way forward. Suddenly a trail of smoke and flames appeared from the engine and the plane lost height, falling rapidly, and crashing into the mud on the edge of the forest, amid loud cheers from the Grenadiers.

One less enemy to worry about, Vincent thought as he turned back to the wire.

• • •

75th Field Company War Diary
October 12, 1917.
Company remained in billets as 3rd Guards Brigade attacked.

• • •

The 3rd Guards Brigade were successful in their advance, gaining their objective. From here onwards, the Guards job was to hold the newly gained trenches and strong points originally held by the Germans and continue bringing up supplies and developing proper communications.

For the remainder of the Guards' sojourn in this part of the line, the rain fell incessantly, overflowing the Steenbeck and Broembeck Rivers and flooding the area, which was pockmarked with shell holes.

By the 17th of October, when the 35th Division relieved the Guards, the area had been well secured, duckboard tracks, bridges and tramlines had been established.

• • •

The stink of burning cloth permeated the billets.

Upon arriving in Eperlecques in Northern France after receiving orders to return south, they had a chance at last to bathe properly and were issued with clean uniforms in exchange for their own filthy ones from the last few weeks. Even though the issued gear had been well cleaned, it rarely got rid of the lice eggs that infested them. The remedy was to light a match and run it along the seams, in an effort to burn the eggs and hold down the next, inevitable infestation. Their bodies constantly itched; the scratching became second nature.

Fritz wasn't the only enemy. Large, corpulent rats, well fed on waste food and even the bodies lying in the shell craters in No-Man's Land, and the lice as well. They and other vermin were constant companions, adding to the torment of the filthy conditions in the trenches. The former spread disease, especially typhus, and the latter were said to cause "trench fever", which plagued the troops with headaches, fevers, and muscle pain.

Now at last they were able to rest in comparative comfort. The headaches and aches they suffered from now were not due to trench fever, but rather to the bad beer consumed in considerable quantities the previous night at the estaminet.

Vincent winced as he thought about it, yet he hadn't enjoyed a few hours out so much for a long time. Sergeant Pring had entertained them with his endless stories, and as he sat at the table, Vincent thought he actually liked the man. The estaminet was busy, packed with soldiers back from the front, truly grateful that they could still walk to the bar and have a pint. So many of their comrades hadn't made it back.

He mused on the dreadful week behind them now. The steady, unrelenting rain. The soaked clothing—outside from the rain and inside from sweat. The exhaustion of heavy labor and the constant fear that accompanied every one of them.

You never get used to that.

They had been told they'd done a great job. The CRE had given them a long rambling talk after the parade last Sunday. He did say though that the Guards Division had been the only one to make significant progress during the recent advance towards the Passchendaele Ridge, and that the support of the 55th, 75th, and 76th Field Companies had been critical to that effort. Lieutenant Colonel Lees told them he was proud of the work they'd done.

But the successes of the Paschendaele advance had been at a very high cost; the Guards Division lost 303 officers and 7,898 other ranks.[108]

At times like this Vincent felt happy with his contribution to what was becoming a close-knit team. Most of them had been together now since training back in Ireland, and a sense of camaraderie had developed which carried them along and made their work more efficient. They had good reason to be proud of themselves.

A week earlier, a message addressed to Major-General Fielding C-in-C of the Guards Division, and written by Colonel Clive Wigram on behalf of His Majesty the King, read as follows:

Dear Fielding,

Lord Cavan has informed the King of the doings of the Guards Division in the recent offensive. His Majesty has read with admiration and satisfaction the story of their splendid achievements, and the King heartily congratulates you and the division on all that has been accomplished in spite of the most unfavourable conditions of weather and mud. As Colonel-in-Chief of the Guards, His Majesty is proud to think that there has been imposed upon the division no task that has not been successfully fulfilled. The King has no doubt that after a well-earned rest, rebuilt and re-equipped, the division will distinguish itself in the future as it has distinguished itself in the past, and His Majesty sends you all his best wishes.

Yours Sincerely,

Clive Wigram,

Buckingham Palace,

17th October 1917

---

108 During the Guards Division's four months in this sector, they and the 29th Division put out of action no less than six German divisions. They had good reason to be proud of themselves.

When the message had been read out to them, Vincent had mixed feelings. He was indeed proud of their achievements, and he knew that the Engineers had performed an essential service in supporting the infantry who couldn't have gone ten yards in that mud without the preparations of his and the other field companies.

Yet he had growing feelings regarding the right of Ireland to Independence. It was something they talked about a lot in the mess tent, and a whole new nationalism was slowly developing in him and a good deal of his friends. They still felt they were doing the right thing by fighting in the war, but when it was over, they hoped that the British Government would push through a Home Rule bill, giving the Irish a greater degree of autonomy than they ever had in 800 years.

CHAPTER 25

"A Day Full of Orders— Countermanded Orders, New Orders, and Lack of Orders."

This is the hymn of mud-the-obscene, the filthy, the putrid,
The vast liquid grave of our armies. It has drowned our men.
Its monstrous distended belly reeks with the undigested dead.
Our men have gone into it, sinking slowly,
and struggling and slowly disappearing.
Our fine men, our brave, strong, young men;
Our glowing red, shouting, brawny men.
Slowly, inch by inch, they have gone down into it,
Into its darkness, its thickness, its silence ...

(Mary Borden[109] extract from "At the Somme: The Song of the Mud")

CAMBRAI
1917

A major attack on the Cambrai region was in the planning stage for many months previously. The ground in that region was most favorable for the use of tanks, and these were to be used en masse in this

---

109 https://www.poetryfoundation.org/poems/57329/at-the-somme-the-song-of-the-mud

particular enterprise. The British believed that the enemy's power of resistance was at a low ebb following the Flanders campaign, and a sudden blow in the French front would demoralize the Germans and also be of assistance to the Italians, who were trying to recover after the disastrous Battle of Caporetto. The planning was kept a closely guarded secret, in order to maintain the element of surprise.

The Guards Division had only been in rest billets for three weeks when orders were received for it to move southward. They were not told the destination, which led to much speculation on the part of officers and OR. The move, by route march, began on the 9th of November.

The plan for the Guards, who were part of the 4th Army Corps, was to storm the Havrincourt—Flesquières Ridge and to advance northward to capture the high ground on which Bourlon Wood and the village of Fontaine-Notre-Dame were situated. There would be no preliminary artillery barrage, to maintain the element of surprise, but tanks were to be used extensively.

To maintain the secrecy of the attack, the commanding general of the Guards, Major-General Fielding instructed his senior officers on the plan of attack, but also to spread the rumor that the division was on its way South to relieve the French, and that owing to scarcity of transport caused by rolling stock and motor vehicles having been sent to Italy, much baggage would have to be left at St. Pol.

• • •

75th Field Company War Diary
November 10, 1917.
Loading wagons and preparing for move. One pontoon and two trestles ditched by C.R.E.'s instructions.

November 11, 1917.

1st Brigade move. Company moves off at 8 am. Route via Moulle, St. Martin, St. Omer, Blendgcques and Hedringham to Clarques, arriving at 4.30 pm. (Distance about 17 miles.)

November 12, 1917.

Company moved off at 8 am. Route via Estree Blanche, Rely, Auchy aux Bois, arriving at Nedonchelle at 1 pm. (Distance about 12 miles)

November 13, 1917.

Company leaves Nedonchelle at 8.45 am. Route via Fiefs, Tangry, La Thieuloye, Monchy – Breton, arriving Chelers at 4 pm. (Distance about 15 miles.)

November 14, 1917.

Chelers: Cutting down kits, surplus stores.

November 15, 1917.

As on 14th. Surplus kit dumped in St. Pol.

November 16, 1917.

Kit inspection, rifle inspection. Collection of salvage around billets.

November 17, 1917.

Company leaves Chelers 8.30 am – route via Tinques, Penin, Viller-Sir-Simon, Givenchy Le Noble, Lignereuil and Ambrines – Magnicourt Road. (Distance about 10 miles.) Arrived at Sars le Bois at 1 pm.

November 18, 1917.

Company leaves Sars Le Bois at 8 am. Route via Denier, Avernes Le Comte, Hauville, Wanquetin, Simencourt, Beaumetz Les Loges, Riviere, Bréthencourt and Blairville, arriving Hendecourt 5.30 pm.

November 19, 1917.

OC attends 1st Brigade conference at Blairville at noon and C.R.E. 's conference at Bassie at 2 pm. Company march out of Hendecourt and Ervillers arriving at Gommecourt at 7.45 pm.

• • •

The Guards and the Royal Engineers had route marched nearly one hundred miles and finally arrived on the evening of 19th, the day before the battle started.

They set up billets at Gommecourt and were fed and finally turned in dog tired and filthy after the march. The nice, clean uniforms issued at Eperlecques were muddy and rumpled, though they would have to do, and the men would still be expected to look smart on parade. The Guards were to be held in reserve until (and if) Bourlon Wood was captured by the IV Corps, on which occurrence, they would move forward and pass through the gap in the enemy's defenses.

• • •

Hands wrapped around their mugs, Vincent and five of the sappers sat around a brazier warming themselves, oblivious to the rain, drinking tea they'd just made.

"No sign of any Frenchies here," McLoughlin smiled, "so I think we can scrap that one."

They knew or guessed some time back that the idea of "relieving the French" was just another rumor, and were preparing to go into battle once again, much closer to home.

"Where the hell are we anyway?" asked Kitchens, a young sapper, newly arrived from training at the Chatham Depot.

"Place called Gommycourt or something like that," McLoughlin said.

"Don't make much fuckin' difference, anyway," said Noel Byrne. "Yez'll be wading around in mud with Jerries shootin' at you, regardless …"

Vincent and this small group had become close to each other, after the shared camaraderie of the various battles they'd been through—except for Sapper Kitchens, that is, but he'd be absorbed under their wing soon enough. This had all become their world.

Unlike the officers, the OR didn't get that much leave, and none had been home since their original arrival in France. The concept of "home" had slipped into the background in their lives, and the day-to-day routine, mostly boring, sometimes terrifying, had become the norm. Just then sergeant Pring came around shouting

"C'mon yez laggards, get your arses off the ground and get y'r gear ready, we're maybe movin' in two hours."

75th Field Company War Diary
Tuesday, November 20, 1917.
Company at 2 hours' notice to move from 10 am. Lt. Crane on reconnaissance of road from Bapaume via Velu to Demicourt.

November 21, 1917.
Company moves from Gommecourt to camp at Barastre. Transport by road via Achiet Le Grand and Bapaume. Dismounted portion of Company march to Hamelincourt and embuss there at 9 pm—arriving Barastre at 3.30 am.

November 22, 1917.
Cleaning harness and rifles.

November 23, 1917.

Reveille 3.30 am. Company leaves Barastre at 6.30 am moves via Bertincourt, Veu, and Boumetz to Doignies, arriving at 10 am. Lt. Crane and 2nd Lts. Lawrie and Reid on reconnaissance of roads and tracks between Demicourt and Graincourt. Major Briggs and Lt. Andressy return from leave.

• • •

Fierce fighting had resulted in the taking of the small town of Flesquiers by the 51st Division, and then advancing forward, they took the town of Fontaine-Notre-Dame. That was on the 21st and the Guards were just arriving in the area.

The 23rd was a frustrating day for the Guards, their senior officers, the men, and the engineering companies. The initial attack (by the 51st Division) had been successful, but the element of surprise was lost, and the IV corps had come to a halt outside Flesquieres. The day was described as one "full of orders—countermanded orders, new orders, and lack of orders."

The Guards had been bussed to Barastre through dense road traffic, making the going very slow. The men were exhausted. The situation was total confusion, but the outcome was that the Guards Division was told to relieve the 51st Division at Flesquieres. The 1st and 3rd Brigades were ordered to move forward as far as lock No. 5 on the Canal Du Nord. The R.E. companies received orders to move forward to Trescault. The Guards then carried out their relief of the 51st Division. The 1st Guards Brigade, to whom the 75th F.C. R.E. was attached, found itself on a line about 4,400 yards long from a point S.E. of Cantaing to the S.E. of Bourlon Wood, which was still held by the Germans.

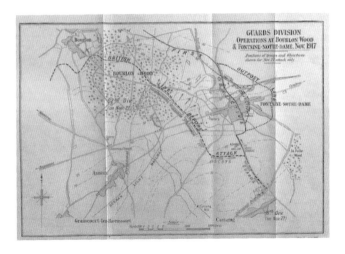

The night of the relief was a quiet one. Apart from enemy shelling of the area, the 24th passed relatively quietly. The town of Fontaine-Notre-Dame had been captured on the 21st, then, in a German counterattack, it had been recaptured.

• • •

75th Field Company War Diary
November 24, 1917.
Company leaves Doignes at 8 am and marches via Hermies, Royalcourt, Metz-en-Cortrai to Trescault arriving at 2 pm. Company bivouacs in tents. No. 1 section to Flesquiere.

November 25, 1917.
Transport remains at Flesquiere. Dismounted to Ribecourt except for No. 1 section. Company works on No.1 R.E. dump Flesquiere, German lighting plant in Catacombs and Dressing Station. No. 2 & 3 sections on road from Flesquiere to La Justice. No. 4 moves camp, work on road, dressing station and German railway running from Flesquiere.

• • •

322

The Catacombs comprised underground tunnels about 60 feet below the surface of the village, carved out of the chalk with large chambers off the main galleries. The galleries were reputed to link up with the surrounding villages and arrangements were made for a former Mayor of Flesquieres to attend and point out the exact run of certain tunnels, which connected with the enemy's territory. They were lit by electricity throughout, and all the chambers were equipped with wire bunks. The troops found their accommodation below ground very comfortable and there was no danger from air bombing nor the heaviest shelling.[110]

• • •

75th Field Company War Diary
November 26, 1917.
Work on road, dressing station and German railway running from Flesquere to Fontaine. Two enemy motor tractors found. One brought back. Work continued on dressing station.

• • •

On the 27th, the 2nd Guards Division carried out an attack on Fontaine-Notre-Dame, but owing to the loss of so many men, even though they succeeded in gaining their objectives, they had to retire back to their original positions. The Engineers were working to support the attack, repairing a German railway to use it for bringing up supplies. All the time they were under heavy machine gun and artillery fire.

---

110 Probably under the Catholic church of Saint Paul du Haut Escaut.

And the weather didn't help either, being extremely cold with heavy snow and rain, oftentimes hampering the work but on the plus side, the heavy rainfall hid them from view from the artillery.

CHAPTER 26

Going Home

I'm goin' 'ome to Blighty—ain't I glad to 'ave the chance!
I'm loaded up wiv fightin', and I've 'ad my fill o' France;
I'm feelin' so excited-like, I want to sing and dance,
For I'm goin' 'ome to Blighty in the mawnin'.

(Robert Service. "Rhymes of a Red-Cross Man")

FLESQUIERE
November 29, 1917

A light dusting of snow lay on the ground, the first of the winter, as they lay Corporal Arnold in his last resting place. He'd been one of the more popular NCOs, always ready to jump in with the other sappers, but ready to lead when necessary. He was a slightly built man, but impressively strong. Fair hair and blue eyes attested to his Saxon origins, but he was of solid Essex farming stock, and his practical solutions to the problems they encountered would be sorely missed over the next few weeks. When the shell landed, he'd been sitting on a tree stump having a smoke, and bang—he was killed outright.

As they stood around his grave, Vincent became aware of the young sapper to his right, coughing. His face had a red tinge to it, and he didn't look all that well. He was new to the company, having just come from the training camp at Étaples. Afterwards, they walked back to the billets together, Vincent quizzing him about where he came from. There was always an interest in newcomers, as there was a freshness about them that intrigued the older hands; there was also a need to look out for these young lads, until they found their feet.

"That's a bad cough ye've got there Donald," Vincent said after introducing himself.

"Yeh, I've had it since the last few days, started in the camp it did, and it's not gettin' any better," he said. "Don't feel that good at all t'be honest … there were a lot of sick lads there."

"Well, the food we get to eat, I'm not surprised more of us don't get sick," Vincent replied.

The following day, Sapper Donald Harmsworth reported sick to the CCS.

• • •

FRANCE
December 1917

75th Field Company War Diary
December 1, 1917.
Company withdrew to SW corner Havrincourt Wood.

Arrived in camp 4 am. Work in afternoon and night on wiring reserve position from Q 23b.8.2. to Q 29 Central. Company returned to camp 9 pm. 55th Field Company R.E. wired to right of us and 76th to left of us.

• • •

Vincent and two mechanics were working on the tractor they had found in Flesquiere, which had been brought back to the workshop. It was one of two left behind by the retreating German troops, but the other was damaged beyond repair, though they'd be able to get a few parts off it. They were Austro-Daimler heavy artillery tractors and the one they towed back was in relatively good condition and just needed stripping down and rebuilding. Vincent was making up some parts and with the spares they'd stripped from the second tractor, they'd have this one in working condition in no time. The weather outside was cold, with a few flurries of snow.

"Looks like it's goin' to be a white Christmas," Bert Johnson said as he got an adjustable wrench on the nuts of the cylinder head.

They were having problems with the metric measurements of the parts but got around it the same way they managed to improvise everything throughout the war.

"Bloody freezing in here," said the other mechanic, John Saunders.

"I don't know, I'm roastin'," Vincent said, as he wiped the sweat off his brow. The other two looked at him, a frown on John's face.

"Are ye OK, Vinnie?"

"Now ye mention it, I'm not feelin' great at all," Vincent replied. "Ach, I'll survive." Then he went over to a chair. "I think I'll sit for a minute and have a smoke," he said as he plonked down on it.

As the day wore on, Vincent felt his temperature rise and his body ached in every muscle, his breathing became labored, and when he tried to smoke a cigarette, the pain was intolerable.

By 2:30 that afternoon, he passed out.

He didn't remember much after that, just vague hazy images of being brought on a stretcher to the field hospital, and the agonizing bumping of the ambulance taking him to the CCS. From there he was brought to another hospital. He could recall people bending over him and mopping his face. Nurses. Then blackness again.

VINCENT: THE LONG SILENCE

Finally, he woke, feeling a little clearer, but the sheets were soaked in sweat. He was in a separate tent with about five others. He lay there, wondering what had hit him, when a nurse appeared, her long gown swishing along the floor of the tent. She came over to his bed, touched his brow with a cool hand and asked him how he felt. He noticed she was wearing a mask over her mouth and nose, and he wondered about that.

"Not too bad now, sister, but I can hardly lift my hand."

"You've had a dangerously high fever. The doctor says you've got purulent bronchitis.[111] He'll be in shortly." Then, hearing someone come in, she said, "Here's Doctor Purcell now."

"Good morning, young man, how're you feeling?" the doctor asked. Vincent gave the same reply, that he felt as weak as a kitten. "I know, you've still a way to go before we have you out of here. You've got what we think is purulent bronchitis. All that yellow stuff you're coughing up … There seems to be a lot of cases. Did you get gassed at any time?" he asked.

"Yes, a few months back," Vincent replied.

"That explains why you're taking it badly," the doctor said. "Mind you, the smoking doesn't help either. Your lungs have been damaged by the gas, and you haven't recovered fully from that yet. It's going to be a long haul for you, but you'll survive."

It wasn't the first time he'd listened to those words.

Vincent was down with what turned out to be an early case of the Spanish Flu. This tiny virus, over the course of its stay on Earth, killed more people than the Great War.

---

111 This was the term originally given to the Spanish Flu, which, though the pandemic wasn't officially deemed to start until March 1918, had been going around the camps since mid-1917. Vincent is recorded as having been in hospital from the 1st to the 15th December 1917.

THE SPANISH FLU

"While it was the general opinion of Philosophers, that all things upon Earth were governed by the Heavens, physicians imputed the Epidemical Catarrhous Semi-Pestilential Fever, to the Influence of the Stars; Whence the Italians gave it the name of Influenza."[112]

So observed Doctor Glass in the Annals of influenza or epidemic of catarrhal fever in Great Britain from 1510 to 1837.

Influenza delle stelle.

The first documented pandemic that fits the description of the flu was in 1580, so it is nothing new. There were four pandemics at least, in the 19th century, three in the 20th century and we have already experienced one this century.

The pandemic known as "Spanish Flu" is dated from March 1918 and continued through 1920. There are, however, records of it as early as 1916 when troops on the Western Front began to come down with this mysterious respiratory illness. It was only later in 1917 that it was realized that this was a rapidly spreading illness that could and did reach pandemic proportions. The conditions were ideal for the spreading of a virus, with many soldiers suffering from the aftereffects of chlorine gas, unsanitary living conditions, stress and overcrowding in camps and trenches, plus malnutrition due to lack of proper food. Smoking was of course endemic in the population in general, leading to lung problems. In order to prevent any mass hysteria during a time of crisis, the Allied Governments tried to censor any reports of a major outbreak of flu. Spain, being a neutral country, had no such reservations, and its press reported widely on the outbreak. This gave the impression that the illness originated there, but in fact the origins are unknown.

The coming and going of people from all over the world provided the opportunity for the disease to spread beyond the base camps and

---

112 https://play.google.com/books/reader?id=vUEJAAAAIAAJ&hl=en&pg=GBS.PA101

hospitals of the troops and become a pandemic of global proportions by the Winter. Raging unabated through 1919, the disease ultimately claimed more lives than the Great War itself.

75th Field Company War Diary

December 11, 1917.

Company moves to billets in Warlus. Transport arrived in afternoon.

December 12–23, 1917.

Company resting. Drill etc. in the morning.

December 24, 1917.

Xmas dinner at midday. Concert in the evening.

December 25, 1917.

Christmas Day: Loading wagons and resting.

December 26, 1917.

Company arrives from Warlus to billets in railway embankment H 13 b.9.0. Horse lines at Oil Factory. G 17 c.5.5.

December 27, 1917.

Company wiring 300 yds. of double apron fence 2 rows deep in Hydrabad Switch.

December 28, 1917.

300 yds. Low wire entanglement breast wire on same line as above.

December 29, 1917.

Company resting.

December 30, 1917.

Hydrabad Switch dug for 300 yds to depth of 1 foot. OC of section and officers go round new line.

December 31, 1917.

Officers and NCOs go round new line taking over from 91st Field Company R.E. Horse lines moved to Lowther Camp. G 10 c.

• • •

When he'd been discharged from hospital, the doctor had recommended Vincent be given leave to go home for two weeks to allow him to recover. The fever and coughing left him weak and exhausted, and he suffered from dizzy spells when he stayed up too long. The cough lingered, still bringing up sputum. He'd never felt so bad. What was needed was rest and good feeding for a little bit.

Vincent returned to the camp on the 29th of December.

• • •

BELFAST
December 15, 1918

As he stepped down from the horse-drawn cab after the ten-minute ride from Great Victoria Street Station to Cranburn Street, Vincent stepped back to admire the new house his family had moved into. It also gave him a breathing space to gather his wits. Not having seen them for just over three years, he ran the gamut of emotions from happiness at seeing his family once again, to deep sadness that his mother wouldn't be there to greet him. She would have shared his pride in himself, at having survived the hell that he'd left behind. Mixed in with all this was a deep sense of excitement at being home again; fear that he may have grown apart from his family, that they wouldn't know what to say to each other; anxiety that he felt more at home now with his fellow sappers in France than with his own kin.

Taking a deep breath, he knocked on the freshly painted front door. They would be expecting him as he'd managed to send a telegram to his father saying he would be coming home for a bit. The door opened, emitting a smell of frying rashers and eggs, and there was Edith, older now, more mature. Behind her he saw Wilfred and Leo, both with happy grins on their faces. Joe and Mina had gone to work, which was perhaps just as well as it would have been overwhelming to meet them all at once. They proudly delivered him into the dining room, where his dada had been reading the paper. Patrick got up and put his arms around Vincent, giving him a bear hug, a rare honor in post-Edwardian Ireland, where shows of intimacy were shied away from.

Edith took his cap and coat and put them on the hall stand. Leo took his kit bag up to the bedroom, and he sat down at the table, famished, ready for some of that delicious smelling fry. Tea was poured and then the innumerable questions, piled up over three years; tales of what happened in the street, their move to their new house—trying to condense three years of their lives into an hour's conversation.

The first day home was great, and exhausting. He fell asleep that night in a real bed, no gunfire, explosions, troop movements, and all the racket of a busy camp in wartime; just nighttime silence broken by the song of an occasional reveler. He didn't get up till ten the following morning, luxuriating in the fresh linen sheets, and the heaviness of the wool blankets against the cold of the December morning.

The prior night, Leo and Joe took him to Kelly's Cellars, a pub down on Bank Street. It was a pleasant walk through the city streets, the shops all dressed for the Christmas festivities, and worth it when he got a great welcome from Frank Short behind the bar, whom he remembered from pre-war days, with a free pint of Guinness "for his service", which made Vincent swell with pride. But it was so different from France and Belgium, where the estaminets were war torn, the clientele rough soldiers having a good time off and letting off steam. Kelly's seemed so refined in comparison. But the thing that got him most was the remoteness of everyone from the war. They had news of it every day, but it had been going on now for nearly three years, and it was old news.

But not for Vincent, it wasn't.

He spent his first Christmas at home since they shipped over to France, what seemed like eons ago. So much had happened in between. It was a happy occasion, Edith doing her best with the turkey, and all chipping in.

But a shadow began to hover over the house as Vincent was due to leave for France again on the 28th. He was at once depressed, and at the same time looked forward to seeing his comrades in arms again. It was hard to focus on anything, and it was almost with a sense of relief that he took the cab to the railway station and began the long journey back to the front. He was suffused with an unshakeable sense of guilt, leaving his family behind, not knowing if they'd ever see him alive again, and yet he was glad to be going back.

The 75th was his home now, no matter what hardships this involved. His friends were all on the front; he shared little in common with the people he met in the bar or on the street in Belfast. They had a different agenda and were fed up with the war and the privations it caused them.

CHAPTER 27

The Beginning of the End

*Six weeks prior, the German supreme command was
making plans for a quick finish to the long-drawn-out war.
Both sides were exhausted, both were getting reinforcements—
the Germans through the capitulation of Russia and the
freeing up of its armies on the Eastern Front; the Allies
were being bolstered by America's entry into the conflict.*

GROSSE HAUPTQUARTIER, KREUZNACH, GERMANY
November 11, 1917

Erich Ludendorff was not a person one would warm to. Nature
had cruelly bestowed upon him a perpetual scowl, and his temperament followed suit, making him a person with few friends.
Furrowed brows, a downturned pouting mouth and cold, steely blue
eyes that seemed to penetrate straight into a person's soul, deterred
anyone who wished to get on his good side. Not that it mattered
to Ludendorff, and in fact he probably regarded his stern visage as
an asset. As First Quartermaster-General of the Imperial German
Army's Great General Staff, he was one of the most powerful men
in the German war machine. He wasn't concerned whether he was
liked or not.

He was the chief policy maker in what was, to all intents and purposes, a military dictatorship, the Kaiser having bestowed almost all decision-making regarding policy and strategy to the German high command.

As he entered the conference chamber of the army headquarters in Kreuznach, all the other occupants of the room stood in deference. His superior, Field-Marshal Paul von Hindenburg, was not present, nor were any representatives of the government.

When all were seated, the murmur of conversation died down; he stared around at the expectant officers facing him, then commenced with his opening remarks.

"Gentlemen, we are at a critical situation in the execution of this war." He paused, letting the silence emphasize his remarks. "As you know, Russia is in the throes of revolution, and has no stomach for a prolonged war with Germany, and so are seeking a peace agreement. When this is signed in the near future, they will no longer be a threat, and we will withdraw most of our troops from the Eastern Front. I would estimate we can add forty-two divisions to our armies in France and Belgium."

He stood, placed both hands on the table and leaned forward, throwing emphasis on his next remarks.

"The British are weakened by prolonged fighting against our superior forces, their troops are tired, and the government is looking for a peace agreement. I think we are close to victory gentlemen. As you also know, the United States of America has declared war on us, but as yet, has almost no army on the European Continent, and while I'm unsure of how many troops they will send, I don't anticipate any arriving before the summer." He paused again and took a sip of water from his glass. "The French are stronger, but tired of war too. In May their armies mutinied, and though Pétain has made concessions, their morale is very low. This is our opportunity. This is it!" he shouted as he slapped the table with his right hand. "But we need to act quickly, before the Americans start to arrive."

The murmuring around the room dissipated as he raised his hands.

"We must attack as early as possible in the spring as soon as it is dry enough for our troops to move quickly over the ground we gain. We have been selecting special *Sturmtruppen*[113] to operate as infiltration groups, breaking up the enemy defense. Some of our finest troops are being readied as I speak, and seasoned infantry and artillery are being brought together, while our best officers are being trained in infiltration methods. As you are aware, we have been perfecting these tactics for some time now, and I believe we can defeat the enemy this time. We will drive the British Expeditionary Force off the continent; the French will have no stomach for further fighting, and it will be too late for the Americans to do anything."

He pushed his chair back and walked over to a large map of Northern France and Belgium hanging on the wall. With a pointer

---

113 Stormtroopers of shock troops.

in his hand, he turned towards the table. Chairs creaked on the floor as the attendees turned to face him.

"What we have to decide is where to carry out our penetration. I believe we should separate the French and British armies, and push the British northwards, toward the coast, into the sea. Do we have any suggestions gentlemen?"

Ludendorff knew two things. The first was that the British, and for that matter, the French would figure out that his army would plan an offensive in the spring. Their thinking would follow the same logic as his own. The second was that the contents of this meeting would leak out, and eventually find its way into the enemy camp. These were certainties. Hence, to obfuscate the enemy's intelligence gathering, he would ask now for a number of possible starting points and make preparations at each one. That would leave the British and French guessing. Crown Prince Wilhelm's chief-of-staff, Von der Schulenberg, suggested the Verdun area, where the BEF and French forces joined up; a logical and strategically effective approach.

General Hermann von Kuhl, who was on the General Staff, stood and walked over to the map. "We should attack in Flanders and take the ports," he said, sweeping his hand across the northern part of the map. "That way, we can prevent them from sending fresh troops, and slow down the American buildup. Then we encircle the British army"—another sweep of his hand— "and they will have no choice but to sue for peace," he continued, and Ludendorff nodded.

This was exactly how he wanted it.

Field-Marshal Rupprecht, the Crown Prince of Bavaria, who commanded his own army group, asked, "What will our objectives be, General?" His dislike for the bourgeois soldier could not be hidden in his voice.

Ludendorff said, somewhat cryptically, "We will punch a hole and let the rest follow." He bestowed his frigid gaze on Rupprecht, returning his antipathy, and then some.

This lack of strategy was to be the rock on which Lundendorff's ship would founder.

• • •

ARRAS
December 28, 1917

As he sat in the carriage of the train, winding its torturous way to Arras, Vincent looked in amazement at the wreckage and debris of war they were passing through. But what really astonished him was the air of defeat that seemed to pervade through the frontal zone.

Soldiers on the roads walked or stumbled along, but he saw little marching. There were many stops on the long journey, and everywhere he sensed the men had lost heart. Winter could do that to you, even when there was no war. The short, grey days, cold, rain, poor rations, and little home leave, combined with the knowledge they were entering into another year of an apparently endless war, would crush even the most optimistic among them.

There were rumors that the British Government were having peace talks, and the idea that all those lives would have been sacrificed for nothing was, to put it mildly, dispiriting.

To put it less mildly, he thought, *it was a fucking disaster.*

• • •

The Battle of Cambrai had exhausted the Guards, and morale was at rock bottom. This was evident in a letter from one lieutenant Lindsay Mackay who was with the 11th Argyll and Sutherland Highlanders.

"1st. January.

Battalion moved back in the afternoon to Simencourt. Roads iced and very slippy. Passed the Guards' transport column en route. Have never seen any transport in such a filthy condition. We took over billets and huts from the Guards Division. Their discipline must have been knocked out of them by the Cambrai show for their huts were in a shocking state - in many cases the planking of the roofs had been taken off and used as firewood. In some the walls had been similarly treated, and the huts were consequently useless."[114]

• • •

STIRLING CAMP
February 2, 1918

The atmosphere in the old Nissan hut that served as an estaminet resembled a dirty pea-soup fog, though the smell of spilt liquor, damp wool, and unwashed bodies was indisputably worse.

The hut was probably the only fully intact building standing in the village of Saint-Nicholas, just north of Arras, surrounded by roofless houses and the remains of the church. Among the bodies crammed in there were four sappers who had been drinking most of the evening, enjoying the release, and rubbing shoulders with men from the other regiments, laughing, singing, and all relaxing after a stint at the front. As they caroused, time passed without anyone taking notice.

Finally, Jimmy Green nudged Vincent and nodded at the old pendulum clock on the wall. It was 9:30 p.m. Their pass was up at 9:00, and bleary eyed, they pulled one of their other mates out of the arms of a young French lady, grabbed Ned Duggan, who was in the process of selling a German "souvenir" he'd "come by" to an Australian

---

114 Excerpt from the diary of Lieutenant Lindsey Mackay.

soldier, and started their wavering walk back to camp. They were singing "Tipperary" as they came up to the gate to be met by Sergeant Pring, who, being on duty, and not able to go out himself that night, took the matter very seriously. Ned had disappeared, and somehow, found his way into the camp without going through the gate.

The next day, Vincent, nursing a stinking headache and dry mouth, presented himself with his mates, sans Ned, who didn't get charged, at Major Briggs' hut, with CSM Pring in attendance. Each had their passes stopped for the next fourteen days.

For each of those days, he reminded himself that he didn't have a headache, had a bit more money in his pocket and was staying out of trouble. *Look on the bright side*, he told himself. *It was good to be back.*

Ned, in the meantime, continued to do a roaring trade in "souvenirs" at the estaminet. The day after they'd been hauled before the CO, Vincent challenged Ned as to how he didn't end up in trouble.

Ned just shrugged. "I've me own entrance into the camp," he replied enigmatically, then added, "I'd made arrangements with the fella at the gate to log me in at nine o'clock. Cost me a bit of whiskey, but y'know, a fella's gotta do what a fella's got to do." He grinned, his bad yellow teeth stained with nicotine. "Ya know?"

Vincent grinned back, and shaking his head walked off.

Life in the camp hummed on.

75th Field Company War Diary
February 16, 1918.

Section 1 revetting railway bank at camp and making accommodation. No. 2 filling in old trenches round Inn strong-point. Finishing bombing straight in Chili Ave. at reserve line. No. 3 water supply, railway duck-boarding and maintenance. Gas proofing, repairing Northumberland Lane. No. 4 wiring from Inn Strong Point to Hyderabad Switch.

(Note: the trenches all had names, and in this area, they were in groups of names, each group beginning with a different letter of the alphabet. Hydrabad, Humid, Hopeful, Hectic, Haggard and so on. DMC.)

Work continued uneventfully on the trenches until the end of February.

March 7, 1918.

No. 1 as on 6th and altering Machine Gun emplacement's and making infantry exits in strong points. No. 2 Lemon trench dugouts and wiring west of Quarry Dump – Central Brigade Sector. (H 18 b and d). No. 4 as 4th.

No. 548378 Sapper Hall R.E. (Reg. patrol No. 3 Acc) died of wounds. Buried at L'Abbeyette. Lewis Gun lectures and instruction by Sgt. of attached infantry commences for 8 OR.

2 sections wiring and digging with working party of 200 on strong point between Hendecourt and Gicheux. Two sections wiring trench covering Blairville.

• • •

On the 21st of March, one of the greatest artillery bombardments of the war, delivering over one-million shells over a five-hour period, began from the German lines, between Arras and Reims in the south. This was closely followed with lightning attacks by the German stormtroopers that pushed the British lines back and then further back; the Bosch were unstoppable. It was beginning to look like the end for the retreating British army. General Ludendorrf's offensive had begun. They called it "*Operation Michael.*" Planning for this last desperate assault had begun four months previously.

• • •

The Treaty of Brest-Litovsk, ensuring peace between Germany and Russia, was signed on March 3, 1918, freeing up fifty divisions of the German army, who were rapidly transported to the Western Front.

On March the 21st, *Operation Michael* started with an attack at the hinge between the British and French armies at Saint Quentin. Later, operations *Georgette* and *Mars* struck further north with the objective of taking the coastal ports.

The British were indeed pushed back, with the possibility of a German victory becoming more likely every day.

• • •

Operation Michael was *the* major part of the offensive, while the others were of a diversionary nature. It was launched from the Hindenburg Line, in the vicinity of Saint-Quentin, France. The intention of General Ludendorff was to break through the Allied lines and advance in a north-westerly direction to seize the Channel Ports, which supplied the BEF and then to drive the BEF into the sea. Then he changed the plan and pushed due west, along the whole of the British front southwest of the River Somme. This was designed to first separate the French and British Armies before continuing with the original concept of pushing the BEF to the coast.

The offensive ended at Villers-Bretonneux, a small town south of the Somme and a short distance to the east of the Allied communications center at Amiens, which was threatened with capture.

However, the Allies managed to halt the German advance. The German Army had suffered many casualties and was unable to maintain supplies to the advancing troops.

• • •

At the same time, the American Expeditionary Force, or AEF, was becoming a major factor in the fighting. Although the first troops, often known as "Doughboys",[115] began to arrive as early as April 1917, under the command of Major General John Pershing, they weren't involved in any action until late October, and then only in a small role. The impact of the AEF really started to make itself felt in the spring of 1918.

By May of that year, over one million American troops had arrived in France through the ports of Bordeaux, La Pallice, Saint Nazaire, and Brest. From these ports they entrained on the French railway system to the front.

At the same time, American engineers were building new ship berths, almost 1,000 miles of additional standard-gauge track, and telephone and telegraph lines.

• • •

Earlier in the month, Vincent had been "volunteered", with John Kelly and six others, into going to Lewis gun lectures and demonstrations. They were happy enough and thought it would make a change from the usual work, and they'd have fun firing the gun on the range. No one considered for a moment that they might just have to use it in anger.

They met with the gunnery sergeant in the mess hut, where he had a new Lewis gun all ready to go. He was a small, wiry individual, with a grey moustache and short-cropped grey hair and bright blue eyes, which he used to great effect as he gazed around the room at this bunch of engineers.

---

115 "Doughboy" is believed to have originated during the American Civil War, from the large globular buttons on the Union uniform that resembled lumps of dough.

God 'elp us, he thought, *if we 'ave to rely on this lot.* Then, as soon as he opened his mouth, he gave away his cockney origins.

"OK, my lads, my name's Sergeant Lockhart, an' by the time we're finished this course, yez'll all be bloody experts with the Lewis gun. We need a team of seven, mostly to carry the spare magazines, but also spare parts." He paused and looked at them. "This, my friends, is a beautiful weapon, it's abou' 'alf the weight of a Vickers gun, easy to transport, good firin' rate, about 500 to 600 rounds per minute, 'n uses 303 rounds, just like yer Lee Enfields. These magazines carry forty-seven rounds an' 'as to be loaded by 'and. By the time I've finished wiv yez, yez'll be able to strip it down 'n put it back together in a minute, blindfolded. An' yez'll just be itchin' to get out and kill some Bosch wiv it." He paused, "Won' you my lads?" Then, giving them an evil grin, he continued, "keep a wad o' cotton wool in yer pocket, it 'elps wiv the cleanin' and yez'll need it for pluggin' yer ears … Now, let's ge' on wiv it."

As he talked, a bit of spit was forming at the corners of the sergeant's mouth, which Vincent couldn't take his eyes off. He looked at John, who'd also spotted it, and it was all they two could do to keep a straight face, as the Sergeant went on '*wiv*' his lecture. He glanced their way, and their smiles disappeared as the blue eyes bored into them.

The sergeant placed the gun on the table and proceeded to slowly dismantle it. He showed them the clock recoil spring, unique to the Lewis, and how to adjust it for temperature and wear. Then the air-cooling system, how gas from the exploding cartridge was used to drive a piston which helped load the next round and discharge the spent cartridge. He explained that the firing system was good enough to get off just a few single rounds, or continuous fire, but that it would start to overheat after eleven or twelve magazines had been used.

"What do we do if it overheats?" asked Vincent.

"Fuckin' piss on it." Replied the sergeant, giving Vincent a baleful stare. "Fuckin' engineers," he muttered to himself.

They spent a week stripping it down, reassembling it, cleaning it, fixing problems, and eventually actually firing the gun.

The 75th could now honestly call itself a machine gun company, a designation they were very proud of.

• • •

75th Field Company War Diary
March 25, 1918.
Sappers working on line near Adinfer. Transport leaves Ransart at noon and marches via Berles – Bois and Pommier to La Cauchie. OC and sappers arrive La Cauchie at 5 pm.

March 26, 1918.
Section parade La Cauchie 2 pm and go up to dig line covering Hendescourt and Windmill Hill. On completion of work, sappers return to billets in Ransart.

March 27, 1918.
Dismounted men wire line covering Hendescourt and on completion of work receive orders to hold the line just wired to support a possible retirement.[116] *Lewis gun sent forward from Transport lines.*

• • •

---

116 The engineers were trained in the use of infantry weapons and were sometimes required to back up the infantry. This seems to have been the case on March 27th, when they received orders to "Hold the line" that they had just finished wiring, to support a possible retreat.

Ned and Sam said they'd prefer to use their rifles, as they laid out the magazines they'd carried up, where they were easily accessible; meanwhile, Vincent and John disassembled and checked the Lewis gun, cleaning the parts and working the mechanisms. Vincent set the recoil spring, and they put it all together again. Nerves had been running a little high as they set up their defense just outside the old cemetery on the outskirts of Hendescourt. The silence was splintered as they had a test firing, then after a few minutes, a few courageous birds began to sing again.

The rest of the company had taken up positions behind the ancient headstones. Vincent wondered idly what the corpses lying below them would think if they could see what was going on at their last resting place. He shuddered as he hoped they wouldn't be joining them. It was late afternoon, as they lay behind a low wall that gave them reasonable cover from being seen by an approaching enemy but wouldn't be much help once the Germans discovered their position. But before that happened, the attackers had to scramble over their own old trenches, then negotiate the lines of barbed wire the 75th had laid down.

The big guns were relatively silent as the troops behind began an orderly retreat, while the Engineers held the line. Further south, and west, the fighting had been very heavy, with the British falling back as the German shocktroops forged relentlessly forward, taking back all the hard-won ground. For the first time, it seemed as if they were losing, and that all the years of hard fighting were coming to an end, with victory in sight for Germany.

It began to grow colder as the afternoon wore on, but thankfully it didn't rain. Sentries were allocated and the rest of them made the best of the situation, as the night wore on. Wrapped in their greatcoats, they tried to get some rest. Sleep came eventually despite the flashes of artillery fire and flares further west of them.

The two at the Lewis gun took it in turns to nap, one always keeping it ready.

• • •

75th Field Company War Diary
March 28, 1918.
Dismounted part of Company continue to hold line covering Hendecourt. At night continue covering of line N. of village.

• • •

Thick stratus cloud was promising rain later in the day, which they hoped should slow the enemy down, when early in the afternoon, they heard shouting and gunfire to the right.

The engineering company holding that section of the line was letting go with everything they had, including a couple of machine guns. Then their own lookouts shouted a warning and seeing a group of grey clad figures about 500 yards away, they opened up with the Lewis gun. They were on the Germans' flank and in a position to provide enfilading fire, which they commenced with gusto. The withering fire from in front, with the 75th's enfilading barrage slowed the enemy down as they tried to negotiate the wire, and finally they fell back in retreat.

The sappers of the 75th FC lay there through the rest of the afternoon, hearts beating, waiting for a second assault.

It never came.

• • •

75th Field Company War Diary
March 29, 1918.
Situation improved and men withdrawn from line into shelters at N. end of village. Continue to wire line and dug "T" heads in old German trench running north towards Ficheux. Three men wounded.

March 30, 1918.
Same as 29th. Transport lines remain at La Cauchie forward billet moved to Blairville (X 4 a.8.7.) and is accommodated in cellars.

March 31, 1918.
2 sections wiring and digging with working party of 200 on strong point between Hendescourt and Gicheux. Two sections wiring trench covering Blairville.

• • •

Vincent's fears of a German victory were ill founded. The enemy had again made the mistake of advancing too far without proper support, as the ground over the area they took was so damaged, the roads all sabotaged and even the water in the wells poisoned, that they were unable to continue the advance. Ludendorrf, unusual for a German General, had no real plan to continue the assault. They did succeed in gaining a distance of about forty miles, in a salient, or curve, that somewhat resembled the scowl on Ludendorff's face when he began to realize his offensive was petering out.

While the stormtroopers were a very successful concept, by the very nature of their *modus operandi* they carried little food or ammunition with them, relying on supplies from the rear. The direction of the German advance was across the wasteland that had become the countryside either side of the Somme. It became equally difficult to move supporting artillery across this moonscape, denying the infantry their necessary support. It was a Pyrrhic victory for Ludendorff.

• • •

Sitting on a headstone in the cemetery, which they had defended so vigorously, smoking a cigarette, Vincent gazed across the once-more-quiet field. The long grass and weeds in this neglected farmland blew gently in the early April breeze, warmed by a gentle sun. Despite all the noise and mayhem, the birds were still performing. As he listened to a thrush singing its heart out, he thought about the vicious fighting that took place over the last few days; tens of thousands of British and Commonwealth soldiers now lay dead, not to mention the German troops who had given their lives. A generous share of the losses were Irishmen, hoping their country would see Home Rule as a result of their sacrifice. He shook his head in sorrow at the futility of it all.

He could see Ned Duggan out there, foraging for souvenirs— helmets, medals, watches, anything the dead Germans no longer needed. These would fetch good prices in the estaminets, especially to the Aussies and new American troops flooding into the war zone.

Good luck to him, Vincent thought fondly. *He's a bloody scoundrel, but he's also a survivor. He'll come through this whole thing in one piece, and who knows what he'll do afterward; but he'll make money and make his way up in the world.*

He got up wearily, stubbed his cigarette out on the headstone, and, realizing what he had just done, apologized to the incumbent. Then he picked up his rifle and trudged back to their billets.

CHAPTER 28

Of Ghosts and Introspection

There are more guests at table than the hosts
Invited; the illuminated hall
Is thronged with quiet, inoffensive ghosts,
As silent as the pictures on the wall...

(Henry Wadsworth Longfellow)

STIRLING CAMP, NE OF ARRAS
April 29, 1918

A tea urn sat in the middle of the bare wooden table, as Kelly, O'Boyle, McLaughlin, Duggan, Vincent, and that young cockney lad who had joined the company a few months ago, Mick Kitchens, sat around it, their mugs filled with well stewed tea.

The rain was pelting down outside the Nissen hut, running in a stream past the door. It was freezing cold, and the hut was infused with a cozy fug, thanks to the wood stove going full belt. A few oil lights gave a low illumination, casting flickering shadows around the hut. They'd no desire to go anywhere tonight, and so they just sat there playing cards and chatting. The conversation drifted back to a month ago when they had buried Edgar Hall, one of the sappers who had been caught in No-Man's Land and took a sniper's bullet in the chest. He'd died the following day.

They'd liked Edgar, who was one of those people who always managed to see the bright side of things, which was an asset in the trenches. He was always up there offering to help the new sappers and would volunteer for anything.

"Anyway, he's gone now," said Ned Duggan. "I hope he's in a better place than this, an' with better tea to drink." As he gulped down the bitter strong tea, screwing up his face. "Jayus, it's awful stuff, this."

"I d … d … did his numbers," stammered O'Boyle.

"What're ye talking about?" Duggan asked him.

"Y … ye know, numerology, I … learned to work out the numbers and w … what t … tuh …they mean," Boyle said in a rush, trying not to let his stammer get the better of him. "H … h … each letter of the a … alphab … bet has a number c … c … corresp … pondin' to its place," he explained. "T … then I h … have this book, which … which explains what it sig … signifies."

The rest of the boys were all looking at him, incredulous.

O'Boyle had the book in his pocket, well thumbed through and dog-eared; he pulled it out and wrote down Hall's name—'*Edgar N Hall*'—and then put the numbers under each letter. He kept adding until it came down to a single digit, which was the number one.

"Show me," said Duggan, grabbing the book. "It'd take ye forever to tell us, John," he said then, ribbing him good-naturedly.

"One, yeh, it says he's independent, and … what's that word, Vinnie?"

Vincent looked at the book. "Innovative," he said. "But look here, it says ones are big risk takers. D'you remember how he jumped out of the shell hole to try and get back to the trench? He should've stayed put," said Vincent. "Look where it got him."

"Ach, I don't know, all this numerology shit," groaned McLaughlin.

And then the discussion turned to the paranormal.

"D'yez believe in ghosts?" asked Ned. "I saw me sister a while back, when we were in the billets in Pilgrim Camp, back there in Proven. She was just standing there, between the tents, looking at me and smiling." He said it gazing into space, recalling the memory. "I got such a shock, I dropped the box I was carryin' and when I looked up, she was gone." He went on to explain he never said anything to anyone, because he thought no one would believe him.

"Well, I can only remember what I saw at the Chateau de Trois Tours," Vincent replied.

"I was talkin' a while back to some Canadians, 'n they told me a story about one of their lads," John Kelly said. "We were chattin' in an estaminet, and they were sayin' that this fella, em ... I think his name is Bird or sumpin'... anyway, he was sharin' a bivvy[117] dug into the railway bank, I think they were in Vimy at the time, with some others, an' he was asleep when suddenly his brother pulls the cover off and tells him to come with 'im. Now, you might say, 'what's wrong with that?' Well, nothin' really, 'cept his brother was killed a year earlier." John paused while this sunk in, then continued. "Well, the brother took him off to a part of the village that was in ruins, and then Bird missed him when he went around a corner, and when he tried to find him, he was gone." John looked around again at the group of his mates. He had the floor. "He looks for him, the brother, but he's nowhere to be seen. So, this guy sits down and waits for the brother to come back, but he never did. Then he falls asleep, he's so tired after all the work during the day."

Another pause. John could tell a good story.

"Fuck's sake, go on," said Sam. "What happened then?"

"Well, the sun had come up when some of his mates woke him up. They'd been looking for him. They told him that a shell had hit the bivvy he was in, and all they found was one of his mate's legs, and a helmet. They thought he'd been in there too. And," added John, "the lads who told me swore upside down it was true."[118]

"Jaysus."

"Yez, never know."

"Strange things happen out here."

"Wot're you lot doing in here!" called Sergeant Pring, who had just come into the hut, banging open the door and shaking off his topcoat.

Outside, the night had come early, with the low dense cloud, and though the rain had stopped, a dense fog was drifting through the camp, dripping off the edge of the buildings. Inside, the warmth was inviting, the table with the lads sitting at it lit by a few lanterns, the rest of the hut in shadow.

"We were just chattin' about ghosts," said Vincent. "You got any good stories, Sarge?"

"Blow me down, ye could pave the roads wiv this stuff," Pring said, pouring himself a cup of tea, and continued. "Yeh, there was a story I heard from some of the infantry lads, who'd been at Mons. It seems that two lads from the same company were in a shell hole, when they saw an ole' woman standing there on the battle-field, right in their line of fire. She wuz dressed real weird like, wiv a bonnet an' all an' a blue dress. She stood right in their line of fire but seemed

---

118 Will R. Bird. *Ghosts Have Warm Hands*. Clark, Irwin and Company, 1968.

unconcerned. They thought she might be a Belgian farmer's wife, but then they realized that the bullets were none of 'em hittin' her. Then a third lad, older than themselves, said it was his old mother, come to get 'im. Jaysus, if that same minute, a shell didn't explode close by, and a piece of shrapnel killed him stone dead."

With that, Kitchens, who, unusually for a Londoner, had said nothing during the discussion, piped up.

"I've 'eard of a secret society in London called The Ghost Club. There was a 'fing in the paper, 'bout it. Charles Dickens wuz a member, and I 'fink, Conan Doyle wuz in it. 'As anyone else 'eard of it?"

"I've heard of it," said Vincent. "I read about it in a paper too, the *Daily Mail* I think, it was a while back though. They investigated supernatural things, and there was somethin' about how they would come to all the meetings, even the ones who were dead. But y'know, we live in a strange world here, dead bodies all round, every time we dig a new trench there's bits of people turning up. One day we're alive and the next we're dead. It seems every few days we're puttin' one of our pals in the ground … I think sometimes they don't know which side of the curtain they're on, whether they're alive or dead."

A thoughtful silence descended on the company, as they looked at each other, wondering who would be next to "cop a packet".

THE GHOST CLUB

For the reader interested in the paranormal, the Ghost Club did in fact exist. It was founded in Cambridge in 1855 and is still in existence. Its origins lay with a group of fellows at Trinity College who met regularly to discuss ghosts and psychic phenomena. It was set up in London in 1862, and had many prominent members at different times, including Charles Dickens, Sir Arthur Conan Doyle, scientists such as Sir William Crookes, Sir Oliver Lodge, the Irish poet, W.B. Yeats, and Sir Julian

Huxley. When Dickens died, it was dissolved, but reincarnated in 1882, and still continues to investigate psychic phenomena to this day.

The study and experiencing of the paranormal was very popular towards the end of the nineteenth century and beginning of the twentieth. The war itself heightened the sense of the afterlife, especially for the soldiers who lived with the everyday possibility of being killed.

75th Field Company War Diary
April 29, 1918.
Same as 28th. OC goes round line with GOC Division to select outpost line for Reserve System.

• • •

Vincent "celebrated" his 24th birthday in 1918 in somewhat subdued circumstances, as they were back in the front line at this stage.

No candles on that cake!

May was spent by the company in La Herliere working on the trenches and preparing wells, roads, and bridges for demolition as the Allies were being pushed back by the German offensive.

CHAPTER 29

The Endgame

We are but chessmen, destined, it is plain,
That great chess-player, Heaven, to entertain;
It moves us on life's chess-board to and fro,
And then in death's dark box shuts up again.

(Omar Khayyam)

June 28, 1918

The steady rains of April eased up as spring morphed into summer. Summer, even in war, lifted the spirits, and the withdrawal of German troops after the Spring Offensive presaged a heightened mood of impending victory; the steady arrival of the Americans helped elevate the temper of the troops.

On June 28, troops from the 80th division of the United States Army joined the Guards Division, going into the front line for their first experience of active warfare.[119]

The following are correspondences from the Guards division:

---

119 This was the first American involvement with the Guards division. US troops had already engaged the German army at the battle of Cantigny May 27, to June 5, 1918.

"Guards Division 'Q' to Transport Officer, 1st Guards Bde.— Draw 6 bottles of whiskey from divisional Soldiers' Club and deliver to Bde. H.Q. for American officers attached."

"G.O.C. 1st Guards Bde. to Guards Division 'Q' – on behalf of all officers of the American Army attached to brigade under my command I wish to express my deepest thanks for the courteous present of whiskey foreshadowed in your message. I am requested to add that these officers accept the gift as proof of the solidarity of the union existing between the American and British nations, which will endure 'til the whisky runs out."

The American soldiers proved their mettle in two attacks in August on Guards posts manned by them, where they successfully drove the attacking infantry back.

The British counter offensive began on August 8, described by General Ludendorff as "A Black Day for the German army."

75th Field Company War Diary
August 21, 1918.

Division attacked in front of Moyenville and reached objective on Arras-Albert railway. 1 sect. on water points. Horse troughs and pumps at sugar Factory Bairy at X 20 and at pod in Adinfer Village. R.E. reconnaissance of captured area by Lt. Ross. 1 section under Lt. Reid made mule track from A 26 b.1.1 to A 9 a.5.5. R.E. stores guided up to all Battn. HQ in forward position on supply tanks. Nos. 2 & 3 sections rejoin Company.

August 22, 1918.

Continued maintenance and improvement to horse water points. Made track improvements to take artillery. R.E. reconnaissance parties.

• • •

By the beginning of September, the Germans had been driven from all the areas of the old battlefields of the Somme.

They were in retreat.

On the 3rd of September the following is recorded:

"The 2nd and 3rd Guards brigades went over the top under a creeping barrage … and—found nothing whatever in front of them save a prodigious number of dead horses, some few corpses and an intolerable buzzing of flies! As they topped the ridge above Lagnicourt, they saw against the first light of the sun, dump after German dump blazing palely towards the east. That was all. They wandered, wondering, into a vast, grassy, uninhabited plain that stretched away towards the Bapaume—Cambrai Road. Not a machine gun broke the stupefying stillness …" [120]

However, this easy march forward ended at the Canal du Nord, where the German army made a stand.

The job of crossing the canal and taking the Hindenburg line behind it fell to the Guards division.

75th Field Company War Diary
September 12, 1918.
Same as 11th and making scaling ladders. Lt. Lawrie MC appointed Adj. R.E. Guards Division.

• • •

IRELAND
c. 1954

I was at school when Vincent had the accident. I do remember that, but not exactly when or what age I was, though I'd say about nine.

---

120 *The Irish Guards in the Great War* by Rudyard Kipling.

We lived in a semi-detached house, or duplex as they are known in the U.S. The residents were good, solid people, policemen, carpenters, nurses and so on. I suppose it would be called nowadays "affordable housing". At any rate, the gutters had become blocked, and being a little short of money and always practical, my dad decided to make his own ladder. Nothing seemed strange about that, but looking back, why would he do that? At any rate, we had witnessed the new ladder, which consisted of two twenty-foot long, four-by-two pieces of timber, with two-by-one pieces nailed between them as steps. He didn't trim the ends or anything else like that—a very simple affair. He'd got it out that day, and put it up against the wall, with the base on the grass behind the house. Being Ireland, the grass was always wet. Then he climbed up with his bucket and trowel to clear the gutter. The base slipped, and down came the ladder, coming to rest when the top went through a downstairs window and hung there. His legs jammed in the rungs, and he was very badly hurt—he could have easily been killed. There followed a long spell in bed before he was mobile again.

Not long after, gangrene set in with one of his legs, and he ended up having it amputated. I've heard that a long-term effect of chlorine gas was poor circulation. Smoking, as that doctor had warned him at the front-line hospital, didn't help either.

Why am I telling this story?

I tell this little story because, when I looked at photos of the trench ladders they made for the assault on the canal, I saw a replica of the one my father made. It was there, in the trenches, where he learned that particular piece of carpentry.

• • •

75th Field Company War Diary
September 13, 1918.
Repair of Boursies – Demicourt Road.

September 14, 1918.
Ditto. 17 of No. 1 section sent to hospital – gassed.

September 17, 1918.
Same as 16th and gas-proofing dugouts. Reconnaissance of Demicourt for water. None found.

• • •

The weather was hot—Indian summer conditions were prevailing, and the animals suffered terribly. The retreating Germans had poisoned the wells, and water became a precious commodity.

The men had first call on the water, but the horses, especially those pulling the heavy artillery pieces forward, were having a very difficult time.

• • •

75th Field Company War Diary
September 27, 1918.
Division attacked across Canal Du Nord. Company made crossing at Demicourt – Graincourt Road. *Started work at 8.30 am – crossing ready for all arms by 12 midday.*

• • •

The task allotted to the Engineers was to get the artillery across the Canal du Nord with as little delay as possible. Before the battle, it had been impossible to build any roads or bridges across the canal, but everything possible had been done to prepare the equipment for immediate installation of crossings.

• • •

75th Field Company War Diary
September 30, 1918.
Making Flesquiere – Ribecourt Road *with 4 Companies 2nd Coldstream Guards. Maintaining canal crossing.*

October 8, 1918.
Marcoing. *2nd and 3rd Division attacked. Guards Division prepared to go through but held line at night. 1 section Div. HQ. Company moved to Marcoing.*

October 9, 1918.
Rumilly. *Division advanced . Company moved with transport to billets in Rumilly. 2 sections work on Masniers – Crevecourt Road. 1 section on Div. HQ. Reconnaissance for water.*

October 10, 1918.
Wambaix. *Company moves to Wambaix. 1 section on Div. HQ Seranvillers, 1 section on Crevecourt – Masnieres Road. One section on water supply Rumilly.*

October 11, 1918.
Quievy. *Company moved with transport to Quievy. One section water supply Bevillers. One section water supply Carnieres.*

• • •

When the Germans had retreated from the Hindenburg Line after the battle of Cambrai, they established a new defensive position to the east of the River Selle. From there, their resistance stiffened.

To continue the assault, the Fourth Army under General Rawlinson had to find a way to cross the river and attack the German defensive positions behind it. Their main target was the area around Valenciennes. From there, the German railway center at Aulnoye would be within artillery range.

After the costly fighting at Cambrai and St. Quentin, there was time for the artillery to come up from the rear and for preparations to be made to cross the obstacles of the Selle River and its surroundings. Moving the artillery and other equipment meant horse drawn transport, but water was nowhere to be found and became an increasing problem for the advancing army.

• • •

75th Field Company War Diary
October 12, 1918.
2 sections erecting water troughs in Erclin River. 2 troughs made and erected. 1 section drinking supply Quievy. 1 section repairing demolished bridge over river at D 19 b.7.7. Bridge completed for single lorry traffic.

October 15, 1918.
Making barrel bridges for crossing of Selle River. Collecting material for heavy bridge.

October 17, 1918.
St. Hilaire. Company with transport to St. Hilaire. Barrel bridges taken to railway at V 28 a 97 and camouflaged. 6 complete bridges stacked. Lts. Ross and Winch reconnoiter river N. of St Python.

October 18, 1918.
Made 4 more barrel bridges and carted to forward dump. 2nd Lt. Winch reconnoiters Selle River with infantry patrol with view to bridging.

• • •

The tasks given to the Pioneers prior to the crossing of the River Selle were (1) to construct footbridges for the infantry before zero hour on the 20th of October, and (2) the construction of pontoon or trestle bridges as soon as possible after zero hour for the passage of field guns across the river to assist the infantry in the event of a counter-attack by enemy tanks. Then, (3) the construction of a bridge at St. Python capable of carrying tanks and heavy vehicles. There was also the possibility that another bridge might be required to relieve any congestion of traffic there might be on the bridge at St. Python.

It was anticipated that the provision of the footbridges would be the most difficult of these tasks as it involved a long carry down the slope from the railway line, exposed to the close-range fire of the Germans. Eight footbridges were to be used, four on the front of each attacking brigade, and at each alternate bridge it should be duplicated if possible, and a spare pier and grid dumped at each bridge in case repairs were needed.

The 75th and 76th Field Companies were allotted the task of erecting the footbridges. This would have to be done in the dark, under possible enemy fire. They had to carry the bridges down the steep banks of the Selle, which were very slippery due to heavy rainfall, and under complete silence. Splashing had to be avoided when the bridges were put in the water. They succeeded in getting their trestles fixed into the bed of the river, but one of them sank into a deep muddy hole.

The British 3rd and 1st Armies, north of the 4th Army, maintained the offensive pressure the following day.

In a surprise joint night attack in the early morning of the 20th of October, 3rd Army formations secured the high ground east of the Selle. Following a two-day pause to bring up heavy artillery, the attack was renewed on 23rd of October with a major combined assault by 4th, 3rd, and 1st Armies; the fighting, which continued into the next day, resulted in further advances. At this stage, the German Army was retreating at a forced but controlled pace. On October 24, the German Army counterattacked at the Canal de la Dérivation but were repulsed and pushed back by the Belgian Army.

On the 26th of October, Erich Ludendorff, First Quartermaster General of the German Army, resigned under pressure from Kaiser Wilhelm II.

CHAPTER 30

Crossing the River Styx

According to Greek Mythology, the River Styx separated this world from the underworld. The ferryman Charon is often described as having transported the souls of the newly dead across this river into the underworld. In ancient times some believed that a coin (Charon's obol) placed in the mouth of a dead person would pay the toll for the ferry across the river.

If they could not pay the fee, they could never pass into the underworld.

> My God this water is cold,
> As we step in off the bank
> My feet are losin' their hold,
> Soft mud, glutinous and dank.
> Let's pull it together my merry men,
> Get this bridge to the other side,
> So we can cheat the ferryman,
> And not pay him for the ride.
>
> (Derek McCann. "Bridging the River Selle")

SAINT-PYTHON
October 19–20, 1918

The night stillness was broken suddenly by the hoarse quack of a duck, somewhere along the river, then silence again. Occasional frogs could be heard grunting, but otherwise an eerie stillness shrouded the oily blackness of the slowly moving water. Even the battered landscape seemed to be holding its breath. The mist swirling around ruined buildings, revealing, then hiding them again. Heavy rain had lashed down all day, but late in the evening it had stopped, and a thick fog descended over the water, wafting in and out of the reeds on the steep grass-covered banks. It resembled the River Styx with Death and the Underworld waiting on the other side.

The German sentries on the far side of the river were listening for any sound of the British using the cover of the dense miasma to stage an attack, but there was nothing.

There was no light, the darkness compounded by the fog was all enveloping. The group of ten sappers and pioneers carrying the makeshift barrel bridge walked slowly forward, with a man in front following the tape. More pioneers followed behind with the planks for the roadway.

At 10 pm the previous night, the 19th, they had put down guide tapes in the drenching rain, and now, with boots covered in rags to prevent any noise, Sergeant Pring leading the way, they found the top of the riverbank, and began their precarious, silent descent, slithering down the steep sides, grunting, muttering silent curses as their feet slipped then gained traction again.

The tapes were the only way they could find the river, waist high and freezing cold in the middle. It was a blessed relief when the barrels floated into the black water, held in position with ropes as they waded across. On the other side, Vincent took his stake, one to each man, and with a club hammer covered in rags, as gently as possible pounded it into the mud. These would be used to hold the bridge in place.

Their orders were to proceed silently, but if the Germans opened fire on them, to lay there with the pontoon and wait until the artillery barrage opened up.

Excellent planning, Vincent thought to himself. *With just a couple of small flaws … If there hadn't been the merciful blanket of fog covering them, they would be sitting targets for the machine gunners; and, to boot, the artillery would be firing at the road about one hundred yards on the other side of the bank; they would be firing blind in the darkness and fog, depending on the calculations of their gunnery officer. If he got his sums wrong, the shells would be landing in the river.*

Pring took out his pocket watch, though he knew it was too dark to see the hands. The ticking sounded loud in the stillness, with just the quiet thump, thump of the hammers. He estimated about an hour to go when the British barrage would start up. They wanted to be out of here by then.

"Quietly lads." He whispered, somewhat unnecessarily.

The others were coming in now, passing across the planks and tying them in place with rope. But when the foot bridges, which would carry the infantry across, were in place, they had to return and bring over trestles for heavier bridges to take the artillery across behind the infantry. Having finished their tasks, the men waded back, their lower halves numb with cold, and then went to carry the heavy, awkward trestles over and down the bank. This was the tricky part—this was what Engineers did best. The trestles had to be perfectly in line, and level to take the roadway of timber planks. Strong and stable enough to hold the heavy 18 pounder field guns that would be needed to support the infantry as they moved forward.

They got one down the bank, and into the river, the pioneers carrying it on their shoulders, the weight of the heavy steel trestle driving their feet down into the mud, one squelching step at a time. That was put in place on the west side.

The next one, they were to be spaced six feet apart, was lifted across and dropped carefully. It disappeared under the water—down a hole! They took deep breaths and went under to try and get hold of it, but it was staying put. Finally, they had to leave it, and come back at daylight. At least the foot bridges were all ready. There would be time at daylight to get another spare trestle in place, when they could see what they were doing.

By 1:45 am, on the 20th, the last bridge was going into position when a German machine gun opened fire. They were firing blind though, and by then the other sappers and pioneers had returned to comparative safety.

• • •

75th Field Company War Diary
October 19, 1918.

Company resting till evening. Company moves to Rlwy. St. Python – Haussy at varying times from 6.30 pm to 10 pm. For purposes of making 8 infantry crossings and trestle bridges for field guns across Selle River. 2nd Lt. Winch and No. 2 section placed tapes from crossing places to railway. This was completed by 11 pm. ½ Company Pioneers with No. 1 section under Lt. Brown and covering party proceeded down tapes at midnight and placed bridges in river without disturbance from enemy, who were holding far bank of river.

October 20, 1918.

All infantry bridges in position by 1.15 am, giving 8 new crossings and 3 undamaged existing crossings. No. 3 section with ½ Company Pioneers under Lt. Ross took in trestle bridging equipment to river side and withdrew just before zero [hour] at 2 am. No. 4 section made crossing on railway for field guns. At 2 am infantry crossed the river without difficulty and No. 3 section commenced erecting bridge for field guns to cross. Company withdrew on completion of their tasks except for maintenance parties.

October 21, 1918.

One section maintaining river crossings. 2 sections on roads in St. Python.

October 22, 1918.

All sections building bridge for 60 pounder guns over River Selle at St. Python. Work commenced at 9 am and completed 4 pm.

• • •

After the hectic days of crossing the Selle, the Germans continued their retreat. The Guards were given a welcome period of rest, which lasted to the end of October.

"... they were washed and cleaned and reclothed with all speed and handed over to their company officers for the drill that chases off the bad dreams.

The regimental sergeant-major, got at them too, after their hair was cut, and the massed brigade drums played in the village square of Carnières, and ere the end of the month, inter-company football was in full swing."

— The Irish Guards in the Great War, Rudyard Kipling

CHAPTER 31

What Passing-Bells …

What passing-bells for those who die as cattle?
Only the monstrous anger of the guns.
Only the stuttering rifles' rapid rattle
Can patter out their hasty orisons.
No mockeries now for them; no prayers nor bells,
Nor any voice of mourning save the choirs—
The shrill, demented choirs of wailing shells;
And bugles calling for them from sad shires.

(Wilfred Owen. "Anthem for Doomed Youth")

VERTAIN

November 3, 1918

A pair of fours, an ace of spades, seven of hearts, and a queen of diamonds, hmmm …

Not being much of a gambler by nature, Vincent put his cards on the table. The betting went on, and Billy Basson won the pot— forty-five cigarettes; not a bad haul, and that was it for the night. Billy went off to bed happy. The others stood and tidied up the room, chatting about the game of poker that had just ended. By the standards of previous billets, this place was pretty good, now that they were on the German side of the Hindenburg line. There was comparatively little damage, save a few wrecked houses, most of the buildings being intact. They were filthy dirty, but that had been taken care of, and the company was finishing up two relatively peaceful weeks. Much needed after the fighting, the taking of the Hindenburg line and crossing the Selle river.

The small village of Vertain was well behind the fairly rapidly moving front line now, in what had become, for the first time in three years, a mobile war.

The old stalemate of trench warfare was finished.

"Have ye read the paper that came in today?" asked John Kelly, looking at Vincent, Sam McLaughlin, and John O'Boyle. The three of them shook their heads.

"No. We've been too busy," Vincent replied.

"It looks like they're talking peace at last. From the way we're chasing Fritz, it looks like they're finished."

"I think the Yanks comin' in, has made the difference."

"Fritz is fuckin' knackered after that last push."

"So are we."

They began to talk about what would be likely to happen, but at the same time they knew the fighting wasn't over yet. There was talk of another assault using the Guards pretty soon.

"I … I'm a b … bit worried ab … about Billy," said John O'Boyle. "S … s … since that s … s … shell got me, I've had a f… few s … st … strange experiences ha … ha … happen to me. Seen s … some …" He trailed off, embarrassed that the others would laugh.

"Go on, John," Kelly said.

"W… well, j … just now, as B … Billy walked out, I … I saw a sh … shadow beside h … him." He looked away. The others didn't know what to say, and so just shrugged.

"It's probably a trick of the light, John," Vincent said, knowing at the same time it probably wasn't.

"M … m … maybe."

"Billy'll be fine. Sure he's a driver, they're always behind the lines."

• • •

On the 2nd of November, the divisional Headquarters moved into Vertain, and they were kept busy setting them up.

Meanwhile, the Guards were moving up to a small town called Villers Pol, where the front was now situated just to the west of the town. Orders had been received for a resumption of the attack on the fourth of November, with the ultimate objective being the town of Maubeuge, seventeen miles further east.

• • •

VILLERS POL
November 4, 1918

On the west side of Villers Pol ran a small river about ten feet wide and not too deep; it had been crossed by a stone bridge, but that was gone in the center, thanks to the retreating German explosives. Nonetheless, the attacking infantry managed to ford it and move forward beyond the town. As there were large numbers of troops and equipment moving forward, it became imperative for the Engineers to repair the bridge as quickly as possible.

Two miles beyond, in a small wood by Wargnies le Petit, a group of Germans were still holding out, and in the church tower, a sniper was playing havoc with the Irish Guardsmen moving forward.

Vincent's section had crossed the river and were waiting for the trestles to be brought up. They sat around, smoking and watching, as half a mile away, the drivers dismounted and were urging their horses through the mud caused by the heavy rain and the hundreds of infantry boots. It was getting foggy following the rain, and Vincent could just make out the figures working with the laden wagons.

"Would ye like me to go and help them with the wagons, Sarge?" he asked his superior, who was also watching them.

"Nah, we were told to wait here, so just 'ang on a bit. We need to get those trestles off as soon as they get 'ere."

Just then, they heard the crump of mortars going off in the wood, down the road by Wargnies, and they realized the Germans were still holding out. There had been sporadic machine gun fire from that direction all day.

To their horror, the shells started landing near the five wagons loaded with the bridge equipment. There were screams of terror from the horses, as they bucked and struggled, knocking the drivers on the ground; and then a couple of rounds landed right among them, and all Vincent could see was flames and smoke and then wrecked wagons.

"Let's get over there!" the Sergeant shouted, waving the section back across the river, but when they arrived, there was chaos. Horses were screaming in agony, in their death throes; all the drivers were hurt. Vincent found Billy Basson lying on the ground, legs gone, almost unrecognizable. He went over and knelt down beside him. He was still alive, but Vincent could see the life force draining from his face, and then he just closed his eyes.

He was gone.

John Kelly arrived at the scene and saw the Sergeant beside Billy. Vincent was sitting on the ground, knees splayed and his head in his hands, in shock. Tears rolled down his face, digging grooves in the muck that covered it. John put his hand on Vincent's shoulder, and they stayed there while the sergeant said a silent prayer close to Billy's ear.

Eons passed in a few moments, while they sat there in shock. The stretcher bearers had already arrived, having been with the advancing troops, and they were taking the other drivers, who were still alive, away to the ambulance station. They came for Billy last; he was beyond help now.

Vincent, John, and Billy had been good mates, ever since they'd helped him get his horses off the ship back in Le Havre, what seemed a lifetime ago.

Now there was just the two of them—Vincent and John.

"C'mon lads, let's get these trestles into place!" shouted Sergeant Pring. He had seen all this before and knew the best thing for them was to get them busy, let the shock wear off.

Slowly, John helped Vincent up and they got to work on the bridge. It was going to be a long day.

• • •

75th Field Company War Diary
November 4, 1918.
Division attacked at Villers Pol. No. 3 section constructed trestle bridge across river North of village. No. 1 section stood by between Wargnies Le Petit and Villers Pol. Trench mortars got drop hits on transport with wagons, carrying Weldon trestle, knocking out 11 horses, 10 being destroyed. Driver Basson was killed at the time. Sapper Ball was wounded. Trestle bridges put across at about 18 hours.

• • •

Fourteen miles further south from where Vincent's company were working, near La Motte farm, the German and British troops were separated by the Sambre—Oise Canal. The objective of the 9th Army was to cross the canal and push the Germans back, but it was a well defended obstacle. The Engineers had made wooden bridges across the locks and some of the men paddled makeshift rafts across.

A platoon from the 2nd Manchester Regiment under Lieutenant Wilfred Owen were using a raft, which Owen was on, to ferry planks across to complete the pontoon bridge. Then a German machine gun sprayed the raft, bullets splintering the wood. One of them slammed into Lieutenant Owen, ending the life of a war poet and probably one of the greatest voices for the men caught up in the chaos of the First World War.

WILFRED OWEN[121]

The sun shone from a cloudless blue sky, warming the streets of Oswestry, in what was an unusually warm and dry March. The men going about their business in the small market town in Shropshire, on the Welsh order, sweated in their stiff-necked shirts and black business suits, customary back then in the halcyon days of the Victorian era. It was March 19th, and the people in the town were looking forward to spring, following another harsh winter.

None of this worried Susan Owen, holding her first born child to her breast, experiencing a love so deep no man would ever know it. The baby was a day old, tiny, red skin, eyes squeezed shut as if he didn't want to accept that he had made it into the real world. She brushed down the soft black hair on his head and kissed it gently. She and her husband Thomas had talked (not argued, mind you) about what they would call the baby; finally settling with Victorian formality on Wilfred Edward Salter Owen. Appositely, whether they were aware of it or not, the etymology of the first name means, "he who wants peace".

---

121 Photo Wikimedia Commons, public domain. Unknown author.

The house Wilfred spent his first four years in, Plas Wilmot, was a comfortable red brick building on the outskirts of the town. His father worked there as a railway clerk and though they lived in a fine house, the family income was small, for the house belonged to Susan's father, Edward. Though he had scant memories of it, it was a happy time for little Wilfred, during which his sister Mary was born in 1895.

Wilfred grew up a devout Anglican, in tandem with his mother, their closeness buttressed by their shared religious beliefs. Although he attended technical schools, Wilfred was at heart a romantic; serious and compassionate. The arts drew his interest, especially poetry and his early poems go back to his teenage years, influenced by the romantic poets, Shelley, and Keats.

His family couldn't afford to send him to university, and while he passed the matriculation exam for the University of London, he didn't have the first-class honors to obtain a scholarship. This led to him staying with the Vicar of Dunsden, near Reading, where he attended classes at University College, Reading. During his time at Dunsden, he became disillusioned with the church mainly for its failure to provide aid for those in need.

In 1913, he moved to France where he worked as a tutor in the Berlitz School of Languages in Bordeaux. And then came the outbreak of war.

Owen returned from France and enlisted with The Artists Rifles Training Corps, appropriately enough, on the 21st of October 1915. After completing training in Essex, on June 4, 1916, he was commissioned as second lieutenant in the Manchester Regiment. He certainly held a very snobbish regard for his subordinates, referring to them as "expressionless lumps", and one imagines he didn't endear himself to the troops under him. However, in June 1917, after falling into a shell hole and suffering concussion, he was caught in the blast of a trench mortar shell and spent several days unconscious lying amongst the remains of one of his fellow officers. He was later diagnosed with what was then called neurasthenia or shell shock and ended up in Craiglockhart War Hospital in Edinburgh for treatment.

During his time there he became acquainted with Siegfried Sassoon, another poet, who had a considerable influence on the younger Owen. He spent some of his time there teaching in Tynecastle High School, in a downtrodden area of the city and was discharged later in the year. From then until August 1918, he remained in England ending up at the Northern Command Depot at Ripon.

In July 1918 he returned to active service in France, despite the fact he could probably have remained in England.

Wilfred felt it important that he join with Sassoon in condemning the atrocities of war, and his poetry told of the horrific realities of trench warfare and the futility of it all. In August 1918, he returned to the front line with the 2nd Battalion, Manchester Regiment. On 1 October, he led his platoon to storm several enemy strong points near the village of Joncourt. For his courage and leadership in this action he was awarded the Military Cross.

Then on November 4th, while Lieutenant Owen was working on a makeshift raft, transferring planks across the Sambre-Oise Canal to help the sappers building a pontoon bridge, a machine gun bullet slammed into his body, and the war was over for Wilfred.

Just one week later, on the 11th of November 1918, an armistice was declared between the opposing sides in the war. Tom and Susan Owen were sitting in their comfortable living room, listening to the church bells ringing in celebration of the end of hostilities. Susan was deep in thought as she knitted, planning a welcome home for her son, when the door knocker sounded. Tom went out to answer and opened the door to the postman with a telegram in his hand ...

• • •

Wilfred's brother Harold had joined the Merchant Navy and was in the naval reserve. He was an officer on board the British cruiser HMS

Astraea and later wrote about an extraordinary and inexplicable experience while the ship was anchored off the coast of Cameroon:

"I had gone down to my cabin, stepped inside, and to my amazement I saw Wilfred sitting in my chair. I felt shock run through me with appalling force and with it I could feel the blood draining away from my face.

I did not rush towards him but walked jerkily into the cabin—all my limbs stiff and slow to respond. I did not sit down but looking at him I spoke quietly, 'Wilfred, how did you get here?'

He did not rise, and I saw that he was involuntarily immobile, but his eyes—which had never left mine—were alive with the familiar look of trying to make me understand. When I spoke, his whole face broke into his sweetest and most endearing dark smile.

I felt not fear, only exquisite mental pleasure at thus beholding him. He was in uniform, and I remember thinking how out of place the khaki looked amongst the cabin furnishings. With this thought I must have turned my eyes away from him. When I looked back my cabin chair was empty ...

I wondered if I had been dreaming but looking down, I saw that I was still standing. Suddenly I felt terribly tired, and I lay down on my bunk. Instantly I went into a deep oblivious sleep. When I woke up, I knew with absolute certainty that Wilfred was dead."

75th Field Company War Diary
November 5, 1918.

No. 4 section to maintain bridge at Wargnies Le Petit. No. 3 section repairing crossing erected day before in Villers Pol. Company moved off at 1430 hrs. to neighbourhood of Amfroipret – owing to obstructions on road, billets were found at Gommegnies for the night.

November 6, 1918.

Company moved to Amfroipret. One section working in village filling craters in road. Lt. Brown made reconnaissance of road as far as Mecquignes.

November 7, 1918.

Lt. Ross and No. 3 section constructed trestle bridge (Walden) at Baviseux. Lt. Lynch and No. 2 section work on railway crossing W. of Baviseux. Lt. Charles made reconnaissance of road as far as Malgarni.

November 8, 1918.

Vertain, Northern France. Lt. Ross and section completed crossing for lorries at railway crossing with sleepers. Lt. Brown with No. 1 section and ½ No. 4 section completed trestle bridge from (?) for 8-ton axle loads. Lts. Lynch and Charles with 1 ½ sections and infantry working parties fill in craters at Amfroipret.

November 9, 1918.

La Longueville. Company moved to la Longueville. Lt. Lynch made reconnaissance of road at La Longueville to Frignes – Maubeuge. Major Briggs DSO MC struck off strength of Company.

November 10, 1918.

Maubeuge. Company moved to N. end of Maubeuge. No. 1 section put trestle bridge down earlier? And prepared to put it in. (Writing is very difficult to read in this section. DMC) 1 platoon 4th Coldstream Guards, No. 2 section and No. 4 section working on road craters. P 6 a.3.3.

November 11, 1918

Capt. Kirby left to command 154th Field Company R.E. Capt. E. H. Grant R.E. (SR) joined Company as 2nd in command and acting OC in absence of Major Briggs. Company working on filling of craters at La Longueville – Maubeuge Road. Hostilities ceased at 1100 hours.

CHAPTER 32

The Futility of War

It's a mighty good world, so it is, dear lass,
When even the worst is said.
There's a smile and a tear, a sigh and a cheer,
But better be living than dead;
A joy and a pain, a loss and a gain;
There's honey and maybe some gall;
Yet I still declare, foul weather or fair,
It's a mighty good world after all.

(Robert W. Service. "Cheer")

The village in Northern France, where once a small, but content population lived in relative harmony in their humble houses—where they went to mass in their church with its fine steeple, where they gathered at the estaminet on sunny Saturday evenings, drank wine and where the old men sat around tables drinking coffee and playing chess—was now reduced to heaps of rubble.

What was left of their belongings were scattered and rotting in the piles of bricks and dust. Their few possessions had been looted by the retreating army. The bodies of dead soldiers had been removed and the streets cleared of rubble to allow the troops to pass through.

The people returned, despondently walking through the streets, wondering what lay ahead of them, and why they had to suffer like this; some began to peel off at where their house had once stood. A few buildings were left relatively whole, among them a barn, with locked doors. Needing someplace to store their pieces of furniture, the men got a bar and broke away the lock. Inside, as their eyes grew accustomed to the dark, they were met with a grotesque tableau; two long dead soldiers, one Australian and one German, were kneeling and facing each other, each with a bayonet thrust into the other.

When the army was clearing the town of bodies for burial, they missed this barn—or perhaps they didn't?

Whatever the reason, this little tableau represented the stage that both sides had reached, beaten to their knees, hundreds of thousands dead … and what for?

The utter futility of it all was not lost on the men who went into the barn.

• • •

A heavy frost lay over the ground as reveille sounded and the men mustered for parade. A strange silence had shattered the cacophony of war.

No gunfire.

They had known there were talks going on and wondered, not without some excitement, what was happening. Then, at 11 am, the Acting CO, Captain Grant, told the assembled men that an armistice had been agreed; the war was over. No more fighting.

It was with confused emotions that Vincent went about his work that day. He couldn't stop thinking about it. He would soon be going back to Belfast for good, to be reunited with his brothers, sisters, and his father. They had been good about writing to him and keeping him up to date with local goings on. He was 24 years old, and unsure as to what kind of work he would get, where he would live and what he would do with himself. After four years of drills, parades, and being told what to do had made its mark, it was hard to even think like a civilian.

As they began the long march through Northern France, into Belgium towards Germany, he suddenly felt a closeness to the other men, a kinship they all had taken for granted, as they looked out for each other. Many of the tired, war-weary, khaki-clad soldiers had been with him since they came over to France in 1915. It seemed like several lifetimes ago. He'd probably never see any of them again and felt a deep sadness at this thought.

Marching through the rubble of what had at one time been thriving market towns, where belongings, furniture and broken bricks were mixed up in dusty heaps as the owners tried to recover what remained of their possessions, he began to see it for the first time. The terrible, biblical devastation they were leaving in their wake. He saw the incongruous sight of a chimney standing alone, the mantle and fire intact and a picture still hanging on the wall. A place where once a husband and wife sat together after dinner, the children kissing them goodnight.

They passed through what had once been rich farming countryside, where the smell of new cut hay had filled the air; replaced now by the stench of death. Rotting corpses and mud, the fields strewn with abandoned weapons, wagons, and the remains of men and animals from both sides buried in a shallow grave of mud. Blackened stumps of trees protruded where once a pretty copse had been. People starving because there were no crops to harvest.

They never deserved this.

Vincent remembered his brother Jim reading to them from the bible when they were young. He recalled especially the Book of Revelations. To his nine-year-old imagination, the frightening beings revealed by John the Evangelist in this story remained forever embedded in his memory. Jim himself was fascinated by it and reread it many times. He had in fact taken the name John Evangelist when he joined the Christian Brothers. Now he was in India, doing what he loved most—teaching, living up to his chosen name.

He pondered on how relevant it was to the world they now marched through.

War, Famine, Disease, and Death.

For the past few months more men were dying from the Spanish Flu than from German guns.

As Revelation 6 opens, John sees Jesus Christ, the Lamb of God, who begins to open the first of seven seals on a scroll, representing God's future judgement of people and nations. In this book of prophecies, John sees what will happen on earth at the end of times when God judges its inhabitants.

When Jesus opens the First Seal, it summons forth a horseman on a white horse, wearing a crown and carrying a bow.

CONQUEST.

"I looked up and saw a white horse standing there. Its rider carried a bow, and a crown was placed on his head. He rode out to win many battles and gain the victory."

Jim had explained to Vincent that in scripture the bow is seen as a weapon of military triumph and the crown the conqueror's headdress.

On opening the second seal, a second rider on a fiery red horse is summoned.

WAR.

"Then another horse came out, a fiery red one. Its rider was given power to take peace from the earth and to make people kill each other. To him was given a large sword."

The third seal is opened and reveals a rider mounted on a coal black horse, holding a pair of scales.

This is the prediction of unbearable inflation caused by scarcity, hunger and shortage of necessities brought on by war.

FAMINE.

"And I looked, and behold, a black horse! And its rider had a pair of scales in his hand. And I heard what seemed to be a voice in the midst of the four living creatures, saying, 'A quart of wheat for a denarius, and three quarts of barley for a denarius, and do not harm the oil and wine!'"

And then the fourth seal is broken.

DEATH.

"And I looked up and saw a horse whose color was pale green. Its rider was named Death, and his companion was the Grave. These two were given authority over one-fourth of the earth, to kill with the sword and famine and disease and wild animals."

The Four Horsemen were surely a metaphor for what had taken place. Vincent understood that they represented the destruction caused by the dark side of man. He realized that this would always be with us, as long as we inhabit the Earth.

They had called the war "the war to end all wars." But it wouldn't be.

This thought left him devastated, that the peace that existed now was only temporary.

• • •

As they marched that day through the French countryside, a fog had descended, swirling around them, sometimes hiding the wagons in front.

In a light clearance of the thick mist, Vincent could have sworn he saw spectral figures of soldiers marching in tandem with them. Some were on horseback, most walking. They were the dead, who were joining in the final march into Germany. One of the men on horses was Billy Basson, who turned and smiled at Vincent. All the others were there: Beale, Millar, Rae, Bean, Livingston, Albright, Thomas, Arnold, Hall, and the sad, lost Lieutenant Ure. There were lads who were still in their teens, middle-aged men, generals and privates, poets and carpenters, British and German uniforms, all together now, taking part in their final march. Then the fog closed in again.

He thought his imagination was getting the better of him, but strange things happened in this war. This epiphany had a profound effect on him, and for the first time he really began to see meaning in the bible. He was living it. Many men had lost their religious beliefs in the black pit of despair that was the horror of war. But as he dwelt on the book, his brother's voice in his ear, he felt the beginnings of a deep understanding.

• • •

And so began their long march, from France, through Belgium, finally reaching Cologne just in time for Christmas 1918 … **Maubeuge, Bersillies, Binche, Charleroi, Fosse, Dave, (then across the River Meuse), Lourriere, Francesse, Doyon, Bermonville, Bohon, Malacorde, Bergeval, Recht, Mürringen, Losheimer,**

Garben, Ramsheid, Blumenthal, Kall, Kalenburg, Kommern, Zulpich, Erp, Gehn, Freisheim, Stotzheim, Lechenich, Liblar … and finally, Cologne.

75th Field Company War Diary
December 2, 1918.
Cologne. *Company marched to Cologne and billets in Braunsfeld suburb. 2nd Lt. N. H. Charles returns from leave.*

December 23, 1918.
Company cleaning stables in Aachener Strasse. Capt. P. R. Pence-Jones MC provisionally posted to 75th Field Company R.E.

December 24, 1918.
Company resting.

December 25, 1918.
Christmas Day celebration.

The rest of the month was spent resting in billets at Cologne.

• • •

The company remained in Cologne until the 24th of February 1919, on which date, Sapper Vincent McCann was demobilized. He returned to Belfast, to his family on Cranburn Street, much to their relief that he'd survived the war. Later, on his father's retirement, they moved to Ballyhaise, Co. Cavan.

Vincent's fighting wasn't over yet. When he returned home, Ireland was in the throes of the "War of Independence" against his former employer, the British Government. He joined the Irish Republican Brotherhood, which later became the I.R.A., and fought for the country's right to self-determination.

But that's another story.

After Ireland gained independence from England, and the inter-party differences had been thrashed out in a vicious civil war, he joined the fledgling Irish Customs and Excise Service, a job in which he remained until his forced retirement in the late 1950s.

Vincent passed away in January of 1971, a few months shy of his 77th birthday.

I hope his spirit was able to revisit the places in Belgium and France where he spent the war and see that they are all now as they once were, before the Four Horsemen rode through them on their devastating journey.

TO VINCENT

So many times, he'd pause to wonder,
How it would be to return?
To where the guns had spat their thunder
The villages left to burn.

Where brave men died and widows cried,
Their families left to cope.
What was it for? He sadly sighed,
For lasting peace, there is no hope.

The places he knew are different now,
No trenches, the wire long gone.
The killing fields lie 'neath the plough,
The woods now freshly grown.

The towns rebuilt with loving care,
The fear and hate cast aside.
We're all friends again, *plus de guerre*
Until once more the Horsemen ride.

He'd love the chance to visit "Wipers",
And stand beneath the Menin Gate,
and listen to the bands of pipers
pay tribute to his fallen mates.

To Talbot House he'd go once more,
to rest amid the garden blooms,
he'd cast aside that bloody war,
And let his soul its peace assume.

(*Derek and Terry McCann. "To Vincent"*)

Acknowledgements

In many ways, this is the hardest part of the book; one that I've left to the last. While the author writes the book, so many people have an input, that it gradually becomes a group effort.

Behind me all the time there is my partner of over 52 years and biggest supporter, my wife Terry. Her unfailing strength is the fuel that keeps me going. I can't thank you enough.

To my sons, Simon and James; thank you both for your military service. You share with my dad the experience of being at war on foreign soil. To Anna, my daughter for her constant encouragement, usually via Facetime from Ireland.

Thanks to my editor, Joe Tower and his business partner Rea Frey for their positive attitude and input; By the way, they do a great podcast at Writewayco.com!

To Dr. Heather Montgomery, Queens University Belfast, who was instrumental in finding the mock trenches at Moore Camp, Kilworth, Co. Cork and shared her experiences of them with us.

To my friend Peter Deller and his wife Ann, in Ireland, for putting me on to the War Diaries and gently pushing me when I slowed down.

To my first cousins, Chris Ray and Father Joe McCann, and the other cousins who have worked so hard at putting the family history together.

To Frank Le Fevre and his lovely family in France, for taking Terry and I to several battle sites, cemeteries and museums, most notably Fontaine Notre Dame, where the guards fought in one of the later battles in the war.

To Frédéric Devys at Le Chateau Philiomel for his wonderful hospitality while we stayed there during our visits to the battle sites at Loos.

Thanks to my friends Mike Kacmarcik and Joe Gardeski and all the other radio hams I hang around with, for their suggestions and support, as well as keeping me sane with all their crazy humor.

To my siblings, who shared my puzzlement over my father's silence, Tony, Pat, Noreen and Ann; thanks not only for being such good family, but dear friends as well.

This book could not have been written without the excellent work by both the National Archives, (UK) and the National Library of Scotland, the former in digitizing the army records and the company war diaries, and the latter for digitizing the trench maps. Thank you.

If I have forgotten anyone, please accept my apologies and thank you for your input.